INDIA AND HUMAN RIGHTS

About the Editor

T.S.N. Sastry is a Reader in International Studies and Coordinator of the Centre for Human Rights, School of Social Sciences and International Studies, Pondicherry University, Pondicherry. He was the first recipient of Ph.D. degree in International Law from Andhra University, Visakhapatnam in 1996.

Dr. Sastry has authored a book, entitled *State Succession in Indian Context*. He has also edited *Fifty Years of Indian Independence and the Polity*, and co-edited *Studies in Human Rights*. He has published as well a good number of research papers in journals of national and international repute. Dr. Sastry has participated and conducted many seminars and conferences.

INDIA AND HUMAN RIGHTS
REFLECTIONS

Edited by

Dr. T.S.N. Sastry

Foreword by

Prof. A. Laxminath

CONCEPT PUBLISHING COMPANY, NEW DELHI-110059

Cataloging in Publication Data—DK
Courtesy: D.K. Agencies (P) Ltd. <docinfo@dkagencies.com>

India and human rights : reflections / edited
by T.S.N. Sastry ; foreword by A. Laxminath.
p. cm.
Contributed articles.
Includes bibliographical references.
Includes index.
ISBN 8180692043

1. Human rights—India. I. Suryanarayana Sastry, T. (Tamma),1961-

DDC 323.095 4 21

ISBN 81-8069-204-3

First Published 2005

Published and Printed by
Ashok Kumar Mittal
Concept Publishing Company
A-15/16, Commercial Block, Mohan Garden
New Delhi (INDIA)

Phones : 25351460, 25351794
Fas : 091-11-25357103
Email : publishing@conceptpub.com

FOREWORD

Human Rights represent one of the most powerful ideas in the contemporary world. In a world of economic globalisation, where individualism, greed and becoming rich which are seen as the most important things in life, and where at the same time the formerly secured moral positions for judging our actions seem to be declining into a morass of post-modern relativism, the idea of human rights provides an alternative moral reference point for those who seek to reaffirm the values of humanity.

Human Rights represent a powerful discourse that seeks to overcome divisiveness and sectarianism and to unite people of different cultural and religious traditions in a single movement asserting human values and the universality of humanity, at a time when such values are seen to be under threat from the forces of economic globalization. The idea of human rights, by its very appeal to universally applicable ideas of the values of humanity, seems to resonate across cultures and traditions and represents an important rallying cry for those seeking to bring about a more just, peaceful and sustainable world. The idea of human rights readily endorsed by people from many different cultural and ideological backgrounds and it is used rhetorically in support of a large number of different and sometimes conflicting causes. Because of its strong appeal and its rhetorical power, it is often used loosely and can have different meanings in different contexts.

The idea of human rights is largely a product of Enlightenment thinking and is, therefore, inevitably contextualised within an essentially western and modernistic framework. This has led to the criticism that human rights thinking and rhetoric are simply another manifestation of colonialist western domination, and to the suggestion that the concept of human rights should not be used. While it is true that much of the contemporary understanding of human rights has been shaped by Western Enlightenment thinking, the same can be said of many other concepts that are frequently used in political debate, such as democracy, justice, freedom, equality and human dignity. To stop using such words simply because of their western enlightenment associations would be to deny their power and importance across cultures and would lead to sterile and limited political debate. The task, therefore, should be to loosen them from the shackles of western modernism and to reconstruct them in more dynamic, inclusive and cross cultural terms. Sometimes human rights become nothing more than a new language for consumerism and self indulgence. The other criticism is that claims of human rights can conflict with each other and, therefore, one is left with the problem of reconciling competing claims. The universality of human rights must not be confused with a static and unchangeable notion of human rights. Human rights must be seen as constructed, rather than objectively existing, the important thing is the process of dialogue, discussion and exchange that seeks to articulate such universal values.

In contemporary society, fundamental and human rights are directed not only against State action, but also against the intrusion of other expansive social systems, such as economy, mass media and religion. Historical and sociological processes make human rights emerge as a central feature of modern society. Fundamental freedoms and human rights are not merely to be considered transhistorically but to be related to the specific and dominant structure of modern society. By institutionalising fundamental freedoms and human rights, the modern society protects its own structure against self-destructive tendencies towards dedifferentiation. At the same time human rights protect the fragile position of the individual within societies like modern India. Without institutional mechanisms that enable and fortify the co-existence of highly individualised persons and autonomous function systems, the risk of regression or dedifferentiation is real. Human Rights protect and strengthen modern individuality, which is no longer constituted by "total inclusion", in a family, corporation or State. Human rights constitute a socio-economic institution which protects functional differentiation against its self-destructive tendencies thus guaranteeing a decent life and equality of access to all State and social institutions.

Indian experience can be viewed as a conflict resulting from a search for a balance between the use of law by elites for purposes of domination and the use of law to moderate elite domination by providing avenues of participation for the disadvantaged. The existence of this duality is perhaps the result of the failure of the masses to understand their legal rights, the restricted access of the masses to the legal system in terms of time and/or financial constraints. The 'civic revolution' as a model of social transformation would make it a logical necessity that law as an instrument of social change is held under constant review (Prof. Yogendra Singh). The efforts of the three wings of the State, viz., Legislature, Executive and Judiciary and the efforts of the public organisations, enterprises and civil society working to advance the movement of democratic law and social change must be linked for more effective implementation.

In the present day context law's uniqueness flows more from its versatility and open endedness of the social forms it structures, than from its purity. Laws flexibility ensnares it in post-modern dialectic of multi-directionality against directionless performivity. Jurisprudence cannot ever be again—at least with good conscience - an abstract study of philosophical models. Its aim is wisdom as to law's being and law's effects.

The primary idea of human rights involves rights against the government. The present day concept/idea includes the rights to be guaranteed by the government. A true sense of priorities would suggest that the essence of liberty which comprises right against the State should not be confused with claims or entitlements which need to be satisfied by State.

Human Rights can play a significant role in securing the accountability of those who wield power and control of resources essential to the satisfaction of basic human needs. Rights to secure the writs of mandamus and prohibition are important checks on the abuse of power. Right of access to information, right to public hearing and freedom of speech and of the press are crucial in checking the governmental lawlessness and abuse of discretion or powers by bureaucratic and government officials.

Hegel once stated that wisdom will only arrive when human has ceased: must this be so? It appears at this time more than ever before that this is the case when human rights are read into Article 21 of the Indian Constitution by the very Supreme Court which was known for its narrow positivist stance. More so the Indian Supreme Court's concern for the prisoners rights and their recognition and enforcement via Article 21 is a tribute for our country's human rights awareness.

The Universal Declaration is intended as a minimum standard which should find universal acceptance in order to prevent the expected "clash of cultures and civilizations". One of the consequences of rights being the point of departure for constitutional law is that phenomenon like social rights (which are in fact duties or responsibilities of the States) have been drafted as individual claims in national constitutions despite their non-justiciability (e.g. Directive Principles and Fundamental Rights). Hardly two decades later, the Universal declaration gained the status of an obligatory (albeit non-justiciable) document for all the countries of the world.

Brian Berry has ably demonstrated why Rawls theory of "justice as mutual advantage", being inadequate to consider the intergenerational question, must be expanded to include the notion of "Justice as Impartiality". Prof. Amartya Sen acknowledges "the influence of Theory of Justice had extended by the early 1980's, beyond the realm of political philosophy to that of welfare economics. Rawls' conception of justice should include the internal justice of the family and the individual, assuring adequate protection of Human Rights, in his wider conception of moral development. The irony of the Rawlsian legacy is that the difference principle and the pragmatic conception of 'overlapping consensus' aroused maximum interest in countries where social welfare policies and human rights protection have been the most developed—whereas in developing countries like India this aspect of Rawls' early work has been virtually ignored.

Martha Nussbaum's approach addressed to Constitution makers offers a most versatile conception of constitutionalism. She offers us a rather thick (as compared with the thin Rawlsian) version of the original position from which the basic structure of the Constitution stands derived. Constitutions ought to deliver.... The social basics of these capabilities (Women and Human Development). Martha insists that constitution ought to espouse capabilities as a "Central goal" such that citizens stand endowed with "choice whether to pursue the relevant function or not to pursue it". Constitutional design ought to respect "citizen's power of choice" and traditional, civil and political liberties. The principle of 'Multiple realizability' of central human capabilities is exposed to a whole variety of individual tastes, local circumstances and traditions. Implementation of the capabilities principles must be left, for the most part, to the internal politics of the nation. Nussbaum further states that international agencies and other governments are justified in using persuasion—and in grave cases of economic and political sanctions to promote such developments which must presuppose a theory of global justice.

The twin ideas viz. multiple realizability and constraints on implementation combined together justify constitutional arrangements that, for example, emplot all kinds of trade-offs between civil and political rights on the one hand and social and economic rights on the other hand.

Prof Upendra Baxi maintains that the trade-off that the Indian Constitution sculpts by its distinction in Part III (enshrining fundamental rights enforceable by courts) and Part IV (the Directive Principles of State Policy that cast obligations, not so enforceable, on the legislature and the executive) violates, centrally, the list of central human capabilities. While we may all applaud with Nussbaum the rare examples of public policy that have developed political action to fulfil some Directive Principles, this is besides the point; the point being the justification of constitutional design that legitimates such trade-offs in the first place. The multiple realizability principle does not navigate Constitution making to any safe harbour; but obviously, what Nussbaum has in view is more substantive than a wish list.

Constitutions, on Martha Nussbaum's approach, are all about the delivery of basic human capabilities; if so, the two principles she advances give away far too much, despite the well-meant insistence that the 'political implementation, must remain to a large extent the job of the citizens. The 'irreducible plurality' of her list is a justified response to 'worries about universalism'. But when this principle addresses the goal of limiting trade-offs among capabilities, its runaway generality becomes problematic. The two discursive traditions unite on human aspiration towards human justice. Justice, as Rawls says, is a way of distributing the rights, duties benefits and burdens among individuals within society. This form of distributive justice should be implemented to empower the people through Rights to make them human.

In the present day context law's uniqueness flows more

from its versatility and open endedness of the social forms it structures, than from its purity. Laws flexibility ensnares it in post-modern dialectic of multi-dimensionalism.

What we need at this juncture is the re-institutionalization of human rights protection to adapt to more and more differentiated and complicated post-modern social, political and legal framework, which includes facilitation of access to right to life, liberty and equality.

Law plays a central role in civil society which cannot flourish where there are inadequate legal assurances of their ability to operate autonomously from government. Legal associations play a central role in the development of civil society by supporting rule of law mechanisms that permit the independent existence of non-governmental entities and by encouraging the development of institutions that foster their growth. A strong civil society also demands and oversees legal constraints on State power and the accountability of State actors. The words 'civil society' means the space of uncovered human association and also the set of relational networks-formed for the sake of family, faith, interest and ideology—that fill this space. Ideally the associational life of civil society is its capacity simultaneously to resist subordination to State authority and to demand inclusion into State political structures. Human Rights advocates argue that civil society creates a 'setting of settings'.

The present book titled *India and Human Rights Reflections* ably edited by Dr. T.S.N. Sastry is a welcome addition to the Human Rights Jurisprudence in India. Contributions by eminent authors made the book unique in the literature on Human Rights. I fervently hope that such admirable efforts by the members of fifth estate will usher in a new era in the realization of human rights through human flourishings in India.

Prof. A. LAKSHMINATH
Dean and Registrar
NALSAR University of Law, Hyderabad
Former Dean, Faculty of Law Andhra University and
Nagpur University

PREFACE

"Human Rights", are the rights, which every individual is entitled to enjoy his life and liberty freely within the jural postulations to have protection. Apart from a set of do's and dont's, they define the moral, ethical, philosophical, sociological, legal values and attitudes in governing the human relationship. They repose their faith in the inherent dignity and well-being of a human person. Human rights are the inalienable rights of man and transcend time and territory in enhancing the quality of life of the human family. Hence they are fundamental virtues of every culture and nation in its governance. As rightly pointed out by Prof. Upendra Baxi these rights are not *"a gift of the west to the rest"* and are not the sole propriety of congregation or a community.

India being a *dharmic* land, human rights are part of its culture and developed on the philosophy of *Dharma* from ancient times. The *Vedic* texts such as the *Vedas, Vedangas, Srutis, Smritis, Dharmasastras* and *Nitisastras* of Manu, Yajnavalkya, Narada, Sukra and Vidhura, *Puranas, Ithihasas,* the *Arthasastra* of Kautilya and the various other literary texts, extensively described the rights and duties to be followed by the 'ruler' and the 'ruled' in different epoch through the concept of *Dharma* for the well-being of the state and society in all its dimensions. Unlike the Western society, which has developed the concept of human rights on the tenets of 'rights', the Hindu philosophy firmly affirmed its faith on duties by teaching the concept of *'dharmo rakshathi rakshathaha'* (protect *dharma, dharma* protects you). Further to regulate the human relations in a just and equitable manner the saints and philosophers declared with a caution to create oneness in the minds of the people that all the human beings belong to one family and all men are equal through the concepts of '*Vasudhaiva Kutumbakam*' and '*Sarva Manava Saubrathauya*'.

After independence, the Constituent Assembly taking into consideration the cultural heritage of India, as well as the philosophical contours of the West and the ideas developed by international law of human rights drafted the constitution in maintaining equilibrium between individualism and social control. Accordingly, justiciable and non–justiciable human rights of the Universal Declaration and the Covenants of Civil and Political and Social, Economic and Cultural Rights have become part of the Constitution of India as 'Fundamental Rights' and 'Directive Principles of State Policy'.

In order to achieve the constitutional mandate of justice, liberty, equality and fraternity, the State has enacted a catena of legislations and established a National Human Rights Commission for the better augmentation of human rights. However, the erosion in moral values and the concept of *dharma* have had a degenerating impact in realizing the goals of the Constitution. In the last five and half decades, the functioning of the polity clearly depicts that its track record is far from satisfactory in fully augmenting both the justiciable and non-justiciable rights, in spite of an activist judiciary trying its best to engage the state on its tenterhooks in realizing the aspirations of the Constitution. The assertion of caste, ethnicity, resurgence of religious fundamentalism, linguistic perspectives, escalating level of violence in various walks of public life, high amount of corruption, gender based discrimination and violence against the tender age of the children, the resurgence of money and muscle power in elections by the political parties for their selfish ends, lack of proper basic needs (such as food, clothing, shelter), inadequate health care, malnutrition, poor infrastructural facilities, illiteracy, inefficient use of science and technology etc., distinctly leave soothing stains on the working of the Constitution as a functional democracy.

In order to bring back the glory of the nation and to revive the ancient culture of human rights various governmental and non-governmental organizations scholars and philanthropists have been reaffirming their faith in the fundamental concept of values, morals, ethics and the concept of *dharma* through the inherent force of human rights to meet the aspirations and to steer the country as a developed nation and to tinsel itself as a sustainable nation in the club of comity of nations.

In that direction, the present volume is a collection of papers of scholars and thinkers reflecting their perspectives on the various nuances of human rights. The authors in their papers made an attempt to contribute their mite of share to re-energize the country through the mechanism of human rights in order to counter the problems and steer the nation to achieve the path of prosperity through the mechanism of human rights in order to wipe out the tears on the face of millions of citizens of this great civilized nation.

I am highly thankful to Professor A. Laxmi Nath, Dean and Registrar, National Academy of Legal Studies and Research University, Hyderabad for his consent to write a scholarly foreword. I am highly thankful to all the contributors for their positive response to put forward their ideas and encouragement in bringing out this volume.

My thanks are also due to Shri J.C. Pillai, Proprietor, M.J.P. Publishers and Tamil Nadu Book House, Chennai for his constant academic and friendly help in various ways and means.

Last but not the least, My thanks are due to A.K. Mittal, Concept Publishing Company, New Delhi for bringing the present volume with utmost care and sincerity.

Dr. T. Suryanarayana Sastry

CONTENTS

1

A PERSPECTIVE ON HUMAN RIGHTS

Subhash C. Kashyap

The concept of Human Rights is not entirely western in origin nor is it so very modern. It is a crystallization of values that are the common heritage of mankind. In India, references occur as early as in the *Rig Veda* to the three civil liberties of *Tana* (body), *Skridhi* (dwelling house) and *Jibasi* (life). Long before Hobbes, the Indian epic *Mahabharata* described the civil liberty of the individual in a political State. Ancient Indian society was a highly structured and well-organized affair with the fundamental rights and duties not only of individuals but also of classes, communities and castes clearly laid down. The concept of *Dharma* was precisely that of rule of law - the supreme law, which governed the sovereign and the subjects alike and covered the basic principles involved in the theory of rights, duties and freedoms. Long before the second century B.C., we find mention of the law of nature, which even kings had to obey on pain of deposition. Also, kings were required to take a pledge never to be arbitrary and always to act according to "whatever law there is and whatever is dictated by ethics and not opposed to politics." Kautilya, the author of the celebrated political treatise *Arthashastra*, not only affirmed and elaborated the civil and legal rights first formulated by Manu but also added a number of economic rights. He ordains that "the king shall provide the orphan, the aged, the infirm, the afflicted and helpless with maintenance; he shall also provide subsistence to the helpless expectant mothers and also to the children they give birth to."

The ancient ideal that has survived in the consciousness of the millions of ordinary Indians has been that of the welfare and happiness of all - *"sarvesham mangalam bhavatu, sarve bhavantu sukhina"* - and of the whole world being one family— *"vasudhaiva kutumbakam"*. We are supposed to pray everyday not only for our own well-being but for the well-being of all mankind. The ancient Indian perspective of a global society is that of a family - giving and sharing - and not of a market place where everything is bought and sold and where the spirit of essential human unity becomes subservient to the supremacy of crude market forces.

Writing and discussions on human rights are very much the in-thing these days both nationally and globally for intellectual discourse as also for discussions among politicians around the world. The foundational norm governing the concept of human rights is that of the respect for human personality and its worth, regardless of colour, race, sex, religion or other considerations. These rights are essential for the adequate development of the human personality and for human happiness. Without getting involved in definitional controversies, therefore, human rights may be said to be those fundamental rights to which every man or woman inhabiting any part of the world should be deemed equally entitled merely by virtue of having been born a human being. Concept of human rights today essentially has political, social and economic connotations. It is founded on the ideal of realization of equality of all men, freedom and liberty for all men and basic to them all, social, economic and political justice for all men. Guarantees of political and civil rights without social and economic rights are incomplete just as the latter alone are insufficient to satisfy the spirit of man. The social and economic rights are primary while the civil and political rights are higher. If the former constitute foundation of the building, the latter provide the elevation. Basic to human rights is the concept of non-discrimination. But, if we look into the pages of the history of mankind, this basic principle of non-discrimination between human beings or of the universality of human rights has not always been so self-evident or accepted as being so axiomatic. There has been a perennial conflict between the elite's perception of their individual liberties and the fundamental human rights of the common people. Also, there has always existed and continues to exist a wide gap between precept and practice, between abstract principles and their application or implementation.

Without taking sides in the old controversies between the school of Natural Law and the school of Legal Positivism, it can be safely asserted that in a modern democratic State all rights flow from, are authorized and protected, and, where necessary, restricted by the organized will of the community. In other words, all rights are given by the people to themselves and the sanction behind them is the Constitution and the law of the land and not any natural, divine or immutable commandment or endowment.

Also, all rights are in the final analysis social, involving as they do relationships between individuals in a society. It is for each society to determine in its discretion what disciplines from time to time it must accept to ensure that the rights of the people at large are safeguarded. It follows as a corollary that while conceptually human rights must be the same for all societies, their implementation would necessarily remain culturally bound and variable. In the actual realization of the rights for its members, each society has to evolve its own model of implementation and protection which may be best suited to its own circumstances and needs. Foreign models can hardly be of much avail.

Western writers would like us to believe that it was the British *Magna Carta* (1215) which for the first time formulated human rights and liberties of the individual against the authority of the State and that it was followed by the Petition of Rights (1627) and the Bill of Rights (1688). It must not be forgotten that in England during all this period, it was a struggle between the barons and landed aristocracy on one side and the king on the other. The people were nowhere in the picture.

The western ideas of rights and liberties were conceived

in a particular socio-political framework, in situation of oligarchy, feudalism and highly restricted franchise. Natural rights and natural law in the context of doctrines of *laissez faire* meant basically the right of each individual to freedom of trade and enterprise, equality of opportunity in trade and business, freedom of contract and free competition. Right to property was put on a higher pedestal than right to life itself. Even slavery was justified under rights to property and to freedom of trade, contract and competition. Slaves were herded as animals in dark cages in the holds of ships and sold to the elite society in Europe and America. The 'trade' was financed by leading merchants of England, Spain, France and other countries. If fifty per cent of the 'merchandise' reached the destination alive, the average was considered not bad.

It seems never to have troubled the conscience of those vexing eloquent on the theories of human rights of freedom and equality that they traded in human beings or held them as slaves, working in their homes and on their farms. That there was anything reprehensible in their hunting the native American Indians and depriving them of their land or in their owning slaves and perpetrating the practice of slavery did not occur even to those who were assembled together to sign the noble Declaration of Independence and proclaim the "self-evident truths" that "all men are created equal" and endowed with "certain unalienable" rights to "Life, Liberty and pursuit of Happiness". All these people presumably thought that in putting to use their human chattel as they liked they were merely exercising their individual liberty to enjoy their 'property' without interference.

That there was anything wrong in the practice of serfdom did not bother the framers of the *Magna Carta* and the Bill of Rights. Also, those who were propounding the doctrines of freedom and democracy at home and priding themselves in their parliamentary institutions did not find anything incompatible in their subjugating whole nations and races of men and following policies of blatant colonial repression abroad. The human rights of their conception were thus meant to be applicable only to the select nobility of the white race and not to all mankind without discrimination of race, sex, colour or creed.

What may be regarded in our times as the inalienable rights of all members of the human family where crystallized in the Charter of the United Nations. It affirmed "faith in fundamental human rights, in the dignity and worth of the human person, in the equality of men and women and of nations large and small". The Universal Declaration of Human Rights adopted by the U.N. General Assembly on 10 December, 1948 may be said to be almost the first ever-international effort to codify the fundamental human rights. The declaration was followed by a series of covenants and conventions. By now, there are over hundred covenants, declarations, treaties, conventions or other such instruments of the U.N. in the human rights area. But, if one looks at the genesis of the human rights movement after the Second World War, it may need to be examined whether it was in its conception and motivation as altruistic or as devoted to the professed noble cause of human rights as it is made out to be.

In recent history, we have been witnesses to Hiroshima, Nagasaki, Vietnam, Iraq, Bosnia, Kosovo etc. One is tempted to ask the deity of human rights: "Oh god! What crimes are not committed in thy name?"

History apart, *the fundamental questions in connection with the concept of human rights today are: whose rights do we mean – of the individual or of society? Who authorises, who takes away and who protects these rights? Who determines when and what constitutes violation of Human Rights? Can the powers who themselves have been the greatest offenders against humanity and exploiters of mankind and who built their own national mansions of affluence and development with the sweat of slaves, indentured labour and colonies be now allowed to assume the role of policing the globe in the grab of protecting human rights?*

There was a time in recent past when international law was supposed to apply to the conduct of what was called the comity of "civilized" nations of the world. The colonies were inhabited by the uncivilized "natives". It was the white man's burden to civilize them. In somewhat similar vein, now in the neo-colonial age of multinationals, market economy and globalization, the developing countries are being subjected to preaching, admonitions and pressures in the name of human rights.

Obviously, western discourses on human rights promotion cannot be expected to be acceptable to us in the context of today's national and international societal conditions and objectives. The contents and contours of the 'natural' and 'unalienable' human rights need continual reappraisal and redefinition against the shifting backdrop of contemporary realities. As with development, so with human rights, the struggle is a continuing one. In the matter of human rights all countries of the world are at best at the developing stage. Even among the so-called developed countries, there is perhaps none where the human rights are not violated or subjected to various limitations. In fact, if we look round the world we find instances of blatant discrimination between human beings and violation of basic human rights. *Racial discrimination, women's inequality, growing rate of crime, unemployment and infringement of civil liberties of individuals are still affecting millions of people in some of the otherwise most advanced, affluent and developed countries of the world. The hard fact to be remembered is that the western countries started preaching lessons of human rights, rule of law, constitutionalism, civil society etc. to others after they had themselves become highly affluent and developed by flouting all these norms and concerns.*

Again as with development, so with human rights, the problem is very largely one of the distribution and equalization nationally and internationally. Sometimes, even modest plans to secure basic human rights for the people of developing countries are thwarted by international monetary and economic pressures. *National and international dadas, gangsters or terrorists use human rights as a weapon against lawfully constituted democratic governments in the third world countries. Leaders of the armaments lobby who specialize in weapons of mass destruction and causing maximum pain, misery and devastation, are in the forefront of the human rights movements.*

While the most blatant violations of human rights in 'friendly' countries with totalitarian regimes are glossed over with impunity, verbal rebuffs, propaganda and sanctions are not the only weapons against those who try to assert themselves. Big corporations acting as go-betweens and tempters attempt to "corrupt ruling groups and to destabilize from the top and subvert from below". The neo-colonialism under the garb of economic liberalization and globalization etc. takes "the shape of mercenaries, multinationals, money and maneuvers". It may be legitimately asked: "Is it fair to expect developing nations to acquiesce in its perpetrating relations of inequality and conditions of discrimination." They may have to do it under compulsions but is it indicative of respect for human rights, equality or freedom?

The only superpower left, the United States does not have the courage to criticize China or Pakistan or Saudi Arabia who hardly had a creditable record of respecting human rights. In every case, the United States is dictated by its own narrow strategic, economic and purely commercial interests and not by human rights record of the countries concerned. For example, faced with a tough competition in the area of textiles, carpets, readymade garments etc. and not being able to beat Indian goods on grounds of quality or prices, the bogey of the use of child labour was raised under the banner of human rights. It is not appreciated that some traditional arts and handicrafts in countries like India are hereditary and require long training right from childhood. In fact, it is part of their vocational education and the father's workplace is their school. *No questions are asked about the use of child labour in China, Korea, Latin American countries etc. That there are a good number of child prostitutes or sex workers – both male and female – in some of the advanced countries of the world does not seem to agitate the conscience of the international human rights activists.*

In all discussions on the subject of human rights, a climate is often sought to be created either by design or through prejudice or ignorance where under the developing countries may appear to be in the dock and on the defensive while the affluent ones can lecture them about. Conflicts arise and Human rights all over the world are, in fact, threatened by:

(i) Excessive concentration of wealth and means of production and distribution and the most extravagant *per capita* consumption pattern in the so-called advanced and developed countries of the world. According to the figures cited in the Constitution Commission Report, over the 30 years from 1960 to 1990 the affluent 20 per cent of the world was found to have enhanced its share of income and consumption to 86 per cent while the poorest 20 per cent had their share reduced to 1 per cent;

(ii) Racial discrimination, new economic imperialism and restrictive trade practices;

(iii) Overt or covert interference by some powers to dictate and determine the national policies and programmes of other countries, using nations as pawns in their global aims and for that purpose to prefer more pliable, docile, subservient and unstable military or other junta governments without popular base;

(iv) The growing and ever increasing gap between the developed countries and the poor developing countries of the world;

(v) The most affluent and powerful countries using the stick of human rights in their trade war to bar the entry into their country of more competitive goods from developing countries.

It needs to be particularly stressed that there is no conflict at all between the protection of human rights and promotion of development plans for building a 'no-poverty society' or going for 'economic liberalization with a human face'. It is wrong to suggest that in developing countries civil and political rights should take a back seat to economic and social growth. The real issue in the developing as in other countries is not of making a choice between the two sets of rights, but of finding an acceptable compromise. The situation calls for a harmonization in which all the basic human rights are accorded their rightful place for the general well-being of the community. It would be wrong to assume that the poor need only bread and the satisfaction of their economic want or that human rights are of no value to them. The poor need both food and freedom. Freedom is their birthright and food obligation of the State towards its citizens.

While the developing countries were engaged in trying to bring issues of right to development as a human right on the centre stage of international deliberations, the western powers were still perfecting their strategy of using human rights as a political, strategic, economic and diplomatic weapon in international relations. *What we witness today in not so much a concern for the rights of human beings as such under national and international law but a struggle in the pursuit of politics, economics, commerce and diplomacy behind the mask of protecting human rights.*

Fundamental human rights in India with their modern attributes and overtones are a development more or less parallel to the growth of constitutional government and parliamentary institutions from the time of British rule. The impetus for the development obviously came out of resistance to foreign rule when the British resorted to arbitrary acts such as brutal assaults on unarmed *satyagrahis,* internments, deportations etc. There was no fundamental law guaranteeing the subjects rights and liberties and they were humiliated and discriminated against in many ways, in their own country. From its earliest stages, the national struggle for freedom in its practical manifestation was largely directed against racial discrimination and to secure basic human rights for all the people. The freedom movement and the harsh repressive measures of the British rulers encouraged the fight for civil liberties and the demand for constitutional guarantees of some fundamental rights.

As far back as 1895, the Constitution of India Bill (described as the Home Rule Bill) envisaged for India a constitution guaranteeing to everyone of her citizen certain basic human rights like freedom of expression, inviolability of one's house, right to property, equality before law etc. Following the Montague Chelmsford Report in 1918, the Indian National Congress made a demand for writing into the Government of India Bill then on the anvil "a declaration of the rights of the people of India as British citizens" including therein, among other things, guarantees in regard to equality before law, protection in respect of liberty, life and property, freedom of speech and press, and rights of association.

The Commonwealth of India Bill finalized by the National Convention in 1925 embodied a specific "declaration of rights" visualizing for every person certain fundamental rights. A resolution passed at the Madras session of the Indian National Congress in 1927 reiterated that the basis of any future Constitution for the country must be a declaration of fundamental rights.

The Motilal Nehru Committee appointed in 1928 by the All Parties Conference, in its Report declared that the first concern of Indian people was to secure fundamental human rights that had been denied to them. The famous Karachi resolution of 1931 on "Fundamental Rights and Social Change" further clarified the goal and added another dimension to the demand for constitutional rights.

Representing the crystallization of the values and concepts held dear in India's varied and rich cultural heritage and having its roots deep in the motivational forces of the national struggle for independence and coming closely on the heels of the Universal Declaration of human rights, inclusion of a bill of rights in the Constitution of India accorded with the contemporary democratic and humanitarian temper and constitutional practice in other nations of the world. Also, it reflected in no small measure the anxiety of the founding fathers to incorporate and implement the basic principles enunciated in the Universal Declaration. In fact, within a year of the adoption of the Universal Declaration of Human Rights, the Assembly incorporated in the Constitution of India the substance of most of these rights. The two parts—the Fundamental Rights and the Directive Principles—of the Constitution of India between them covered almost the entire field of the Universal Declaration of Human Rights.

The Indian constitutional format in respect of human rights was remarkable as a significant and unique attempt at conflict resolution for the delicate balance it sought to achieve between political and civil rights on the one hand and social and economic rights on the other or between the individual rights and social needs. The whole scheme was based on a philosophy postulating a dialogue between individualism and social control. The Constitution makers believed in the equal importance of the two sets of rights as a cardinal tenet of their philosophy. Human Rights for them were indivisible and civil and political as well as social and economic rights had got to co-exist to make for true human happiness and lead to the fullest flowering of each human personality not only in individual but also in wider community interest.

Human rights issues having been highly emotive in India, Members of Parliament have been quick to take note of any instances of arbitrary or high handed executive interference with individual rights or violations of the liberties of citizens or operation of weaker section and have raised these issues in the Houses of Parliament. Discussions on human rights issues have contributed a great deal to keeping the administration on its toes and ensuring that any cases of blatant violation of fundamental human rights particularly of the less privileged sections of society did not go unnoticed.

Vicious and motivated propaganda is unleashed against India in the matter of human rights violations. More than eyebrows are raised in the name of child labour. Armed forces are accused of atrocities on civilians while dealing with infiltrators, terrorists and insurgents. The police are blamed for employing primitive and barbaric methods of crime investigation. While not all the accusations are entirely unfounded, everything has to be seen in perspective. First and foremost a country has to defend itself, its freedom and territorial integrity and then it has to give the highest priority to providing security and protecting the dignity of its citizens.

The very aim of terrorists is to destroy the rule of law through calculated violence against both the individual and the State. Innocent citizens are abducted, tortured, raped, killed and brutalized. Political leaders, workers and the relatives are eliminated to prevent all democratic political activity. Government officials are killed to silence the administration. Members of the judiciary and the press are intimidated to create a break down of the legal system and of independent journalism. Intellectuals, educationist, journalists and community leaders are abducted and killed to silence dissenting opinion against terrorism. The systematic religion based extremism by terrorist elements has resulted in the exodus of 250,000 members of other religious communities including Hindus, Sikhs, Buddhists and Christians from the Kashmir Valley to other parts of India. Indeed, as many as 50,000 Muslims also felt compelled to flee the Valley to seek safety and succour in other parts of India. The spectre of cross-border terrorisms threatens the survival of democratic civil society. It was imperative to bring massive pressure of world public opinion against terrorists and subversives and for not protecting them in the name of human rights. A situation cannot be allowed in which human rights are seen to be the preserve of the practitioners of terrorism while those dealing with the menace courageously, under extremely difficult circumstances are falsely condemned for violation of human rights. Human rights must not be used for sectarian ends and their genuine promotion can only be achieved if we all work together to create an environment of trust, understanding and friendship.

Let us look at the problem from another angle and face facts. We may deliver discourses in defence of human rights. But, in the context of the way our population keeps growing, the way the poor children in some parts get literally sold for a few hundred rupees, thousands of people get killed everyday in natural and man-made calamities, accidents, orgies of violence etc., and hundreds and thousands meet premature death due to reasons of undernourishment, disease and poverty, the value attached to human life in India (unless it is one's own) is very small. In any case it is nowhere like what it is for, say, an American. The yardsticks for measuring human rights violations have necessarily to be culture and country specific. Poverty has a culture of its own. When the real struggle for millions is for sheer survival, when there are no schools for miles together and there are some 110 million children in the 6-14 age group for whom society has failed to provide any schooling or non-formal education, where families live in abject poverty, somebody has to discard hypocrisy and call a spade a spade and say whether it is better for the children to die of hunger, get sold, join the force of street beggars or to do some honest work for a living, presuming that some such work opportunity is available.

The intelligentsia must be able to unmask the marauders masquerading as protectors of human rights nationally and internationally. Free thinking intellectuals with no axe to grind are expected to consider the theme without any preconceived notions in all its facets, with an open mind, freely, frankly, critically and fearlessly.

2

AWAKENING OF HUMAN RIGHTS UNDER THE ANCIENT TEXTS

RAGHUNATH PATNAIK

Human rights are those minimal rights by virtue of which one enjoys maximum natural rights against the State or any public authority. In the early period people fought against tyranny of ruling powers for which time and again rules and laws were created to bind the rulers to follow the norm. In course of time such enjoyment of right turned to become mere ideology as there were neither agreed catalogue of such rules or any machinery for their enforcement. Later people succeeded to establish the concept of human rights expressively through *Magna Carta* of 1215, Petition of Rights of 1628, Bill of Rights of 1688, American Bill of Rights of 1791 and the French Declaration of Rights of Man of 1789. In the gradual metamorphosis of social change, human rights became the milestone for seeking protection against the capricious acts of rulers.

However, in India people believed that the philosophy behind the origin of concept of human rights is not western but was considered to be as an accepted principle of Indian culture from time immemorial. In the ancient Indian civilisation during the *Vedic* period of *brahminical* society rights of individuals were recognised through higher moral values of *dharma*. It may not be out of place to mention here that the term 'Human Rights' although is of twentieth century origin, yet people in India had believed that it is as old as the history of human civilization and was known to them as 'Natural Rights' or 'Rights of Men'. Conceptually the moral values of *dharma* [righteousness], *artha* [wealth], *kama* [desire] and *moksha* [salvation] were designed to create harmonious social order by striking a balance between inner and outer as well as spiritual and material aspects of life, had an upper jurisprudential value than the positive law. Such aspect of moral value and humanitarian traditions was impelled from *Vedas, Puranas, Mahabharata, Bhagwat Gita* and other religious scriptures and aimed to free people from traces of conflicts, exploitations and miseries. Even the 'Rulers' enacted Laws in subordination to such natural tenets. It was believed that Laws must aim for helping mankind in enjoying liberty and fundamental freedom and for dignified living from omnipotent police State or dictators. The *Vedic* India practised the strong tradition that *sarve vabantu sukhinoh: sarve shantu niramayah: maa kashchit dukhah bhag vabet!* [let everyone be happy; let everyone be free from all evils; let nobody suffer from grief] and the principle that *vasudheva kutumbakam* [all are of one human family].

The Rights of Man were also found in *Rigveda* in which adequate framework for the regulation of the behaviour of the ordinary person as well as the Sovereign are found. It prescribed two principles known as *dharma* and *danda*. The social responsibility of the King was fixed to perform a supreme duty of protecting his subjects from disorder and anarchy and he was very much subordinated to the law unlike his subjects. The *Rigveda* also envisages three Civil Rights viz. *Tana* [Body], *Skridhi* [dwelling place] and *Jibhasi* [Life]. The *Arthasastra* prescribed certain economic rights and ordained that the King shall provide maintenance to the orphan, the aged, the infirm, the affected, the helpless, afflicted expectant mother and children. It was also the duty of the State to support education and other welfare of its subjects.[1]

The ancient Indian concept of Human Rights and the Humanitarian Laws were based on war regulations and were adopted either before, during or after the war.[2] For example, the warfare was based on the principle of equation of armed units, such as army consisting of elephants, horses, chariots or footmen were combating with opposing like category. Even in use of destructive weapons principle of parity was followed, for instance, Lakshmana in *Ramayana* and Arjuna did not use *Brahmastra* and *Pashupatastra* to avoid indiscriminate destruction of innocent lives. Manudhrama prescribed that places of religious worship and individual houses not participating in war were ousted from targets of warfare. So also persons who are sleeping, not in possession of war weapons or armour or is fighting with another person were not to be slanted.[3] During those days war was considered to be *dharmayudha* as in *Mahabharata* the enemies never killed the sick nor the wounded but were captured and treated as prisoners of war and as subjects of their own.[4]

The humanitarian ideas were quite popular in India and were seen in the form of abolition of Slavery in 1811, abolition of *Sati* in 1829, abolition of Infanticide in 1830, establishment of Torture Commission in Madras Presidency in 1855, introduction of Widow Remarriage in 1856 and Prohibition of Child Marriage in 1929.[5] Even Mahatma Gandhi dreamt about establishing a *Rama Rajya* in India in which he emphasised for social and economic justice for all and for ensuring dignity for men.[6]

Distortion of Human Rights

With the invasion of *Aryans* the history and civilisation of indigenous people in India began to distort the ideas of rights and responsibilities. Gradually victory and enslavement won by force or fraud were justified and selective human killing were based on the principle of might is right. Gradually the doctrine of *karma* [work] and the theory of transmigration of soul were cunningly formulated to perpetuate inequality. People become victim of orthodox contradictions and caste and religious acts which were beyond the limits of the civil society and became sacrosanct to them.[7] In those days, one of the intriguing feature was that the violator of the human rights remained invisible as there was no evidence to nab him or such acts were believed to be based on religious prejudices for which there was social acceptance. During the Buddha period caste system was rejected by the Buddha followers and they practised non-violence, non-hatred and friendliness of all.[8] During that time secular education was introduced so that people from all walks could learn universal freedom and tolerance. Later some non-*Vedic* sect saints like *Nath, Yoga, Alvar* [Tamil saint],[9] *Siddhakara; Sufi* saints like Kabir, Tulasidas, Tukaram and *Baul* saints of Bengal like Jaidev, Chaitanya became prominent in propagating *bhakti* [the path of devotion] movement,[10] the spirit of mutual understanding, tolerance, co-operation and human equality.

Conclusion

Achieving and preserving human rights in a movement of a vital right from the ancient period and should be continued despite opposition from self-serving individuals or governments. The prophetic voice in this regard is awakening of the mind to change the attitude and conduct of individuals towards other fellow individuals. The pursuit of human right activities must aim to provide a patina of decency by pre-empting disparities in defence of preserving human rights. It is considered that education is the only single most factor for awakening the people for implementing beneficial changes in the society and more so in the field of quality of life one leads in that society. Therefore, innovative methodologies are required to be implemented so as to provide culturally relevant literature to preserve and protect individual human rights. The importance of such education is not just the knowledge but as the method of applying the same in practical life to subserve the purpose.

References

1. Manu; Quoted from Dhayani; S.N., *Fundamentals of Jurisprudence – The Indian Approach,* Edn. 1992 at p. 45.
2. Code of Manu [200 BC to AD 100]; *Mahabharat* [1000 BC]; Kautilya's *Arthasastra* [300 BC] and Sukracharya's *Sukranitisar.*
3. *Encyclopaedia of Social Work in India,* Vol. II [Government of India Publications Division], New Delhi, Edn. 1987, pp. 90-95.
4. *Purananuru* [Tamil] Song 9 [Commercial Printings], Madras, Edn.

1923 at p. 23. Following the principles, Chandragupta Mourya set free prisoners captured in war; See, R. Shamsastry, *Kautilya's Arthasastra* [Mysore Printing and Publishing] Mysore, 1967 at p. 168.

5. B.S. Baliga, *Studies in Madras Administration,* Vol. 1 [Government of Madras] Edn. 1960, pp. 258-261.
6. M. Sundara Raj, *Awakening of Human Rights,* [Oxford University Press] Edn. 2000, at p. 18.
7. Hindu Caste System in the context of Human Rights had undergone strides for stratification of society; *Mahabharata – Santi Parva,* quoted from K.M. Sen, *Hinduism* [Penguin] Edn. 1961.
8. Emperor Ashoka not only followed but also preached non-violent humanitarian and humanist values of Buddhist philosophy.
9. S.N. Dasgupta, *A History of Indian Philosophy,* Vol. III, Edn. 1940.
10. Prof. Satish Chandra, *Cultural Interaction in South Asia,* Hamdard Institute of Historical Research, New Delhi, Edn. 1993 at p. 103.

GENESIS OF HUMAN RIGHTS IN INDIA

SUNIL DESHTA AND LALIT DADWAL

Introduction

Human beings are rational beings. They by virtue of their being human possess certain basic and inalienable rights, which are commonly known as human rights. These rights of human beings are not derived from being a national of certain State, but belong to them because of their very existence and are based upon the attributes of human personality. They are derived from the inherent dignity and worth of human being. As rightly observed by Jacques Maritain,[1] "The human person possesses rights because of the very fact that it is a person, a whole, master of itself and of its acts, and which consequently is not merely a means to an end, but an end, which must be treated as such." The expression 'dignity of the human person' means nothing if it does not signify that the human person has the right to be respected, is the subject of rights, possesses rights. To have human rights, one need not do anything special than be born a human being.

They are based upon the belief that all persons are born free and with equal dignity. Being the birthrights, these are inherent in all the individuals irrespective of their caste, creed, religion, sex and nationality.[2] Human rights and fundamental freedoms allow us to develop fully and use our human qualities, our intelligence, our talents and our conscience and to satisfy our spiritual and other needs. They are the sum total of the opportunities which ensure adequate development and expression of individual personality. Without such opportunities man cannot lead a decent life.

Evolution of Human Rights in India

The concept of human rights as it is understood today has evolved over the centuries. Though the expression "Human Rights" seems to have modern face, human rights are as old as human civilization. Human rights have existed, in however, nascent a form, ever since man, as a gregarious animal, has lived in communities, families, clan, tribe, village, town or nation and now in an independent world community.[3] Looking at the concept of human rights from a historical perspective, it would be seen that it is neither entirely western in origin nor so modern. It is the crystallization of values that are the common heritage of mankind.

While introducing the concept of human rights, a well known scholar says,[4] "human rights is twentieth century name for what has been traditionally known as Natural rights or, in a more exhilarating phrase, the rights of man." Woven into the wrap and woof of human history, the concept of human rights has a variable and dynamic one. It has in fact varied from generation to generation and evolved with the changing times and under the constantly shifting conditions. The concept of human rights or natural rights was not unknown to ancient thinkers. The rights of man have been the concern of all civil societies from time immemorial but that is different thing that they were not recognized by the specific name, 'Human Rights'. They had a place in almost all the ancient civilizations of the world.

Human Rights in Ancient India

The concept of human rights is not alien to the Indian political thinkers and philosophers. They have expressed concern to secure human rights and fundamental freedoms for all human beings everywhere since the very early times of *Vedic* age.[5] Philosophy of human rights had already occupied a place of prime importance in ancient Indian Brahmanical society. The Indian thinkers are of the view that it is not justified to limit the origin of the concept of human rights to only western civilization. What the west has discovered today in the field of human rights has been an accepted principle of India's rich legacy of historical tradition and culture since time immemorial,[6] which is evidenced by the declarations made in the Vedas. The relevant declarations are:

> *Ajyestaso akanishtas ete*
> *Sam Bhrataro va vridhuhu sowbhagaya*[7]
> *Samani prapa saha vaha ann abhagaha*
> *Same yoktre saha vaha yunajmi*
> *Araha habhimiva Abhitaha.*[8]

These *Vedic* provisions forcefully declare equality among human beings. The last of them impress that just as no spoke of a wheel is superior to other, no individual can claim to be, or regarded as, superior to others. Equality of all human beings and the duty of each individual to strive for the happiness of every other individual as also the equal right over food, water and other natural resources are found incorporated in these declarations.[9]

In ancient India, Law, which was structured on the philosophy of *dharma,* did not have much scope for religious discrimination. We learn from the *Mahabharata* that *dharma* was ordained for the advancement of all creatures as well as for restraining creatures from injuring one another.[10] In the *Bhagavad Gita* righteousness has been described as the essence of *dharma*. The *Upanishads* speak of *dharma* as the foundation of the whole universe, through it one drives away evil.[11] In the *Vedic* era, king or monarch was not above law and on violation; he could be punished like any other citizen. The *Vedas* and *Smritis* have spoken highly of equality of brotherhood e.g. *vasudeiva kutumbakam* (the whole world as one family).

The modern utopia of a global village is more or less akin to this concept.[12] It is quite interesting to pinpoint here that the immoral epics, *Vedas, Ramayana* and *Mahabharata* demonstrate the deep commitment and faith of our sages towards justice. All the four *Vedas* insist on equality and respect for human dignity.[13]

In the whole eighteen *Puranas,* Vyasa has said two things: doing good to another is right, causing injury to another is wrong.[14] The references with regard to equality can be in *Vedas* to the effect that *'Ajeyeshthaso ak nisthas yetsa bhraterona sobhagaaya'*[15] which means 'no one is superior or inferior. All are brothers; all should strive for the interest of all and should progress collectively'. Manu says, "the king should protect and support all his subjects without any discrimination in the same manner as the earth supports all living beings."

Whether it is *Mahabharata* or *Arthashastra* or Manu *Dharmashastra* or *Narada,* there is great emphasis on the institution of kingship and *Rajdharma* in order to escape from political disorder, social chaos and injustice. Kings were required to take a pledge never to be arbitrary and always to act according to "whatever law there is and whatever is dictated by ethics and not opposed to politics".[16]

There was, however, a downfall of human rights jurisprudence in post-*Vedic* age. But with the rise of Buddhism and Jainism there was a revival of human rights jurisprudence. Influenced by the teachings of Buddha, Ashoka worked extensively for the protection of human rights. His chief concern was the happiness of his subjects. Torture and inhuman treatment of prisoners were prohibited under Ashoka's administration.[17] Ashoka had been successful in the establishment of a welfare State and basic freedoms were available to people. King used to dispense justice to the people. The study of *Mudra Rakshas*[18] shows that dispensation of justice was considered as one of the important duties of the rulers.[19]

Hence, it is abundantly clear that ancient Indian jurisprudence stood for enlarging and encouraging human freedom, liberty and equality for all people. It has developed common ideals based on human unity and harmony which transcends diversities of race, colour, language, religion, etc.[20]

Human Rights in Medieval India

During Muslim era in India, especially in the pre-Mughal period, there were series of cultural, social and political stressed and strain on the style and way of life of Hindus. The Muslim rulers in India were fundamentalist and despotic who forced upon the Hindus their own laws, customs and religious practices. Hindus were not treated in law on par with the Muslims—the latter being the conquerors and the former being the *Kafirs*—the non-believers of Islam, special disabilities like *jazia*, were imposed on Hindus. Both in theory and practice, there was discrimination against Hindus *vis-à-vis* Muslims.[21] Muslim rule in India was not founded on the basic principles of human dignity, equality and justice, and was essentially autocratic, theocratic and irresponsible, devoid of the idea of rule of law, morality, justice, tolerance and social harmony.[22] So the significance of Muslim rule in India from the point of view of human rights was counter productive to harmony, justice and equality and the concept of human rights got lost on its way in the dark and narrow alleys of the middle ages.[23] It was, however, at a later stage that muslim State in India became considerably modified in its form.

Some of the Moghul rulers, especially Akbar the great brought about a basic change in the style of Moghul administration. He adopted a policy of tolerance and non-discrimination towards Hindus and saw that no injustice is committed in his realm. Hence, it is not wrong to say that, with Akbar a new era begin in Moghul History of India in the field of human rights with his policy of universal reconciliation and tolerance.[24] His policy of tolerance and non-discrimination towards Hindus was followed by his son Jahangir too.

During the reign of Aurangazeb, the concept justice was made less intricate and more expeditious than in the former reigns. Corruption in judiciary was made a crime for the first time. If delay in justice resulted in loss to a party, the aggrieved party could be compensated by the judge himself.[25]

The right of an accused to be released on bail did exist during Mughal rule in India.[26] Similarly the right to benefit of doubt was known to Muslim jurisprudence in the administration of criminal justice. The benefit of doubt was known as *shuba* (doubt) which entitled an accused to be acquitted.[27]

It cannot, however, be denied that the Aurangazeb was the most cruel, fanatic and despotic ruler. He made earnest efforts to convert Kashmiri Pandits to Islam with the use of his governmental machinery. The ninth Sikh Guru Teg Bahadur had to sacrifice his life, and in 1675 A.D. Guru Gobind Singh (Tenth Sikh Guru) had to sacrifice his four sons in fighting against injustice and repression to save Hindus from conversion. Finally, the *Bhakti* movement evolved in later periods ultimately revived and regenerated the old Indian values of truth, righteousness, justice and morality.[28]

The inalienable, immutable and everlasting natural law found its exponent in the great saints like, Sankara, Ramanuja, Madhava, Tulsidas, Kabir, Nanak, Swami Ram Krishna, Swami Dayananda Saraswati, Raja Ram Mohan Roy and others who reinterpret the *Vedic Dharma* to re-establish the supremacy of Indian *Vedic* values over alien ideals and philosophy.[29] The philosophy of these social reformers and leaders was nothing but a reinstatement of natural law with religious fervour to enthuse people towards the path of *Dharma,* enlightenment and unity at a time when Hindu society was dominated and divided by foreigners.[30]

The cult of Sufism prevalent in medieval India spread the message of secularism by the symbiotic synthesis of the core values of different religions to bind the pluralist society. Saints and holy persons propagated the message of the Sufi saints to emphasise that the difference between human beings is man-made, all being born equal.[31]

It may be recalled that from time immemorial Indians have called their culture by the name of 'human culture' (*Manav Dharam/Manav Samriti*). No gain saying the fact that human dignity had universal appeal and Indian culture had tried to be so comprehensive as to suit the needs of every human being, irrespective of age, colour, sex or caste.[32]

Human Rights in Modern India

The transition from the medieval to modern period has resulted in a prodigious change in the Indian history. With the advent of British rule in India, a new era started which created ripples in the political and legal spheres leading to imposition of British political and legal culture on India. The British Government in India had not only deprived the Indian people of their freedom but had based itself on the exploitation of the masses, and ruined India economically, politically, culturally and spiritually. Resistance to this four-fold disaster was manifested in the form of demand for fundamental freedoms and civil and political rights for the people.[33]

The British Indian rulers discriminated against Indians in matters of their political and civil liberties and rights. They resorted to arbitrary acts such as brutal assaults on unarmed *satyagrahis,* internments, deportation etc., against Indians fighting for national independence, equal justice and economic equality.[34] After witnessing the colonial rule, every Indian was of the firm opinion that the recognition, protection and implementation of human rights are not only basic but also inalienable for them for leading a civilized life. It is, however, after the national struggle for freedom that a concrete movement for claiming the human rights for the people of India took shape in which people from different walks of life joined together to achieve *swaraj* (independence) for themselves.

Raja Ram Mohan Roy (1772-1823), one of the greatest rationalist and creative thinkers of his age led India in the earliest period for her transformation from feudalism to modernity. His rational mind made him a poignant critique of those religious rituals of Hinduism like, *Sati* and Child marriage, which patronised and promoted societal violence against women in the name of religion. His opposition of polygamy, and his advocacy for equal rights of women including the right of widows to marry and right of women to property also came from his firm belief in the supremacy of reason.[35] In this context, it would not be out of place to mention that, for his catalytic thoughts and actions, Ram Mohan can reasonably be regarded as the founding father of human rights movement in modern India.

To revive the philosophy of human rights in modern sense, concerted efforts were made by the Indian National Congress, which demanded basic human rights in the Constitution of India Bill, 1895. Constant resistance to the foreign rule manifested in the form of demand for fundamental freedoms, civil and political rights for the people. The rights like freedom of expression, right to property, equality before law and inviolability of one's own home, figured in this Bill. Congress as early as in 1918 in Bombay session demanded declaration of rights of people of India and again demand of these basic rights were reiterated in Nehru Committee Report in 1928. The Congress in the resolutions of 1917 and 1919 asserted demand of civil rights and equal status with the English men. In 1922, Congress aimed at achieving *swaraj* to shape dignity of the country. The Sapru Report (1945) incorporating the proposals of fundamental rights did not find favour. Simultaneously, the freedom struggle had reached its climax and demand for independence gained momentum. In a landmark development, the British Cabinet Mission in 1946 recognised the need for a written guarantee of fundamental rights in the Constitution of India and envisaged a Constituent Assembly for framing the Constitution of India.

The Constituent Assembly pledged to draw Constitution for the country wherein shall be guaranteed and secured for the people of India justice: social, economic and political, equality of status and of opportunity before the law; freedom of thought, expression, belief, faith and worship, vocation, association and action, subject to law and public morality.[36]

India got independence on 15th August, 1947. The Constituent Assembly accomplished the Herculean task of drafting the Constitution, which was enacted and adopted by the people of India on 26th January, 1950. The genesis of the vision, need, recognition, protection and enforcement of human rights which lies in the freedom struggle of Indians for more than a century culminated in the form of fundamental rights and Directive Principles of State policy on which the mammoth structure of Indian Republic stands today.

The aspirations of people of India found expression in the Indian Constitution, which enacted a nearly complete catalogue of human rights around the time when the international scene was witnessing the framing of Universal Declaration of Human Rights. The human rights content of the Indian Constitution is a complex amalgam of civil and political rights along with economic, social, religious and minority rights.

The Preamble, Fundamental Rights,[37] Directive Principles of State Policy,[38] newly added Fundamental Duties[39], reservation for scheduled castes and tribes, special provisions for Anglo-Indians and other backward classes,[40] are important constitutional provisions from the human rights point of view. Now, the concept of human rights is no longer a philosophical conception, it has become a functional reality. The study of human rights with reference to Indian Constitution reveals that the Constitution enshrines almost all the human rights provided in the various international conventions, covenants and treaties, such as Universal Declaration of Human Rights, 1948, the International Covenant on Economic, Social and Cultural Rights, 1966. etc. It is pertinent to mention here that our constitutional makers, having incorporated a long list of fundamental rights, have also provided effective remedies for the enforcement of these rights. Articles 32 and 226 have adequate provisions for the enforcement of fundamental as well as other legal rights of the individuals through judicial means. These articles are the novel provisions in the Constitution of India and have no provisions in the Constitution of any other country.

Apart from the aforesaid constitutional provisions, various statutes have also been enacted by the Indian legislature with a view to protect and promote human rights. These legislations seek to protect different aspect of human rights. Some of the important legislations enacted by the Union are, Protection of Human Rights Act, 1993; National Commission for Minorities Act, 1992, National Commission for Women Act, 1990; Protection of Civil Rights Act, 1955; Scheduled Castes and Scheduled Tribes (Prevention of Atrocities), Act 1989; Immoral Traffic (Prevention) Act, 1987; Bonded Labour System

(Abolition) Act, 1976; Juvenile Justice (Care and Protection of Children) Act, 2000; Child Labour (Prohibition and Regulation) Act, 1986, etc. India has also adopted a number of legislative measures for the social security of the labour, which have been greatly influenced by ILO's standards.

When there is any discussion on human rights in the country, the role of judiciary in giving a concrete shape to these rights through its activism cannot be ignored. The enforcement of human rights by the judiciary has now become an integral part of our jurisprudence. By virtue of Articles 32 and 226, the Courts have greatly extended the ambit of judicial review and devised new methods and strategies by opening the doors of justice to the poor and downtrodden through public interest litigation (PIL). Under the emerging and expanding concept of PIL, the traditional rule of *locus standi* that a petition under Article 32 can only be filed by a person whose fundamental right is infringed, has now been considerably relaxed. In a number of cases the Supreme Court has used Public Interest Litigation as a prime tool to build up its own jurisprudence, a jurisprudence with social relevance compelling the governments and other instrumentalities to discharge their constitutional duties of protecting the poor, downtrodden, exploited and victimized categories of people including, prisoners, under trials, workers, bonded labourers, women and children against social and economic injustices and ensuring realization of basic human rights. It can fairly be concluded that judiciary in India through the innovation of Public Interest Litigation or Social Action Litigation has broadened the concept of social justice and has gone much ahead in structuring, expanding, protecting and promoting the human rights.[41] By putting strenuous efforts the courts are trying to translate the constitutional philosophy of human rights jurisprudence into reality. The judiciary has been rendering judgments which are in tune and temper with legislative intent while keeping pace with time and jealously protecting and developing the dimensions of fundamental human rights of the citizen so as to make them meaningful and realistic.[42]

By giving a liberal and comprehensive meaning to 'life and personal liberty' the courts have formulated and established a plethora of rights, such as right to privacy; right to travel abroad; right to livelihood; right to shelter; right to live in; pollution-free environment; right to medical care; right to education; right to live with human dignity; right to speedy trial; right to education; right to live with human dignity; right to speedy trial; right to free legal aid; right against inhuman, cruel and degrading treatment; right against solitary confinement; right against handcuffing, bar-fetter; right to compensation etc.

This latest judicial trend reveals that Indian Courts are quite enthusiastic in using the law as a tool of social revolution. What is being realized is that the process of social change through law involves not only the legislature but courts also interact and reach through interpretative device. That is why judiciary is expected to act as a catalytic agent of social control and hammer out human rights jurisprudence in the light of the philosophy envisaged by the Constitution.

References

1. Jacques Maritain, The Rights of Man, quoted in Maurice Cranston, *What are Human Rights?* (1962), p. 6.
2. Nagendra Singh, Human Rights in Changing World, (1st edn.), p. 85.
3. R.P. Dhokalia, Human Rights as objects of Thought and Expression of Global Conscience, *Banaras Law Journal*, Jan-Dec., 1992, Vol. 26, Nos. 1 & 2, p. 5.
4. Maurice Cranston, *What are Human Rights?* (1962), p. 1.
5. S.C. Khare, Human Rights and United Nations, (1978), p. 193.
6. Furqan Ahmad, "Human Rights and Developing Nations : Provisions, Problems and Perspectives", in Prof. Z.A. Nizami and Devika Paul (ed.), *Human Rights in Third World Countries* (1994), p. 107.
7. No one is superior (*ajyesaso*) or inferior (*akanishtasha*). All are brethren (*bhrataraha*). All should strive for the interest of all and should progress collectively (*Sowbhagayanam va varidhulu*). *Rig Veda–* Mandala 5, Sukta - 60, Mantra - 5, cited in inaugural address of Justice M. Ramajois, in Judicial Colloquium in Bangalore, 24-26 Feb., 1998.

8. All have equal rights in articles of food and water. The yoke of the chariot of life is placed equally on the shoulders of all. All should live together with harmony supporting one another like the spokes of a wheel of the chariot connecting its rim and the hub. *Atharvaveda – Samjuana Sukta,* cited in inaugural address of Justice M.Ramajois, in Judicial Colloquium in Bangalore, 24-26 Feb., 1998.
9. *Ibid.*
10. Dhirendra K. Srivastava, *Religious Freedom in India,* (1983), p. 25.
11. A.S. Altekar, *State and Government in Ancient India,* (1985), p. 51.
12. Prabha Chawala, *Equality and Justice in East and West,* (1980), p. 85.
13. S.N. Dhyani, *Law, Morality and Justice,* (1984), p. 87.
14. *Ibid.*
15. *Rigveda,* Mandala-5, Sukta-60, Mantra –5. cited in inaugural address of Justice M. Ramajois, in judicial Colloquium, in Bangalore, 24-26 Feb., 1998, p. XVI.
16. Subhash C. Kashyap, *Human Rights and Parliament,* (1978), p. 19.
17. Nagendra Singh, *India and International Law,* 1969, p. 10. also see, Paramjit Jaswal and Nishtha Jaswal, *Human Rights and the Law,* (1996), p. 5.
18. *Mudra-Rakshas* was written by Vaishaka Dutta who was contemporary of Chandra Gupta.
19. E.J. Rapson, *The Cambridge History of India,* (1921), vol. 1, p. 436.
20. *Supra* note 12, pp. 3-4
21. S.M. Maqbul Ahmed, *Islam and Medieval and Modern Societies,* (1965), Vol. I, pp. 394-398.
22. Asaf, A.A. Fyzee, *A Modern Approach to Islam,* (1981), p. 29.
23. S.N. Dhyani, *Fundamentals of Jurisprudence: The Indian Approach,* (1997), p. 43.
24. *Ibid.,* p. 259.
25. J.N. Sarkar, *Mughal Administration,* 1920, p. 107.
26. Martin Ennals, "The Struggle for Human Rights", in A.R.Desai (ed.), *Violation of Democratic Rights in India,* (1986), vol. I, p. 37.
27. *Ibid.*
28. P.L. Mehta and Neena Verma, *Human Rights Under Indian Constitution,* (1999), p. 18.
29. *Supra* note 24, p. 98.
30. *Ibid.*
31. J.S. Verma, "The Spirit of the Indian Constitution" in *New Dimensions of Justice,* 2000, p. 143.

32. Sanjay Joshi, "The Right to Equality, Life and Liberty Under the Constitutional Law of India" in Abdulrahim P.Vijapur (ed.), *Perspective of Human Rights,* (1999), p. 83.
33. S. Subramanian, *Human Rights : International Challenges,* (1997), p. 122.
34. *Supra* note 24, p. 101.
35. Jaytilak Guha Roy, "Human Rights Movement in Modern India" in Abdulrahim P.Vijapur (ed.), *Perspective of Human Rights,* (1996), p. 83.
36. C.A.D., Vol. II, p. 296.
37. Fundamental Rights are - (1) Right to Equality (Articles 14-18); (2) Right to Freedom (Articles 19-22); (3) Right against Exploitation (Articles 23-24); (4) Right to Freedom of Religion (Articles 25-28); (5) Cultural and Educational Rights (Articles 29,30); (6) Right to Constitutional Remedies (Article 32).
38. Articles 36 to 51
39. Articles 51-A
40. Articles 330 -342.
41. Ajay Kumar Singh, "Role of Judiciary in the Promotion and Protection of Human Rights" in Abdulrahim P. Vijapur (ed.), *Perspectives on Human Rights,* (1999), p. 79.
42. A.S. Anand, " Judicial Review—Judicial Activism Need for Caution", *J.I.L.I.,* Vol. 42, (2000), p. 157.

4

FREEDOM MOVEMENT IN INDIA
A HUMAN RIGHTS PERSPECTIVE

B. KRISHNAMURTHY

The State which has come into being as the protector and promoter of the welfare of its subjects, paradoxically has in many a case turned out to be major violator of the human rights of its own subjects. In such a situation, it becomes inevitable for the subjects to rise in revolt against the 'State' and the 'government' of the day, to put an end to those violations and to restore and regain their lost rights. From this angle, the freedom struggle in India against the colonial domination of the British and other European powers, can be termed as an effort to restore the human rights of the Indian people, which were being violated systematically by those European colonial masters. An attempt is being made in the following pages to study and analyze, how the British colonial rule deprived the Indians of their rights and the way in which the leaders of the freedom movement tried to recover and regain these rights to the general Indian public.

The British came to India as traders, but, capitalizing on the disunity and struggle for power among the Indian rulers and potentates, succeeded in securing several parts of the Indian sub-continent under their control. At the initial stages, there territories were ruled by the Governor General, who was the representative of the British East India Company in India and later by the Viceroys, who represented the British Crown.

The process of the centralization of the Indian administration and judiciary started with the introduction of Regulating Act of 1773 and continued for 85 long years. This followed by 89 years of decentralization (1858-1947). This resulted in 174 years of systematic and atrocious suppression and oppression of human rights of the Indian subjects, who were actually suffocated under these processes and procedures.

The most notable point of the Indian political scenario under the British rule was that the decision making power had been shifted to London, four thousand miles away from the Indian soil. As a result, the Indians had lost their political decision making rights and were reduced to the status of second-class citizens in their own land. The British never hesitated to project themselves as rulers and to designate and discriminate the Indians as the ruled. Higher positions in the government, administration and the army were reserved for the English people and the Indians were recruited only to the low positions like clerks, interpreters and sepoys. At a later stage, this has created a severe heart burning among the English-educated Indian elite. It was quite natural that the Indians boycotted the Simon Commission, which was appointed to go to India to make an on-the-spot evaluation of the progress attained under the Government of India Act of 1919, since no Indian was included in such a process.[1]

The British never bothered about the Indian customs and traditions and denied the native rulers their right to adopt a male child, in case they were having no male issues. They adopted the 'doctrine of lapse', through which they tried to annex the territories of those rulers, who died without legal heirs. Again, they never cared about the Indian sentiments, while taking decisions like the partition of Bengal (1905), which they tried to justify on the basis of administrative convenience.[2] Moreover, the British involved India into wars, which they waged with the other powers, to achieve their national interests and imperialistic goals.

The trading company, which was elevated to the status of the rulers of India, conducted its business of administering the country with profit motive and this system of economic exploitation was unashamedly followed by the royal representatives as well. The British sincerely believed in the concept of 'eminent domain', which ensures the authority, power and sovereignty of the 'State' over the resources within its boundary and extended it to their Indian colonies, thereby pronouncing that all the Indian resources were vested with the British colonial masters. Economic policies, which were beneficial to England were thrust upon the Indians, which cost them dearly. 'Colonies for the colonial masters' was the motto and guiding principle of the British colonial policy.

As mentioned earlier, India was involved in the imperialistic wars with the Eastern powers, which were funded by the Indian exchequer. The wealth of India was systematically drained and funnelled out of India to Britain. The Indian agriculture and handicraft as well as household industries were deliberately suppressed. *Rayatwari* and *Jamindari* systems were introduced which served the interests of local bigwigs and worked against the well-being of peasants and poor people. The Indians were required to grow cash crops like cotton and indigo, which were in demand for the English industries as raw materials. This had seriously affected the native food production and resulted in periodical occurrence of famines and food shortages.

The Indians, who were known for their transoceanic commercial contacts with different parts of the world, were reduced to the status of agents and junior partners of the British commercial enterprises in the East. Their once-thriving shipping industry was crippled by putting and imposing several hindrances. Heavy taxes were imposed upon the Indian products so that they could not compete with the British manufactured goods. The British monopolized the Indian markets and flooded them with cheap, machine-made goods from home.[3] Every sector of production suffered due to the British greed.

In the socio-cultural spheres also the rights of the Indians were severely and severally violated. Racialism and the feeling of racial superiority of the colonial masters manifested in the restrictions they have imposed on the native population.

Reserved clubs and promenades were very much rampant in cities like Calcutta and Delhi, into which natives were not allowed. Such was the case of high-class compartments in the Indian Railways. For the same offence, the Whites were punished with leniency, while the punishments meted out to the natives were quite severe. Again, for the same nature of work, the Whites were paid more and the locals had to be satisfied with lesser wages. All these go to prove that racial discrimination was rampant under the British colonial rule.

Moreover, the native religion was ridiculed and the Indians were denoted as 'copper-coloured pagans'. Their religious practices and rituals were looked down upon. The State encouraged the conversion activities of the Christian missionaries and patronized their activities through offering favours to the converts in the government's services.

Again, the culture and literature of the Indians were ridiculed by the colonial masters. Lord Macaulay, who introduced the English education in India, is reported to have said that entire literature in the Sanskrit language could not measure up to a single page of English literature. The natives were regarded as uncivilized barbarians.

Thus, the British colonial masters have ridden roughshod over the Indian political, economic and socio-cultural rights in all spheres of life. They later were told that they did not deserve self-rule and that the British rule was a blessing-in-disguise for them. India was bleed white by the colonial leaches. Basic rights such as right to life and livelihood, right to equality, right to expression and association were denied to them. The religious freedom, right to belief and the right to practice their own religion of the natives were severely restricted and impinged upon by the colonial State.

II

In such an atmosphere, the leaders and people of India, who were well-aware of the loss of their human rights in the hands of the colonial masters, decided to take up on the alien rulers and were determined to secure back their rights. At the earlier stage, the Indian National Congress, which was established in

1885, worked as a petitioning body. They had high belief in the justice and sense of fair play of the British and through memoranda and petitions they tried to bring to the knowledge of the rulers, the sad plight of the Indians and sought remedial measures. However, very soon, they have realized that their belief on the English Gentlemen was wrongly placed.

Next stage came when the Extremist elements in the Congress such as Bal Gangadhar Tilak clamoured: "*Swaraj* (self rule) is my birth right and I shall have it". This was followed by a short stretch of militant nationalism during which some brave sons and daughters of our land, made a valiant effort to drive the colonial masters away from India through inflicting a sense of fear in their hearts.

The entry of Gandhiji into the liberation movement has electrified it. Indeed, he transformed the elite movement, which it was although, into a mass movement. Several new faces entered into the Indian political scenario such as Jawaharlal Nehru. These leaders clamoured for *'Purna Swaraj'* and for the introduction and implementation of the rights of the individuals. Annie Besant's treatise on 'Home Rule' movement and Motilal Nehru Report of 1927, listed certain rights that were to be conferred upon the Indian subjects by the British colonial masters. As such, the leadership of the Indian freedom struggle was attuned to the human rights dispensations and shortcomings of the alien rule and they followed several strategies to achieve their goal of recovering the due rights of the people. As they felt quite rightly that the British could not perpetuate their anti-people regime without the active support and participation of some among the Indians themselves, they initiated Civil Disobedience as well as Non-Cooperation movements.

As the revenues from the Indian empire was misused or not used properly on the agricultural and industrial growth and public welfare of the Indians, the leaders have advocated No-Tax Campaign, as an instrument of showing and demonstrating their disapproval of the Government. Gandhiji considered Salt Tax as the "most inhuman toll tax that ingenuity of man can devise", as it hit the poor hard and determined to violate the oppressive Salt laws through his 'Salt *Satyagraha*' programme in 1930.[4] Initially, the colonial masters have failed to understand the significance and future implications and impacts of his famous 'Dandi March'. Actually, by demonstrating his right to produce salt, Gandhiji had thrown the gauntlet in front of the British and their self-proclaimed sovereignty over India, since production of salt is being considered, as one of the sovereign rights of the 'State'. The earlier indifference of the British that "the Mahatma could go on boiling sea-water till Dominion status was attained" soon changed into nervous apprehensions.

The leaders of the Indian freedom movement looked up on the British imperialism as an economic venture and determined to strike it down with the weapons of 'boycott' and collective public burning of foreign goods, especially the mill-made textiles. On the other hand, they encouraged the use of *Swadeshi* (home made) articles and especially the *Khaddar* (hand-spun cloth). The 'spirit of *swadeshi*' and its goal were very clearly brought out by Lala Lajpat Rai when he said: "The logic of losing business is more likely to impress this nation of shopkeepers than any argument based on the ethics of justice."[5] While the British harped on theme of 'legacy' of British rule in India, Lalaji in his famous book *What England owes to India?*, argued that the industrial revolution in England owed its success to the raw materials and flow of wealth from India.

Again, in their effort to deprive the British of the profits of the shipping industry, the leaders like V.O. Chidambaram Pillai of Tamil Nadu established 'Swadeshi Steam Navigation Company', in their effort to compete with the English ship-owners and to relieve the native merchants from their clutches.

The greatness of the leaders of the freedom movement lies in the fact that while fighting for the restoration of rights of the people, they have simultaneously fought against the social evils of the day, which had kept various sections of the society weak and vulnerable. Leaders like Gandhiji and Ambedkar tirelessly worked against untouchability and for the well-being of the socially and economically downtrodden people. They strived for the introduction of prohibition of the production, sale and consumption of liquor or *arrack,* which was the root cause of the economic deterioration of several thousands of households. They raised their voice against the social evils perpetuated by the religion and the age-old tradition on women and other vulnerable sections of the society and worked ceaselessly for their upliftment. In short, the leaders of the freedom tried to attain and achieve *sarvodaya*—the welfare of all—of every individual as a unit in the masses.[6]

III

The colonial masters tried to suppress the freedom movement with an iron hand and in the process the human rights of the Indians were violated in the most cruel and inhuman ways. The leaders and active participants were put behind bars for unduely long period and under inhuman and blood-cuddling atmosphere.[7] Bal Gangadhar Tilak was accused of sedition for his writings on *Kesari* and *Maratha* and was deported to Mandley. The jail sentence and its hardships had actually crippled his health and spirits. Lala Lajpat Rai, yet another towering personality breathed his last due to the lathi-blows he suffered, when he led the masses during the boycott of Simon Commission. Thousands of leaders and their followers were sent to *Kalapani* or the cellular jail in the Andaman islands, where they had to undergo untold sufferings.

The case of V.O. Chidambaram Pillai, who, as mentioned earlier, started the Swadeshi Steam Navigation Company and thereby challenged the monopoly of the British ship-owners in the Eastern waters, was more horrific. During his imprisonment, he was made to pull the oil-pressing machine, in which usually cattle are used.

The people were denied of their freedom of expression, freedom of association, right to religion and other such fundamental freedoms. On April 13, 1919, the British army officer O'Dyer fired upon people who congregated in the Jalianwala Bagh for certain religious purpose. An incident, which Nehru termed as "a long horror and terrible indignity", resulted in the loss of 1202 lives and left 3,600 wounded and some permanently disabled.[8]

Brave sons of India like Bhagat Singh were hanged to death. Those who have taken active part in Bose's Indian National Army and tried to liberate their homeland through force were severely dealt with. Those who sang 'Vande Mataram' and demonstrated with national flag on their hands were mercilessly beaten and incarcerated. Women freedom fighters' modesty was outraged unashamedly. Thus, the Indian people were denied of their right to expression, right to peaceful demonstration and so on.

Again, the freedom of press turned out to be the major casualty under the British colonial rule. The native English as well as regional language press was crippled and chained by numerous draconian press laws enacted and ruthlessly enforced by the central as well as presidential governments. The voices of the people who echoed the popular will were thus choked. The publishers, editors and printers of the nationalist press were hunted down and were put to untold and unheard sufferings. Writings of the nationalist poets and literary figures were branded as 'seditious literature' and were banned.

IV

The last straw on the Indian camel was mounted when Britain tried to pull India into the Second World War against its will. The leaders severely criticized this move and condemned the callousness of the British Government. While on the one hand, the British proclaimed that they were for democracy and invited every power to join them in their war against the dictatorship of Hitler and others of his ilk, on the other, they refused to offer freedom to their colonial possessions. This stand taken by the British was considered by the Indians as a clear display of double standard and highly condemnable.

In 1942, Gandhiji started Quit India Movement, thereby giving a final warning to the British people to leave the Indian shores for good.[9] The alien government continued to suppress the movement with all muscle power at its disposal. However, at the end of the war and subsequent ascending of Labour Party under Atlee to power, the British Government had decided to offer freedom to India. Thus, India had attained freedom from the British colonial yoke on August 15, 1947, and the centuries-old human rights violations of the Indian people in the hands of the British colonial masters were brought to an end.

V

"Freedom for a nation and a people may be, and is, I believe, always good in the long run, but in the final analysis freedom itself is a means to an end, that end being the raising of the people in the question to higher levels and hence the general advancement of humanity" opined Nehru in 1939.[10] It is believed that without freedom no individual can achieve equality or aspire to rise to higher levels of accomplishments and realize his/her full potentials.

If we measure the achievements of independent India with this yardstick and ask ourselves whether we have achieved equality among more than a billion of our population and raised them to higher levels of accomplishments, our answer may not be an emphatic 'yes'. Undoubtedly, India has achieved a lot, but what remains to be done is quite daunting. The human rights situation of the vulnerable sections of our society continues to be pathetic and deplorable. This has made some people to emphasize on the need for 'second freedom struggle'. However, we have political freedom now and a Constitution which was drafted with all good intentions and which guarantees political, economic and socio-cultural rights to all sections of our society. It just calls for its implementation and enforcement in the letter and spirit. As such, the need of the hour is dedication and self-service from all sections of our society to the cause of *sarvodaya,* the welfare of all of our people. It calls for the spirit of sacrifice and sense of nationalism, which was the hallmark of the leaders and participants of the freedom struggle against the British colonial masters.

References

1. Edmund Muller and Arun Bhattacharjee, *India Wins Independence*, Ashish Publishing House, New Delhi, 1988, p. 90.
2. *Ibid*, pp. 44-47.
3. *Ibid*, p. 1.
4. Asha Rani, *Gandhian Non-Violence and India's Freedom Struggle*, Shree Publishing House, Delhi, 1981, pp. 192-193.
5. J. C. Johari, *Extremist and Militant Nationalism*, Akashdeep Publishing House, New Delhi, 1995, pp. xii-xiii.
6. V. T. Patil, *Nehru and the Freedom Movement*, Sterling Publications, New Delhi, 1977, p. 243.
7. Jogesh Chandra Chatterji, *In Search of Freedom*, Firma K. L. Mukhopadhyay, Calcutta, 1967, pp. 85-90.
8. R. P. Chandola, *History of Indian Freedom Movement*, RBSA Publishers, Jaipur, 1988, p. 119.
9. Abul Kalam Azad, *India Wins Freedom*, Oriental Longman, Madras, 1988, p. 83.
10. Jawaharlal Nehru, "The Unity of India", *Foreign Affairs*, Vol. 16, No. 2, January 1938, p. 231.

5

HUMAN RIGHTS AND THE INDIAN PSYCHE

JUSTICE DAVID ANNOUSAMY

Situation of Human Rights in India

Human Rights were solemnly proclaimed as universal by the United Nations on December 10, 1948. At that moment itself 6 out the 55 members then forming the United Nations had reservations and abstained from voting in favour of the declaration. In fact, there has been opposition to the very idea of human rights in Europe itself, the most noteworthy opponents being Jeremy Bentham and Karl Marx.

Thereafter a large number of countries have joined the international body. They have in principle accepted the declaration. But some of them have in the course of time expressed reservations bordering sometimes on opposition. They found that the declaration was based on the western philosophy of life and was not acceptable in its entirety to their ethos. Consequently regional declarations happened to be framed like the African Charter of Human Rights, the Declaration of Bangkok etc.... The champions of universality were sad over these developments but in order to save the declaration from total collapse they had to compromise in the World Conference on Human Rights in Vienna in 1993 where it was decided that national and regional particularities have to be borne in mind.[1]

As far as India is concerned no conceptual difficulty was voiced. Rights as enunciated in the declaration have been embodied in the Indian Constitution either as fundamental rights or as directive principles of state policy. The Supreme Court of India has converted most of those principles into fundamental rights enforceable in courts in declaring that they are implicit in one or the other of the fundamental rights as listed in the Constitution. The Court has gone recently a step further in holding that any provision contained in an international instrument was enforceable in municipal courts provided it has been accepted by India and is not inconsistent with the Constitution.[2] So, as far as principles are concerned, India is in full agreement with the declaration and legally prepared to implement it.

However if we look at the actual implementation the picture is not as rosy; it is rather grim. Weaker sections of population are yet to taste the benefit of the socio-economic rights. Child bonded labour, battering of women, humiliation of lower castes are of daily occurrence all over the country.

Even in the matter of protection of life and of personal liberty the record is rather distressing. Custodial deaths in suspicious circumstances are frequently reported. No effective steps are taken by the government to prevent them, even though guidelines are not wanting. As far as personal liberty is concerned, there is a pernicious provision in the Constitution itself authorizing preventive detention by a simple administrative order. Such a provision was introduced by the Britishers for the first time by The Bengal State Prisoners Regulation III of 1818. This was then extended to other provinces. Then each province started having its own statute on the subject. The last piece of British legislation is the Restriction and Detention Ordinance III of 1944.

Congressmen were at the receiving end of the preventive detention measures. They have been advocating the total abrogation of such a provision of arbitrary detention. But after independence the Home Ministry prevailed upon Patel, the then Home Minister, to retain the provision, which they argued, was necessary on account of the law and order problems in the aftermath of partition. The new Indian leaders yielded but they did not like to make a direct statement in the Constitution allowing preventive detention. They instead achieved their objective indirectly in making provisions regulating preventive detention, as if its existence was normal, in paras 4 to 7 of Article 22. Thus preventive detention got constitutional recognition.

With the help of those provisions the Union Government has made successively several enactments, the last *avatar* being called POTA. State governments are not lagging behind in this field; they have each their own Acts. With the enormous powers given by these Acts the police and other prosecuting agencies can easily lodge in prison a person for a period of one year through an administrative order without having to follow the elaborate procedure prescribed by the Code of Criminal Procedure to protect human liberty. Politicians also find these provisions handy to send behind the bars their opponents for flimsy reasons. Preventive detention is a blatant violation of Articles 1, 3 and 9 of the Universal Declaration. It is not resorted to in civilized countries except in time of war.

On the whole as compared to European countries the situation in India in respect of human rights is not very brilliant even though there is no expression of conceptual reluctance, or opposition in principle like in other non-European countries. Why this pitiable performance? Rights matured slowly in Europe and were proclaimed in successive waves in the course of two centuries; here they were all ushered in at one stroke. It is also to be remembered that in Europe, at least in some countries, people fought for rights; for us, rights were offered on a platter, there is not the same enthusiasm. These factors though relevant do not explain the so low performance in the matter of rights, especially of civil and political rights more especially of personal liberty where there is also no question of cost involved. We have, therefore, to explore whether there is any cultural resistance to human rights in India.

Sources of Human Rights and Indian Culture

For this purpose we have to review the cultural background of emergence of rights in Europe and compare it with our position in the field. The European country with the longest history of human rights formulation is England. The first piece of legislation is the code of Ethel red (ninth ccentury), followed by the code of laws of Edward the Confessor (eleventh century). They filled the vacuum of law and curtailed the tyranny of the powerful towards the downtrodden. A big step forward was accomplished by the Magna Carta (1215) containing 63 articles of which two are extracted below to give an idea of the situation then prevailing in England and of what the new legal instrument purported to achieve:

> *"No free man shall be imprisoned, outlawed or banished unless by the judgment of his peers or the law of the land."*
>
> *"The free peasant or small land-holder should not by any fine be deprived of his land, nor the villain, or serf, of his carts, ploughs, and implements of husbandry."*

The next step was the Habeas Corpus Act, 1679 and finally the Bill of Rights of 1689. Then the scene of action shifts to America. The State of Virginia proclaims the first declaration of rights in 1776 followed by other States. The declaration of independence of America contains the affirmation of some essential rights. Then we have the famous declaration of the rights of man and the citizen of France in 1789 which had much impact on the rest of the world. This was followed by the bill of rights in America and the incorporation of the French declaration in the Constitution, both in the year 1791.

All those instruments were inspired by the spate of writings on political philosophy in various countries in Europe. From those writings one can easily gather the cultural basis of human rights. Four ideas are found to have been the leading factors. They are: existence of a natural law, reason as the basis of that law, the specificity of man in the creation, the individual character of human rights.[3] Let us now take up these elements seriatim and compare them with our views on the same.

First, the Natural law. The adjective '*natural*' appears along with rights in many places in the French declaration. In the American declaration we find the word '*self evident*' tagged to rights. The idea behind natural law is that positive laws, viz Customs, Roman law and Canon law were inadequate. Above these positive laws there are other laws inherent to the nature of man, which are binding on all men. This idea which dates back to Greeks has developed in the course of time in Europe and gathered strength in spite of some opposition. Blackstone, the well known British jurist of the seventeenth century would go to the extent of saying that only laws which are in accordance with nature deserve to be obeyed, that human laws should not be allowed to contradict natural law.

In India we have espoused the same idea long back in a firmer manner. *Dharma* is the set of moral laws which govern men like the physical laws governing the universe and which are like the latter permanent in nature. Those moral and physical laws are interlinked. Any violation of moral laws by men would perturb the universe. The matter should be set right unavoidably. So linking law to the nature of man and stating that men are governed by laws, which flow from his nature, is something common to both the civilizations. But what is taken into account in India is the nature of the whole universe including men whereas in Europe they confine to the nature of man.

The second element of human rights in Europe relates to the manner of discovery of that natural law. The Europeans attempt to find it with help of reason. It is, therefore, by thinking that one would discover the law. That law should be reasonable, viz. acceptable to all minds. It is not however the result of the common thinking of people. It is propounded by some thinkers and considered as natural law when it appears evident to all.

This method of discovery of natural law makes it liable to change with the evolution of the mentality of people. This explains the growth of human rights. The first set of rights, namely civil and political rights, is meant for man as an individual. In the course of time a second generation of rights (economic social and cultural rights) appeared taking care of man as a social being. This was followed by a third generation of rights more subtle, more delicate like the right of privacy, the right of information claimed by man as a person. Though one may feel happy about recognition of more and more rights, such a quick proliferation raises difficulties of implementation.

In India the natural law is discovered by great seers having great knowledge of man and society, well versed in the *Vedas,* living in isolation, involved in deep thinking, and having no material interest of their own. Their enunciation of law is considered as sacred. One may think that such a method may lead to the stratification of laws and to the danger of law becoming outdated. This however did not happen till India was not invaded. There has been a continuous chain of seers from the sixth century BC to the sixth century AD. Thereafter there have been authoritative commentaries. This kept the law moving though the basic principles remained the same. For instance one may notice that Gautama legislated for a pastoral society, Manu for an agricultural society, and Yagnavalkya for a commercial society.

So between Europe and India there is a substantial difference in the way the natural law is formulated. Adherence to basic values characterizes the Indian law whereas social changes are more quickly reflected in European law. This is of course fully true if we consider only the old Hindu law. The modern Indian law is more on the European pattern. But only the educated elite adheres it to whereas the bulk of the population remains attached to old values. Courts though upholding the new law as embodied in the Constitution are also leaning sometimes towards old values.

The third element of the western political philosophy sustaining human rights is the specificity of man. Each man is an eternal soul though encapsulate in a perishable body. All other creatures are basically different from him because they are deprived of soul. They are meant to serve the needs of man. This conception has led to give a very high place to man, to human life and to his dignity.

The Indian concept is quite different. Man is of the same

substance as the other creatures though superior to them in some respect. There is a hierarchy among living beings. The whole universe is God and man is only a part of it. This led Hindu civilization to give consideration to other creatures as well, to avoid killing them. A vague belief in metempsychosis adds to the respect of animals. Some people go even to the extent of making full funeral rites to monkeys. In the *Ramayana* we witness an alliance between men and monkeys and a joint military action. It is only with the help of monkeys that Rama succeeded in rescuing Sita; Hanuman is placed among deities. Some animals like snakes are still worshipped. The Indian mind is not prone to accept fully the specificity of man as conceived in Europe. Instead it is well prepared to accept rights relating to environment

The pre-eminence of man and the high importance attached to him in Europe being absent in India; there is necessarily not the same enthusiasm for the rights of man. However it is to be stated that European countries are now slowly realizing the close link of mankind with the rest of animal kingdom. The scientific community has been distancing more and more from the religious viewpoint that man was substantially different from animals. Its firm opinion is that man is only one of the branches of the evolutionary tree. Modern science has found that intelligence is not the exclusive attribute of man, that all animals have got some form of intelligence and also conscience, varying of course according to species, that great apes have an intelligence and conscience very close to those of men. Following this trend, New Zealand proposes to make a law giving great apes rights against imprisonment and torture.

It is being realized that blind pursuit of human interests may lead to the deterioration of the earth, which will ultimately prove detrimental to man. The strongest proponents of human rights themselves are veering round the idea of harmony with nature by proclaiming the human right for a healthy environment which will entail balanced ecology and protection of animals and trees against their destruction by man. So, on this point the European and Indian viewpoints are coming closer. But the initial idea of specificity of man which gave impetus to the emergence of rights in Europe will be necessarily missing in India and that will have necessarily some effect in the implementation of rights.

The fourth component of human rights is the consideration of man as an individual shorn of his link with any group. The State itself has come to be regarded as the sum of citizens. There have been deliberate efforts to abolish groups, which individuals belonged to for various reasons. Man was thus freed from his various allegiances of the past and considered for him. This of course gave much strength to human rights. But that leaves the individual fully exposed to the tyranny of the State, as there is nothing in between. On the other side the State has to ensure that all his needs are met.

In India the position is quite different. Though the individual man has got rights and obligations, groups like family and caste still play an important role in his life. Through the system of castes a hierarchy is created between men, which prevents them from thinking in terms of equality. Groups, therefore, constitute obstacles for the development of individual rights. At the same time they provide assistance for him more effectively. Lying between the State and the individual they protect him eventually from arbitrary action by the State.

In fact the individual being weak and fragile may find it difficult to deal all alone with the anonymous State machinery and would land in helplessness. So groups are necessary; even in Europe they did not altogether disappear though the individual has emerged stronger. New groups got formed the most pre-eminent of them being trade unions. Associations with various objectives and spiritual or quasi-religious bodies are flourishing. Nevertheless the cult of the individual persists.

So if we consider the main cultural factors, which contributed to the emergence of human rights in Europe, we find that they differ from our traditional values and social set-up. India could have also formulated a declaration of its own based on its peculiar culture like other non-European countries. But in the euphoria of independence, the elements of the universal declaration were adopted without much concern for their applicability.

Elements of Indian Culture favourable to Rights

It is however to be stated that conditions which have generated rights are not absolutely essential for the implementation of rights once they have been declared constitutionally and have the backing of courts. It is enough that there exist conditions, which would allow development of rights now that they are sowed. We shall, therefore, examine whether there do not exist in our culture some elements, which properly revived could well sustain efforts for the promotion of rights.

The *Vedic* teachings would preach equality of all human beings. The concept of *svadharma,* viz. *dharma* inherent in every being and forming part of the overall *dharma* would require the protection and self-realization of each human being, whatever his position in life. Therefore, the concept of *dharma* does not reduce the human being to nothingness. Its purpose is only to regulate and perpetuate life on the earth.

The Buddhist reform attempted to remove inequality between human beings, more particularly the one created by caste and sex prejudices. Its message had an impact on the society; counter reformists endeavoured to erase it; but its appeal is still present. The spectacular conversion of Ambedkar to Buddhism is there to remind us of the hope raised by Buddhist thought.

The encounter with the West has prompted reforms in Hinduism, the most known being the Brahmo Samaj of Ram Mohan Roy. The Indian National Congress insisted very much for a declaration of rights at the time of elaboration of the Government of India Act, 1935. Jawaharlal Nehru envisioned a society built on a rational basis and took steps towards that end after independence.[4] In the South (especially Tamil Nadu), Periyar, emphatically anti-Brahmin, has launched a movement of self-respect extolling the value of man and which is still alive.

We shall now refer to some basic ancient texts to identify the elements, which may be favourable to the development of human rights. The *Arthasastra* in Book IV relating to suppression of criminals prescribe ofcourse harsh measures. But there is side-by-side insistence on human considerations. For instance the suspect shall not be liable to arrest after three nights after the commission of offence, except when tools of crime are found with him.

After interrogation the accused that does not confess his guilt will be put to torture only if his guilt is found to be probable and of grave nature. Torture is to be given on alternate days and one only each day. For women there will be only half the torture. In no circumstance a pregnant woman or a woman within one-month delivery will be tortured. Similarly the following categories of persons shall not be put to torture: a minor or aged or sick or intoxicated or insane or overcome by hunger, thirst or travel, or who has overeaten or whose meal is undigested or who is weak. A magistrate inflicting torture or punishment wrongly shall be subjected to the same treatment by the king.

In chapter X of the same book, substitute penalties in the form of fine are provided in the place of cutting of limbs for various offences. The closing article of that chapter is worth being reproduced in our modern penal code. It reads as follows:

> " *After taking into full consideration the person and the offence, the motive, seriousness or lightness (of the offence), the consequences, the present (effects), and the place and time, the magistrate shall fix the highest, the lowest and the middle in the matter of punishment, remaining neutral between the king and the subjects*"[5]

These few instances quoted above would disclose the existence in the *Arthasastra* of concern for man, for weaker sections, and care for fair play and due process.

Let us now turn to *Manusmriti* itself considered as responsible for the cruel hierarchy in the fabric of Indian society. We may gather therein also several provisions, which would get approval from the staunchest human rights activists. First there are many precepts in respect of the welfare of weaker sections like the following ones:

> *" Children, old men, poor dependants and sick persons, must be considered as rulers of pure ether... "*[6]
>
> *" Where female relations are made miserable, the family of him who makes them so very soon wholly perishes; but when they are not unhappy, the family always increases "*[7]

In the matter of penalty for offences committed, though Manu prescribes some severe punishments, he makes clear that they are to be resorted to only as the last resort. Before meting out corporal punishments, the king should try first gentle admonition, then harsh reproof and thirdly deprivation of property. Manu dwells on exemption of punishment and suggests penance and expiation. One full chapter is devoted to this matter indicating in detail the kind of penance to be undergone for each offence. It is suggested therein that if having performed any expiation one does not feel a perfect satisfaction of conscience, he should repeat the same devout act until his conscience is perfectly satisfied. It is even provided that those who are unable to undergo penance may get released from their guilt by open confession, by repentance, by devotion and reading the scripture or by alms giving. In this way there is no imposition of penalty by the authority but option for penance by the guilty person himself. He is thus relieved totally of his guilty conscience, his dignity is intact, and he is not a punished convict. All these provisions show a great consideration for the inner feelings of man.

As regards justice and due process Manu is second to none, as the following verses would show:

> *"As a hunter traces the lair of a wounded beast by the drops of blood; let the king investigate the true point of justice by deliberate arguments"*

"Let him fully consider the nature of truth, the state of the case, and his own person; and next, the witnesses, the place, and the time; firmly adhering to the rules of practice."[8]

It is also worth referring to an important ethical work in Tamil language, known as *Thirukurral,* which appeared in the far south of the country, and which has been translated in many languages both Indian and foreign. That work which dates back to the second century AD is universal in conception. It has no reference whatsoever to caste system. It does not claim the authority of any religion; it is based on reason. It deals with man in general and his worldly life only. It has become the perennial source of inspiration for all subsequent Tamil writers.

In part III of his book related to wealth, he deals with the relations between the king and the people. More particularly in three chapters devoted respectively to the kingly greatness, the right sceptre, and the cruel sceptre he enunciates the duties of the king and insists on perfect justice and the necessity of the rule of law. He condemns the bad king in the following words:

The one who plies the murderer's trade, more cruel is the king
Who all injustice works, his subjects harassing[9].

He also lays stress on the importance of due process in the administration of justice as it would appear from the following couplet:

Who punishes, investigation made in due degree,
So as to stay advance of crime, a king is he[10]

Apart from these general provisions regarding the duties of the king, he has also adverted to some specific rights. Dealing with the right to learn he says:

Want of knowledge, mid all wants the sorest want we deem
Want of other things the world will not as want esteem[11]

Turning to the right for food he becomes very vehement and says :

> *If he that shaped*
> *the world desires that men should begging go*
> *Through life's long course,*
> *let him a wanderer be and perish so* [12]

He is not for the free distribution of food at the doorstep of the needy. He is more modern in his approach and advocates the right to earn one's livelihood as follows:

> *Nothing is sweeter than to taste the toil-won cheer,*
> *Though mess of pottage as tasteless as the water clear* [13]

This rapid survey shows that there are in Indian culture many features, which are favourable to human rights. But it is objected that in all the old texts there is no declaration of rights in clear terms but only enunciation of principles and enumeration of duties cast on the king. This objection is not a valid one. First the rights are now constitutionally proclaimed. What was suspected to want is a congenial cultural background in which rights may thrive? It is now seen that such a background exists. Secondly a duty cast on a person creates a right in favour of another person. Even nowadays a right is sometimes expressed in the form of duty. For instance the right of equality is expressed in the Constitution of India as a duty for the State whereas the same is expressed in the French declaration in the form of a right. So what is important is not the manner of formulation but the substance and the machinery for implementation.

To sum up, our cultural background is not averse to human rights but is even favourable to them. What is necessary is to revitalize the indigenous cultural elements, which are supportive of rights.

Turning back to our record of implementation, which is far from being satisfactory we have to acknowledge that there are prejudices, established practices, vested interests, and lack of money and of political will which stand in the way. But here is an inherent force in the human rights arising out of human aspirations, which the democratic set-up allows to harness. With the legal and international support the rights enjoy now they may very well thrive on the Indian soil. However a well thought out programme of action may be necessary. One should not attempt the promotion of rights as a whole. An order of priority has to be established, taking into account the importance of the right, the cost of its implementation, its cultural appeal. A five years or ten years minimum programme may be prepared and implemented fully. The United Nations Commission should also confine to gauge the performance of each nation with reference to that minimum. Thus the way will be cleared for a steady progress of human rights, avoiding unproductive controversies.

On account of cultural divergence some groups of countries have reformulated the universal declaration. We have not chosen that path. We have entered in our statute book the rights as formulated in European countries. But they will be interpreted by our courts in accordance with our culture and emerge with a local flavour. There are some features in human rights, which are common to all men; there are some others, which are peculiar to each culture. Such rights as have connection with culture will necessarily vary in their conception and implementation from one country to another.

References

1. David Annousamy: "Internationalisation of Human Rights" in *Studies in Human Rights,* V.T. Patil and T.S.N. Sastry (eds.), 2000, p. 40.
2. Vishaka and Others *vs.* State of Rajasthan and Others (1997) 6 S.C.C., 241.
3. Introduction Historique au droit, Norbert Rouland, 1998, p. 605.
4. James Chiriyan Kandath : "India and Human Rights: Concepts and Contexts" in *Studies in Human Rights,* V.T. Patil and T.S.N. Sastry (eds.), 2000, p. 396.
5. *The Kautiliya Arthasastra,* Part II, R.P. Kangle, translator, Book IV, Chapter 10, verses 17-18, p. 283.

6. *Manava Dharma Sastra,* translation by G.C. Houghton, IV-184.
7. *Idem.* III-57.
8. *Idem.* VIII-44-45.
9. The Sacred Kurral of Tiruvaluva-Nayanar, translated by Rev. G.U. Pope No 651, 1886 (Reprinted) 1984.
10. *Idem.,* No. 561.
11. *Idem.,* No. 841.
12. *Idem.,* No. 1062.
13. *Idem.,* No. 1065.

6

PERSONS, RIGHTS AND DHARMA

S.S. RAMA RAO PAPPU

The concept of a person is one of the most complex and difficult concepts to understand. It is complex because one can study persons from several dimensions—the scientific, the metaphysical, the religions, the social, etc. Science, specially biology, studies persons dissecting their anatomy and physiology, comparing humans with higher animals, studying the relation between physiological states and mental phenomena, isolating their unique DNA, etc. Religion throws its own insights on persons. Who is a person? Is he a spark of the Divine? Or is he a fallen creature from the Heaven? Is he more privileged than the rest of the creation? Do persons survive death? Metaphysics raises very interesting questions concerning persons. Some of these questions are: Who is a person? What are the necessary and sufficient conditions that make a being a person? Is God a person? Are foetuses persons? Are corporations persons? Can one be a person without a "soul"? Finally, social philosophy steps in and asks how "human beings" can become "human persons?" and the role society plays in transforming Homo sapiens into human persons. In common usage, we do not ordinarily have occasion to say "Jones is a person" unless there is some doubt whether the speaker is referring by the proper name 'Jones' his dog, or cat or his chimpanzee, all of which are named 'Jones.' This gives us a clue to one of the ordinary meanings of the word 'person,' in that the concept of a 'person' negates animals, things, objects, etc. From a scientific point of view, someone is a person in the biological sense, if he is a member of the Homo sapiens, and possesses the human DNA. Likewise, from a metaphysical point of view, an individual is a person if he has a soul, a self, if he possesses reason, etc.

In Western thought, the ethico-social conception of a person took two directions. First, there is the influential Kantian conception of a person according to which every member of the Homo sapiens, in so far as he is rational, is morally an end-in-himself. Kant's second formulation of the Categorical Imperative that "man, and in general, every rational being exists as an end in himself and not merely as a means to be arbitrarily used by this or that will," gives all human beings unconditional worth. The Kantian conception of human persons as ends-in-themselves is revolutionary will be clear if we contrast it with the Greeks who thought that some human beings are naturally born slaves, as "living instruments of the conduct of life," as Aristotle stated. Why is it that every rational human being is a moral person in the Kantian world but not so in the world of Aristotle? Contemporary social philosophers argue that though a slave in Aristotle's conception could be a rational being and could possess the same biological features as the Master, slaves are not considered persons because they lack rights. If we give the Greek slaves all the rights of the citizens, they become full-fledged persons; conversely, if we take away the rights from the Greek citizens, they too become slaves. Western thought, at least since Hobbes, conceived that what makes a human being a human person is the possession of rights. According to Hobbes, an individual possesses rights even in a state of nature "to protect his life and members" and "to possess, use and enjoy all that he would, or could get." What makes a "human" a "human *person*" is his right to self-preservation. Animals, for example, on the Hobbesian theory do not have a right to self-preservation. Like Hobbes, Locke also postulated that social and political institutions are not important for the possession of rights, and human beings are all born with rights. "The state of nature" says Locke, "has a Law of Nature to govern it, which obliges everyone; and Reason, which is that Law, teaches all mankind, who will but consult it, that being all equal and independent, no one ought to harm another in his life, health, liberty or possessions."[1]

For Locke not only persons are born with rights, these rights are also inalienable, meaning that no one can take them away. According to Hobbes and Locke, people can possess "natural rights" even in the absence of social and political institutions and that each individual is the possessor of rights and these rights are inalienable.

If, in Western thought, rights make humans into "persons," in Indian thought it is *dharma* or obligations, which qualify humans to be persons. A person in Indian thought is conceived as a *dharmic* individual or *obligatory person*. According to Western liberal thoughts, humans are born with certain natural and inalienable rights. In Indian thought, humans are born with certain "natural obligations." Sometimes the Indians use the term *rna* or debt to characterize the nature of these obligations. The concept of *rna* is stronger in its connotation than the concept of *dharma,* in that the nature of the obligation which *rna* connotes is more binding than the nature of obligations which *dharma* implies. The debts, which I have to discharge, leave me with no choice; but some of my obligations can be so weak that I may conveniently ignore them. For instance, the mortgage debts, which I owe to my bank, have a compelling nature because (a) I have voluntarily incurred them; (b) I have signed a contract, which specifies my obligations, and so on. On the other hand, my obligation to feed Mr. Kingsley, a starving person in Swaziland is weak because (a) the obligations are too general, (b) he is a total stranger to me, (c) I have no special obligations to him like the special obligations I owe to my parents, and (d) I did not make any promise that I will feed him, etc. In Indian thought, three debts (*tri rna)* are explicitly recognized. These are (a) debts to ancestors, (b) debts to the gods and (c) debts to the sages.

Like the Western liberals who faced the problem of explaining how any one can be "born" with certain natural rights, the Indian thinkers also faced the problem of explaining how anyone can be born with certain "natural" obligations. After all, it may be argued, that one of the important characteristics of the concept of obligation is the notion of voluntariness. Forced obligations cannot be called "obligations." They "obligate"; people are "obliged to" but there is no "obligation." Now a new born baby cannot do anything voluntarily and thus incur obligations.

In answer to this, the Indian thinkers resort to the metaphysics of *karma* and *punarjanma* (rebirth). The obligations which humans find them as soon as they are born look like "forced" obligations but they are not. They have incurred their obligations as a result of voluntary choices and promises, which they have made in a previous birth.

Even if the metaphysics of rebirth sounds mysterious, the notion of being born with obligations is not mysterious. Social living as a form of life consists of innumerable obligations. Some of these obligations re-voluntarily incurred by us; some of them are not. Thus, I may incur an obligation to pay the college tuition of a friend's son because I have made a promise to my friend; but I have an obligation to support my parents, though I have never explicitly made such a promise. My obligation to support my parents is already part of the social system to which I belong. In the process of growing up, I discover my obligations, accept them and impose them on myself.

In Indian thought, then, humans are born with obligations, into a "*dharmic* world" or a world of obligations. But what is *dharma*? When is a human a *dharmic* individual? *Dharma* in Indian thought combines in itself both the virtue-ethic of Greeks and the obligation ethic of the Kantians in Western thought. As a virtue-ethic *dharma* enjoins humans to attain the four human perfections *(purusharthas)*, viz. *artha* (wealth), *kama* (pleasure), *dharma* (righteousness) and *moksha* (liberation). As an obligation-ethic, *dharma* emphasizes the notion of duty and enjoins human persons with innumerable "do's" and "don'ts". *Purusharthas* or human perfections are not human ideals placed in such a high pedestals, which few can attain. They are grounded on human nature, on the desires of humans. The obligation to pursue the *purusharthas* is universal; this obligation is not forced on any one; nor do they bind human persons. Rather, humans seek the *purusarthas* because it is human nature to pursue these ends.

When we move from *dharma* as a virtue-ethic to *dharma* as an obligation-ethic in Indian thought, we land into the "world of obligations" proper. There are a large number of obligations, which our world imposes on us. These obligations have been classified in Indian thought into two categories (a) *sadharana dharmas* (general obligations) and *visesa dharmas* (relative obligations). *Sadharana dharmas* pertain to humans-qua-humans; they do not refer to a particular individual's station in life or his status or role in society. Indian lawgivers have different lists of what these general obligations are. Manu, for example, recognizes the following general obligations for humans (a) *ahimsa* (non-injury), (b) *satya* (veracity), (c) *asteya* (non-stealing), (d) *sauca* (cleanliness) (e) *indriya nigraha* (control of senses).[2]

Visesa Dharmas or relative obligations, on the other hand, pertain to the individual depending on the circumstances or one's station in life. Thus there are obligations which pertain to four *varnas* (*varna dharma*), the four "orders of life (*asrama dharma*), those which pertain to one's offices, positions (like *raja-dharma* or obligations of a king); those which pertain to social roles (like *pati/patni-dharma* or the obligations of a husband/wife to each other; those which pertain to the age and time one lives (*yuga dharma*), etc.

Before we turn to the question "who is a *dharmic* individual?" we should note the following features of the Indian world of obligations. First, as we have already stated, humans in Indian thought do not voluntarily incur their obligations, empirically at least in this life. Rather, humans find themselves in a world of obligations; they discover what their obligations are. Thus our obligation to seek human perfections (*purusharthas*) is part of our "nature"; we do not choose our nature; thus these obligations are not typically voluntary. It is also obvious that we also do not choose our general obligations like telling the truth or being kind; we already find them in our social life and we impose them on ourselves. Even the 'relative obligations" (*visesa dharmas*) are not voluntary in Indian thought. I do not choose the obligations pertaining to my *varna* because I am born into my *varna* and I do not have the freedom to move from one *varna* to another. Likewise I cannot choose not to perform the duties of a householder (*grhastha*) because I am an adult and married and hence the obligations of a householder are binding on me.

As a corollary to the above, we may also state that not only humans find themselves in a world of obligations; they also cannot ordinarily release themselves from them. (Becoming a *samnyasin* or a "renounced individual" is different and we shall discuss it later). Ordinarily, even if an obligation is incurred voluntarily, the individual cannot release himself unless the third party to whom the obligation is owed releases him of his obligations. If the obligations of humans arise as a result of human laws and human norms, then the people who can change or repeal these norms and laws alone can release others from their obligations. Now, in Indian thought, *dharma* is conceived as an eternal law or as an eternal norm and hence no one is competent to release humans of their obligations. Therefore, humans are not only born into a world of obligations; humans also cannot change, alter or repeal any of their obligations.

Second, because individuals through any specific voluntary act do not generate the obligations, they do not also generate correlative rights. Thus, if I have made a promise to you to do X, I incur an obligation to you to do X and it also confers a right on you to demand X from me. But where my obligations are not the result of voluntary actions, they do not also entail corresponding rights on others. As a matter of fact, Indian social *dharma* is a pure world of obligations. No one has any rights; everyone has only obligations.

Third, obligations in Indian thought do not have the character of what we may call "obligations *in persona*," i.e. obligations to specific persons. They are rather "obligations *in rem*" or obligations to others, to groups, to society at large.

Take, for example the *pati-dharma* or the obligations of the husband, for example, Rama. The obligations of Rama as a husband to his wife Sita are not his obligations of Rama as an individual to Sita, another individual; but they are the obligations of Rama-as-a-husband to Sita-as-a-wife.

This leads us to a consideration of the concept of 'person' in Indian social thought. Our discussion of obligations so far may lead one to think that in Indian thought it is "obligations" which make humans into 'persons'; just as in the West it is the rights, which differentiate mere humans from human persons. This, however, is not quite correct.

To be a person, in Western thought, is to be a unique individual with clearly defined rights. In Indian thought, on the other hand, persons have not been individuated as unique individuals with specific obligations. An individual, in Indian thought, is what McKim Merriott calls a "dividual." There is, however some similarity between Western and Indian thought on the question of "becoming a person." In Western thought, anyone (or anything!) can be made into a person by conferring rights. Thus, foetuses, corporations, States, etc. have been made into "corporate person" "legal persons" etc. by conferring rights on them. Children, slaves, insane people, etc. likewise have been deprived of their personhood by annulling their rights. In Indian thought too, people are not the only individuals who have obligations; inanimate things too have their obligations. Just as it is the *dharma* or obligation the king to protect his subjects, it is also the *dharma* or the obligation of water to flow downwards and the *dharma* or the obligation of the sun to rise in the East every morning! Even if we think that only people have obligations, Indian thought emphasized "obligations *in rem*" and not "obligations *in personam*." Thus the obligation of Rama does not belong to Rama as a unique individual, which he voluntarily incurs to specific individuals. Rather, Rama's obligations are Rama-as-a-husband's obligations to his wife; Rama-as-a-son's filial obligations; Rama-as-a-king's royal obligations, etc. Theoretically, therefore, Rama as a proper name is not irreplaceable by another proper name, though practically the individual who has the obligations-as-a-husband, king, son, etc., turn out to be only one individual denoted by the name 'Rama'.

To summarize our discussion so far (a) Indian social thought did not individuate persons, (b) individuals discover their obligations and do not voluntarily incur them, and (c) both human and non-human beings can have obligations. From these assumptions one wonders how Indian thought can conceptualize the notion of a person. It seems to me that a possible way in which we can get the notion of a person without abandoning the Indian assumptions is by making a distinction between "having" or "discovering" one's obligations and "accepting" them. Inanimate objects "have" their *dharmas,* like the *dharma* of water to flow downwards but water cannot "discover" what its *dharma* is nor can it accept or reject this *dharma.* Humans (and similar beings) alone can "have" obligations, "discover" what they are and "accept" or reject them. It is of course possible—for example, in the case of children—to have obligations without knowing what they are. Children, however, discover their obligations gradually while growing up into adulthood. What is, however, not possible in Indian thought is for a person to know or discover what his or her obligations are and reject them, the reason being that one's *svadharma* or personal obligations are founded on one's *svabhava* or essential nature. He who rejects one's obligations, therefore, is one who rejects one's own *svabhava.* This is however impossible, for how can one reject one's own human nature? Acceptance of the world of obligations, therefore, is a natural, spontaneous process and it is in accepting these obligations "ordinary people" become "persons."

There are, however two classes of cases where humans are outside the world of *dharma.* These are the psychopaths and the *samnyasins.* The psychopath, no doubt, is born into a world of *dharma,* but as Herbert Fingarette points out,[3] he does not accept his obligations; he does not care, he does not show concern about them. The *samnyasin,* on the other hand, transcends the world of obligations. What distinguishes the *samnyasin* from the psychopath is that the *samnyasin* performs his obligations without accepting them, cares for others without his ego-involvement and shows concern for the world with a withdrawn self. *The samnyasin* discharges his obligations, but not because they are binding on him but out of a sense of supererogation. He is in the world of obligations, but he does not have obligations; he performs all the obligations but there are no obligations which he has to perform.

References

1. John Locke, *Second Treatise of Government*, 1690, chap. 2, section 6, ed. by Thomas P. Peardon (Indianapolis Bobbs-Merrill, 1952).
2. *Manavadharmasastra*, X. 63.
3. Herbert Fingarette, "Acceptance of Responsibility," in *On Responsibility* (New York : Basic Books, 1967), pp. 17-45.

7

THIRUKURAL AND THE PROTECTION OF ENVIRONMENT

HUMAN RIGHTS PERSPECTIVE

A. DAVID AMBROSE

Right to Environment as a Human Right

The main purpose of United Nations, among others, is to promote the universal respect of and observance of Human Rights and Fundamental Freedoms for all. Now human rights enjoy universal recognition and cry for protection and implementation. The enjoyment of basic human rights like the right to life[1] is dependent upon man's environment, both natural and man-made, says the preamble of the United Nations Conference on the Human Environment.[2] Principle 1 of the Declaration lays down that 'man has the fundamental right to freedom, equality and adequate conditions of life, in an environment of quality that permits a life of dignity and well being...'[3]

Referring to Art. 35(3) and Art. 55(1) and (2) of 1977 Additional Protocol to the Geneva Convention on Humanitarian Laws of Warfare of 1949, Judge Nagendra Singh says:

> *"it would be correct to state that the right to environment in so far as it relates directly to human existence and human survival is of the same category and potency as the right to life and peace..."*[4]

Art. 1 of the 'Legal Principles for Environmental Protection and Sustainable Development'[5] says, "*All human beings have the fundamental right to an environment adequate for their health and well being*".[6] The adoption of the resolution[7] on the need to ensure a healthy environment for the well-being of individuals by the General Assembly without vote also supports this view. In the Nuclear Test Case,[8] New Zealand pleaded that the action of France violated the right of all members of the international community to the preservation from unjustified artificial radioactive contamination of the terrestrial, marine and aerial environment and in particular of the environment of the region in which the tests are conducted.[9] Municipal courts of various countries have recognised the right of the environment as a fundamental human right. For example, in India, the right of the people to live in a healthy environment has been recognized by the Supreme Court in *R.L. and E. Kendra, Dehradun* v. *State of U.P.*[10] Similarly the Andhra Pradesh High Court in *T. Damodhar Rao* v. *The Special Officer Municipal Corporation of Hyderabad*[11] held that the right to life cannot be enjoyed without protection and preservation of the environment. The Supreme Court in *Subhash Kumar* v. *State of Bihar*[12] held that the right to life enshrined in Art. 21 includes the right to enjoyment of pollution free water and air for the full enjoyment of life. Thus the right to environment is considered not merely as a political or moral right but as an enforceable human right.[13]

Thirukural and Environmental Protection

Even though at the time of framing of the Constitution of India, there were several Union and State enactments which covered a wide variety of environmental issues like protection of forests and wild life and pollution of water and air, the framers of the Constitution did not give much importance to environmental protection as they were not then aware of the significance of environmental protection. As a result, the Constitution drafted in 1949 did not even contain the expression 'environment' and there was no reference to environmental protection. Only in 1976, about a quarter of a century later, the expression 'environment' found place in the Constitution by the Constitution (42nd Amendment) Act, 1976. And only in the year 1986, Environmental Protection Act, 1986 was enacted. However, even several centuries before, Thiruvalluvar, the Tamil poet had referred to environmental protection, directly or indirectly, in his various *Kurals* under various headings, thereby proving that *Thirukural* is truly a 'world scripture'.

Protection of Mother Earth

Environment is composed of land, water, sky and forest that surround us. Environmental Protection therefore means, in short, the protection of our mother earth. It is preserving the nature. It is our duty to safeguard the nature of this earth in which we all live in. Thiruvalluvar emphasises this in the second *kural* of the chapter on Pulaal Marutthal by saying, '*Porulachi potratharku illai*' which means 'property yields no benefit to those who do not cherish it'. There will not be any benefit to us from our mother earth if we do not cherish her. It can be said that only to emphasises this point that Thiruvalluvar had said so. Based on this message, Art. 48 of the Constitution of India provides that 'the State shall endeavour to protect and improve the environment'. Further Art. 51A(g) imposes a duty on every citizen to protect and safeguard natural environment.

Protection of the Forest

> '*Manineerum Mannum Malaiyum Ani Nizhal*
> *Kaadum Udaythu Aran*' (Kural 742)
>
> (A fort paramount is set in space among mountains, contained by canals and streams, and covered by thick forests).

In the above quoted *Kural,* Thiruvalluvar says that a fort is that which has an unceasing supply of water, plains, mountains and cool shady forests. Here 'fort' signifies protection. A fort to a nation protects the nation from threats both natural and man-made. In the above said *Kural,* Thiruvalluvar says that cool shady forests protect the nation from all calamities. The uses of forest are plenty. Many animals make forests as their home. Forests play an important role in bringing rains. Meaning that without rain the world will experience misery, Thiruvalluvar says as follows: *Thuliyenmai Gnalathiku Yeartru* (Kural 557).

Thus *Kural* points out clearly the importance of forests in the protection of the nation from the misery of being without rain. Acknowledging this, the Government of India has passed two acts, namely (The Indian) Forest Act of 1927 and Forests Conservation Act of 1980. By Sec. 2(2) of Forest Conservation Act 1980 non-forest use of all types of forests is prohibited. Realizing the significance of the forests, National Forests Policy was declared by the Government of India in 1952 according to which the forests should occupy 33 per cent of the land surface against 23 per cent of that time.

Wild Life Protection

Mannuir Ombi Arulalvarku illenba
Thenuir Anjum vinai (Kural 244)

(from the pain of ignorant darkness
fear not evil to self or surroundings).

If one protects the life of other creatures and remains compassionate to them only then the evils which man's soul dreads will never afflict them says Thiruvalluvar while emphasizing the significance of being compassionate. From a close perusal of this *Kural,* it can be inferred that the life of all creatures should be protected which in turn will bring honour to man. Further in the *Kural, Arivinan aguvathu undo prithin noi.*

Thiruvalluvar asks what benefit has he derived from knowledge who does not strive to keep off pain from another as earnestly as from himself? Killing animals for business and trade is also condemned by *Kural.* In *Kural* 256 it is said no one would sell flesh for making money. It can be discerned that

Thiruvalluvar emphasises generally that life of all creatures should be protected, and animals should not be killed for trade purposes.

In this connection it is pertinent to note that the two previously mentioned articles, Art. 48 A and Art. 51 A(g) emphasize that wild life should be protected. Keeping this in mind, the Government of India has enacted Wild Life Protection Act, 1972 through which, sanctuaries, Natural/National Parks, etc., have been created for the protection and conservation of wild animals. In addition, the Prevention of Cruelty to Animals (Amendment) Act, 1982 also protects the animals. At the International level India has strongly condemned the killing of animals for trade purposes.

Water Pollution Control

The importance of water is very well stressed by Thiruvalluvar in ten *Kurals* coming under the heading *'van sirappu'*. In the last *Kural* under this heading being the 20th *Kural,* Thiruvalluvar says *'Neer indri amiaythu ulagu'*, meaning that in the absence of water , duties of life cannot be performed. Highlighting the significance and importance of water, he thus says further,

> *'Van nokie vazhum ulagu'* (Kural 542)
>
> (Life on earth thrives on rain from clouds, and society looks for good governance to survive).

and

> *Iru punljum vaaitha malaiyum varu punalum*
> *val aranum nattirkku uruppu'* (Kural 737)
>
> (A country beams in prosperity where hills and dales, streams and springs,and strong forts guard and adorn its frontiers).

By these *Kurals* what we means is that three types of waters – the two types of waters from above and below, and water issuing from hills, are the constituents of a kingdom and all living things thrive only when there is rain i.e. water.

It is true that water is essential for any nation. But how should that water be? It should be clear like crystal says *'mani neerum'*. By saying that the water should be clear like crystal and not turbid, it is meant that the water should not be polluted. Because water that is polluted cannot be crystal clear and polluted water will be turbid only. Here two things are stressed. One, water (all the three types) is very much essential for the nation. Second, that water should be unpolluted and clear. Realizing the importance of the prevention and control of pollution of water for human existence, the Indian Parliament has passed the Water (Prevention and Control of Pollution) Act of 1974 and almost all the State governments have adopted and implemented the Act.

In the case *M.C. Mehta* v. *Union of India*[14] the Supreme Court of India had ordered the closure of the tanneries in Kanpur district of Uttar Pradesh, as these tanneries were polluting the waters of the River Ganga by discharging their industrial effluent in the river, in spite of being asked not to do so for several years.

Land Conservation

In order to point out further the relationship between water and land says Thiruvalluvar as thus *'Nilathiyalbal neer thriththatragum...'* (*Kural* 452). The meaning of this *Kural* is that the water changes its quality and partakes the nature of the soil. Therefore, it can be concluded that the quality of the water changes according to the nature of the land (soil) and if the land is polluted, the water will also be polluted. If the land is good then the water will also be good for consumption. This fact highlights the necessity to safeguard the quality of the land (soil) against any degradation or pollution. Recently some of the tanneries near Ranipet in Tamilnadu were asked to close down by the High Court of Madras in view of environmental protection as their industrial effluent discharges polluted the land of that area. Industrial chemical wastes poison the soil. So water in those areas becomes unfit for human use. Further no vegetation can grow in that soil due to the chemical poison in such soils. It is to be noted here that the

Supreme Court of India has prohibited starting of any new prawn farms as the salinity of the water and soil is increased by marine water prawn culture therby making the land and water in that area unfit for use.

Environment and Development

While speaking about the qualities of a State Thiruvalluvar says thus:

> *Perum porulal pettakathu agi arung kettal*
> *Aatra vilaivathu nadu* (Kural 732)
>
> (A country with a treasure of wealth and bountiful crops, lures and keeps its people, free from the pain of want).

According to Parimelazhakar the meaning of the words *'Arungkettal Aatra Vilaivathu'* is that prosperity, free of destructive causes and according to Kaaligar, 'harmless great growth in prosperity'. From the above interpretations and meaning, given by Tamil scholars it can be concluded that 'harmless growth' is stressed in this *Kural*. 'Harmless Prosperity' can be interpreted to give two meanings; one is that there should not be any harm to the prosperity i.e. growth or development. Second is that there should not be any harm out of prosperity. The joint reading of the line *'Nizhal neerum innatha inna'* (Kural 881) that means shade and water though pleasant at the movement are not really so if they cause disease, and the Kural

> *Peelipei sakaadum achirum appandam*
> *Salamiguthu peyinn* (Kural 475)
>
> (Be it the feathery light peacock's flume, an excess load breaks axle of the cart carrying it).

Meaning, that the axle of a cart though loaded with only peacock's light feathers will break if it has been greatly overloaded, makes one to wonder whether Thiruvalluvar only stressed that prosperity should not bring harm to the nation.

Prosperity and development is necessary for any nation. The State can exploit its natural resources for its development. But, if the natural resources are over exploited in the name of development then it can bring harm to the environment. Therefore, development should not be at the expense of environment. This is nothing but the current international principle concerning environmental protection is generally called as 'sustainable development'. May be Thiruvalluvar has highlighted this present international principle of sustainable development then itself.

Environmental Impact Assessment

Environmental Impact Assessment (EIA) is a process evaluating the effects of the proposed development projects, plans or policies on the quality of environment. EIA helps administrative authorities to choose correctly from among various options for making environmentally sound decisions. In exercise of the powers conferred by sections 6, 8 and 25 of the Environment (Protection) Act 1986 Government of India has formulated certain rules regarding EIA. On 27th January, 1994 the Ministry of Environment and Forest has issued a notification making EIA Statutory for 29 different activities in industries, mining, irrigation, power, etc.

EIA is just created in the lines of Thiruvalluvar's principle *'varum munn kakka'* (Kural 435).

> *Azhivathom Avathom agi vazhipayakkum*
> *Oothiyamum suzhuthu seyal* (Kural 461)
>
> (Analyse the costs, yields and profits involved;
> before acting on a proposition).

Says that let a man first reflect on what will be lost, what will be acquired and what will be his resultant gain and then act. Further the Kural says, *'yenni thuniga karumam'* (*Kural* 467). The inescapable conclusion is that the principles highlighted in these *Kurals* just refer to EIA of present day.

Conclusion

The need for environmental protection was first emphasised only in the year 1972 by Stockholm Declaration at the international level. References relating to environmental protection were included in the Indian Constitution only in the year 1976 — a quarter of a century after framing our Constitution. Only by 1986, the Environment (Protection) Act, 1986 was enacted and the importance of environmental protection was accepted in India. Thus only towards the end of the twentieth century environmental protection was given due importance by the world community. But the fact that Thiruvalluvar, who gave us the 'holy book' *Thirukural,* has stressed the importance of environmental protection even several centuries before, can be clearly understood from this short Chapter. Scientists have opined that the degradation of the environment is the reason for the recent natural disastrous like failure of rains, unseasonal rains, acid rain etc. if we do not pay enough attention to the protection of the environment then we cannot escape from the disasters arising out of environmental damages. It would not even be possible to measure the damages. Let us protect the environment and be wise by always honouring the voice of the *Kural* and the following noble message

> *'munnurva kavathu izlukiyann thanpizhai*
> *pinnura irangi vidum* (Kural 535).
>
> (Lacking foresight in sloth, the unwary
> rue their follies in times that follow).

References

1. See principle 6.1 of the Seoul Declaration of International Law Association (ILA) 1986.
2. Declaration of United Nations Conference on the Human Environment (Stockholm) U.N. Doc. A/Conf./48/Rev/(1972). Reprinted in selected documents on International Environmental Law (Oceana, N.Y) 1975, pp. 3-5 *et seq*. 33.
3. *Ibid.*

4. Nagendra Singh, 'Right to Environment and Sustainable Development as a Principle on International Law', *Journal of the Indian Law Institute.* Vol. 29 (3), 1967, p. 289 at p. 291.
5. Adopted by the World Commission on Environment and Development (WCED) experts group on Environmental Development during 18-20 June 1986 at Peace Place in the Hague, *ibid.,* at p. 309.
6. *Ibid.*
7. U.N.G.A Res. 45/94 of 14th December 1990.
8. *New Zealand* v. *France,* ICJ Reports 1974, p. 457.
9. New Zealand Application, 9 May 1973, pp. 14-16.
10. AIR 1985 SC 652 at 656.
11. AIR 1987 AP 171 at 181. The Court said 'the enjoyment of life and its attainment and fulfilment guaranteed by Art. 21 of the Constitution embraces the protection and preservation of nature's gifts without which life cannot be enjoyed. The slow pollution and spoliation should also be regarded as amounting to violation of Art. 21 of the Constitution.
12. AIR 1991, SC 420.
13. Nagendra Singh *supra* note 4 p. 289 also see J.N. Saxena, 'Environment Protection. A Much Neglected Human Right' in R.P. Anand, Rahamatullah Khan and S. Bhatt (ed) Law, Science and Environment (New Delhi,1987) p. 250 at 254: W. Paul Gormley, ' The Right to Safe and Decent Environment'. *IJIL* Vol. 28 (1) (1988) p. 1-32.
14. *AIR* 1988, SC 1037-48.

8

HUMAN RIGHTS
DEVELOPMENT AND RESPONSE OF THE SUPREME COURT OF INDIA

R. VENKATA RAO

The word "Development" has its origin in the Italian work "*VELUPURA*" which means to unwrap, to disentangle, to rid of some thing. The opposite of "develop" is "envelop" which means to hide, to cover up, to put up constraints—that we do when we envelop something. When we develop something, we do the reverse—we remove these constraints, whatever they may be. The word develop is a positive term meaning progress, and when applied to a human being, indicates a comprehensive growth which enables an individual to feel that he/she is as much a part of mankind as anybody else.[1] The Noble laureate Amartya Sen observes that development consists of the removal of various types of unfreedoms that leave people with little choice and little opportunity of exercising their reasoned agency. Development requires the removal of major sources of unfreedom: Poverty as well as tyranny, poor economic opportunities as well as systematic social deprivation, neglect of public facilities as well as intolerance or overactivity of repressive States. Development is a process of expanding the real freedoms that people enjoy.[2]

The Supreme Court of India, which has original jurisdiction in any dispute:

(a) between the Government of India and one or more States: or

(b) between the Government of India any State or States on the one side and one or more other States on the other; or

(c) between two or more States:

has, in the first twenty five years of its existence, more or less acted along the traditional lines. But overcoming the problem of inertia, the Apex Court after 1975 has started making forays by focusing more on the Constitutional objectives and goals. Justice, Social Economic and Political, equality of status and opportunity and liberty in the holistic sense—all to uphold the dignity of the human being—have been of the State—the Legislature and the Executive have been failing to fulfill the constitutional mandate, the Supreme Court through its activism has been coming to the rescue of the common man. Two things are primarily responsible for this:

1. Expansion of the doctrine of *Locus Standi* and ushering in the era of Public Interest Litigation.
2. New meaning to Article 21(Right to life and Liberty)

Normally litigation in Courts is centered on violation of Private rights. A person whose right is violated alone can go to a Court of Law. In India, many persons whose rights are violated suffer in silence resigning themselves to their fate. These persons continue to suffer because of their poverty. Their poverty makes the Courts inaccessible to them. They are prices out of the legal system. To fulfil the constitutional mandate, the Supreme Court of India has opened a new leaf by expanding the traditional doctrine of *locus standi* and by introducing Public Interest Litigation: Public Interest Litigation means—where a person who has suffered a legal wrong or a legal injury or whose legal right or legally protected interest is violated, is unable to approach the Court on account of some disability or it is not practical for him to move the Court for some other sufficient reasons, such as his socially or economically disadvantaged position, some other person can invoke assistance of the Court for the purpose of providing judicial redress to the person wronged or injured, so that the legal wrong or injury caused to such person does not go undressed and justice is done to him.[3]

Safeguards have been built to prevent Public Interest Litigation from becoming Publicity Interest Litigation. Article 21 of the Constitution of India guarantees right to life and personal liberty—"No person shall be deprived of his life or personal liberty except according to the procedure established by Law." The Supreme Court by construing the expression "procedure established by Law" as meaning a procedure which is "reasonable, fair and just" in Maneka Gandhi's Case[4] has liberated it from the narrow confines of A.K. Gopalan.[5] Ever since, the magic *mantra* of "reasonable, fair and just" has been invoked to provide succour to the hapless.

Realizing that development requires the removal of major sources of unfreedom, the Supreme Court by its innovative judgments in the following areas has responded well to the cause of development:

1. Poverty:

   Asian Workers Case, Pavement Dwellers Case, Sanjit Roy's Case

2. Poor Economic opportunities as well as systematic social deprivation :

   Neeraja Chowdhary's Case, Bandhua Mukti Morcha's Case

3. Neglect of public facilities:

   Unnikrishnan's Case

4. Intolerance or overactivity of repressive State:

   Rudul Sah's Case, Neelabati Behara's Case

   The above list is only illustrative and not exhaustive.

Poverty

In the Case of *PUDR* v. *Union of India*[6] (*Popularly known as Asiad Workers Case*), workers were engaged in the construction of stadia and when minimum wages were paid to them by the authorities, these workers, who were mostly migrant labour used to pay Rupee 1 per day to Jamadaar (Middle Man) who was responsible for their employment. People's Union for Democratic Rights observing all this filed PIL petition in the Supreme Court arguing that workers were not being paid their minimum wages. The authorities stated that they couldn't be faulted as they have discharged their obligation by paying minimum wages. They said the workers were voluntarily paying Re. 1 per day of their own accord. Article 23 of the Constitution of India prohibits forced labour. The Supreme Court observed that no human being would like to part with his hard earned money unless he is forced to do so by dint of circumstances. The Court noted that forced labour does not mean use of physical force all along. Force necessitated by economic compulsion also would attract the " Forced Labour" in Article 23. This revolutionary interpretation initiated a new order of development.

In *Sanjit Roy* v. *State of Rajasthan*[7] (*popularly known as Rajasthan Famine Workers Case*) where the State of Rajasthan enacted a legislation excluding the workers engaged in Famine Relief operations from the scope of minimum wages act on the ground that its coffers are empty, the Court examined the Constitutional validity of the said legislation. The State advanced the argument that more workers can be engaged and more families can be benefited if less minimum wages are paid. The Supreme Court while striking down the legislation observed that the State itself couldn't become the exploiter taking advantage of the poverty of the people. If the State is allowed to become the exploiter, it would send wrong signals to private individuals, the Court observed.

Poor Economic Opportunities as well as Systematic Social Deprivation

In *Olga Tellis* v. *Bombay Municipal Corporation*[8] (*popularly known as Pavement Dwellers Case*), where the Bombay Municipal Corporation authorities removed all the pavement dwellers without showing them any alternative avenues, the Supreme Court observed that "an equally important facet of the right to life is the right to livelihood, because no person can live without the means of living, that is, means of livelihood and that deprivation of livelihood would not only denude the life of its effective content and meaningfulness, but it would make life impossible to live."

Taking judicious cognizance of the plight of the meek and weak, the Court very rightly observed in *Neeraja Choudury* v. *State of M.P.*[9] that bidding farewell to the thought of welfare of the downtrodden after passing welfare legislation is making a mockery of the goals and objectives of the said legislation. There should not be any implementation gap, the Court exhorted. The Court said:

> "It has to be appreciated that mere passing of welfare legislation on for the upliftment of the downtrodden, the meek and weak is by itself not sufficient, though undoubtedly the legislation is the first step in the right direction. What is really important is that every law enacted, particularly welfare legislation for the benefit of weaker section of the people, must be implemented in the proper spirit for achieving the noble object or which such legislation is passed. Implementing the law has, necessarily to be effected through human agencies. Unfortunately, frailties of human nature and degeneration of human character often add to the existing problem instead of solving them."

Referring to the implementation of the provisions of the Bonded Labour system (Abolition) Act, 1976, the Court both in Bandhua Mukti Morcha[10] and Neeraja Chowdhury observed that mere identification and release of bonded labour is not enough. It is just a beginning. A thing well begun is half done, goes the adage. But the half would be undone if the rehabilitation aspects is ignored. The meaning of the rights guaranteed under Article 21 and Article 23 of the Constitution has been laid bare when the Court said that any failure on the part of the State to rehabilitate the bonded labour would result in the violation of the said Articles. If the slavery of the bonded labour is bad, the formal freedom without any guarantee of the basic necessities would be worse and bereft of any meaning. Slavery with survival for what it is worth rather than the so called freedom leading to a certain death would be preferred—this is in consonance with the basic instinct of any living being—to protect one's own life. In *Bandhua Mukti Morcha,* the Court observed:

> " The other question arising out of the implementa-tion of the Bonded Labour System (Abolition) Act is that of rehabilitation of the realized bonded labourers, and that is also a question of the greatest importance, because if the bonded labourers who are identified and freed, are not rehabilitated, their condition would be much worse than what it was before during the period of their serfdom and they would become more exposed to exploitation and slide back once again into serfdom even in the absence of any coercion. The bonded labourer who is released would prefer slavery to hanger a world of 'bondage and illusory security' as against a world of freedom and starvation. The State government must, therefore, concentrate on rehabilitation of bonded labour and evolve effective programmes for this purpose.

The Court continued the same vein in *Neeraja Chowdhury:*

> "...Without rehabilitation, they would be driven by poverty, helplessness and despair into serfdom once again. Poverty and destitution are almost perenniel features of Indian rural life for large numbers of unfortunate illustrated humans in this country and it would be nothing short of cruelty and heartlessness to identify and release bonded labourers merely to throw them to the mercy of the existing social and economic system which denies to them even the basic necessities of the life such as food, shelter and clothing. It is the plainest requirement of Article 21 and 23 of the Constitution that the bonded

labourers must be identified and released and on release, they must be suitably rehabilitated. The Act has been enacted pursuant to the Directive Principles of State Policy with a view to ensuring basic human dignity to the bonded labourers and any failure of action on the part of the State government in implementing the provisions of this legislation would be the clearest violation of Article 21 apart from Article 23 of the Constitution."

The Court without beating its luminous wings in the void has been realistic by striking a note of caution that rehabilitation has to take place in a hostile social milieu. With the vested interests dead set against transformation, the task becomes difficult. Perhaps, that makes the association of social action groups, voluntary social service agencies, and dedicated young men and women in the rehabilitation. Psychological physical and economic rehabilitation of the bonded labour are more relevant and meaningful.

Neglect of Public Facilities

Rights to life guaranteed under Article 21 does not mean right to any type of life. Though all living organisms have life; it is the quality of life that places the human beings at the highest in the pedestal. Birth, growth and decay are the attributes of any life. It is dignity clothing the human life that distinguished the life of human beings from others. Life bereft of disunity is not life at all. The Supreme Court in the Case of Unnikrishnan[11] observed that the right to education and to be read as a part of right to life guaranteed under Article 21. A person will be able to lead a dignified life only when he is educated. The Court took care to observe that by right to education it means right to basic education and not higher education. Thus the Court could correctly identify the linkage between education and development. In fact this path breaking decision is responsible for the introduction of the 93rd Constitutional Amendment Bill in the Parliament recently making education a fundamental right.

Intolerance or Over Activity of Repressive State

The State for a long time used to take shelter under the anachronistic doctrine of sovereign immunity, always seeking justification under the premises, 'the King can do no wrong'. The Supreme Court again rose to the occasion and stated that in a system governed by rule of laws, 'the King can do no wrong' would mean the king shall do no wrong. In number of cases the Court made the State accountable and liable for its wrongful acts. Two cases would illustrate the point.

The first is the case of *Rudul Sah* v. *State of Bihar*[12] from which the Supreme Court of India has commenced the era of compensatory jurisprudence. In this case, Rudul Sah was found to have been "Illegally detained" without any statutory justification for a period of fourteen years after his acquittal of criminal charges at a Sessional trial. Considering this as a flagrant infringement of the petitioner's fundamental right under Article 21 not to be deprived of his life or liberty except according to the procedure established by (fair, just and reasonable) law, the court directed the Government of the State of Bihar to pay compensation to Rudul Sah. The genial seeds of penalizing the Repression State were laid thus in this Case.

The second is the Case of *Nilabati Behara* v. *State of Orissa*[13]. This is a case relating to lock up death. A young man was arrested allegedly for having committed the offence of theft and later his dead body was found on a railway track. When the investigation revealed that the youth succumbed to injuries inflicted in the Police torture, the Supreme Court on a petition filed by a the mother of the young man, observed that where human rights and fundamental rights are violated by the officers of the State, the defence of sovereign immunity will not be applicable. The Court directed the State to pay compensation to the mother of the victim. The Supreme Court of India, through its activism, has been striving to remove the UNFREEDOMS, which are the stumbling blocks for attaining development. Its recent direction to the government to initiate an effective food distribution policy to put a stop to the paradox of starvation deaths when millions of foodgrains are lying stacked in the godowns of the Food Corporation of India is a clear example of its concern for development. The Supreme Court has become active only because the common man has become active. Common man should sustain his activism through strong civil societies so that development does not take the back seat.

References

1. Prof. K.D. Gangarde: Gandhian Path to Development: Paper presented at the National Seminar on Sustainable Economic, Social and Political Reforms in the Information Age. India International Centre, NewDelhi, Jan. 2001.
2. Amartya Sen: *Development as Freedom* (Oxford University Press 2000) p. 3.
3. S.P. Gupta v. President of India, AIR 1983 SC, 75.
4. AIR 1978 SC 597.
5. AIR 1950 SC 27.
6. AIR 1982 SC 1473.
7. AIR 1983 SC 328.
8. AIR 1986 SC 180.
9. AIR 1984 SC 1099.
10. AIR 1984 SC 802.
11. (1993) 1 SCC 645.
12. AIR 1983 SC 1086.
13. (1993)2 SCC 746.

9

HUMAN RIGHTS AS JURAL POSTULATES

AN INDIAN PERSPECTIVE WITH SPECIAL REFERENCE TO ECONOMIC RIGHTS

V. HEMALATHA DEVI AND VIJAYA LAKSHMI

Introduction

Human beings like any other form of life are part of the nature and acquire certain claims, liberties, powers and immunities, which can be titled as 'rights'. These rights do not owe their existence to any law but they are the gifts of nature.[1]

All human beings are born with equal and inalienable rights and fundamental freedoms. Recognition of the inherent dignity and of the equal and inalienable rights of all members of the human family is the foundation of freedom, justice and peace in the world. As a common standard of achievement for all people and all nations, to the end that every individual and every organ of society, keeping the Declaration[2] constantly in mind, shall strive by teaching and education to promote respect for these rights and freedoms.

Human rights are of crucial significance and are basic to human welfare and prosperity. Human rights are inseparable from human beings since human existence without right is of no meaning. Every individual must enjoy certain freedoms, which are fundamental to his growth and purposive life.

Human rights include not only civil and political rights

but socio-economic and cultural rights. In a democratic country like India which seeks to maintain a happy equilibrium between individual freedom and social control by eliminating vices of unbridled private enterprise through social and welfare measures, the Directive Principles of State Policy wherein Economic Justice is included to serve a useful purpose.

In this Chapter an attempt is made to discuss the human rights in India with a particular reference to economic rights as jural postulates propounded by Roscoe Pound.

As the economic rights are incorporated under the provisions of Part IV i.e., Directive Principles of the Constitution which are non justiciable, how to make them justiciable in order to bring socio-economic justice enshrined in the Preamble of the Constitution through Rights' based approach is also discussed in this Chapter.

Among the advocates of sociological method Roscoe Pound stands prominent. He was responsible for the growth of the functional attitude in juridical sciences. According to Pound, sociological jurisprudence should be sure that the making, interpretation and application of laws take account of sociological facts. According to Pound every society has certain basic assumptions upon which its ordering, though for the most part there may be implicit rather than expressly formulated. Certain of these assumptions may be identified as the jural postulates of the legal system as embodying its fundamental purpose.

The postulates are working hypotheses and for satisfying social or individual claims. Rights are the legally protected interests. The common law still bears the impress of individual rights. For the purpose of this chapter private and social interests are taken into consideration.

PRIVATE ← INTERESTS → SOCIAL

PRIVATE ↓

Individual's 'Interests' of Personality to be protected by law

↓

Physical Integrity
Reputation Freedom

SOCIAL ↓

Are the claims or demands or desires thought of in terms of social life and generalised as 'claims of social group'.

↓

- In the general security and ğeneral progress.
- In the security of Social Institutions in individual life.
- In general morals.
- In the conservation of social resources.

Social interests in general morals include variety of dimensions like prostitution, drunkenness and gambling. Conservation of human resources wherein the right to resources is involved. General progress deals with economic and cultural progress.

Jural Postulates Propounded by Roscoe Pound

The postulates were formulated originally in 1919 and modified in 1942. In a civilized society:

I. Men must be able to assume that others will commit no intentional aggression upon them.

II. Men must be able to assume that they may control for beneficial purpose what they have discovered and appropriated to their own use, what they have created by their own labour and what they have acquired under the existing social and economic order.

III. Men must be able to assume that those with whom they deal in the general intercourse of society will act in good faith and hence:

   (a) Will make good reasonable expectations which their promises or other conduct reasonably create;
   (b) Will carry out their undertakings according to the expectations, which the moral sentiments of the community attach thereto.
   (c) Will restore specifically or by equivalent what comes to them by mistake or failure of the preposition of a transaction or other unanticipated situation whereby they receive at another's expense what they could not reasonably have expected to receive under the actual circumstances.

IV. Men must be able to assume that those who engage in some course of conduct will act with due care not to cast on unreasonable risk of injury upon others.

V. Men must be able to assume that others who maintain things or employ agencies harmless in the sphere of their use but harmful in their normal action elsewhere and having a natural tendency to cross the boundaries of their proper use will restrain them or keep them within their proper bounds.

These five postulates are synthesis between means and ends, reality and ideal, power and social accountability, which ought to regulate the conduct of men in a civilized society. These postulates are relative, may change and be reformulated according to the circumstances, times and places. Jural postulates once adopted are maintained until new facts show that they are no longer applicable (1919 and 1942).

Making, interpretation and application of laws take account of sociological facts. In order to achieve that end there should be a factual study of the social effects of legal administration, social investigations, a preliminary to legislation, a constant study of the means for making laws more effective etc.

Again in 1942, after an era of transition from agricultural to Industrial society, certain other postulates are added:

I. That a person will have security as a jobholder;
II. That society will bear the burden of supporting him when he becomes aged, and
III. That society as a whole will bear the risk of unforeseen misfortunes such as disablement.

These are to be followed by legislators and judges for evaluating, balancing and harmonizing various interests.

International Perspective

Human rights are of crucial significance and are basis to human welfare and prosperity. They are inseparable from human beings since human existence without right is of no meaning. Every individual must enjoy certain freedoms, which are fundamental for growth and purposive life.

Universal Declaration of Human Rights, 1948, which consists of 30 Articles, provides certain provisions for economic justice.

All human beings are born free and equal in dignity and rights....[3] Everyone has the right to life[4], right to own property[5], right of equal access to public service[6] economic rights[7], right to work, free choice of employment, just and favourable conditions of work and protection against unemployment, equal pay for equal work, just and favourable remuneration[8], right to standard of living adequate for his health and well-being of himself and his family including food, clothes, housing and medical care, security in the event of unemployment, sickness, disability.......[9] etc., and right to education[10].

Indian Constitutional Perspective

"WE, THE PEOPLE OF INDIA, having solemnly resolved to constitute India into a [SOVEREIGN SOCIALIST SECULAR DEMOCRATIC REPUBLIC] [11] and to secure to all its citizens:

JUSTICE, social, economic and political;

LIBERTY of thought, expression, belief, faith and worship;

EQUALITY of status and of opportunity;

and to promote among them all.

FRATERNITY assuring the dignity of the individual and the [unity and integrity of the Nation][12] ;

IN OUR CONSTITUENT ASSEMBLY this twenty-sixth day of November, 1949, do HEREBY ADOPT, ENACT AND GIVE TO OURSELVES THIS CONSTITUTION."[13]

The Indian Constitution through its Preamble emphatically declares that the Socialist Democratic Republic of India shall be committed to the ideal of socio-economic justice. Fundamental rights and directive principles of State policy of the Constitution are the brain and heart of the Constitution.

A Constitution framed in the middle of the Twentieth century could hardly be without a chapter on Directive Principles of the type of the Indian Constitution has. The establishment of political democracy is a fundamental aim of the Constitution. But, that itself is not enough. The sustaining forces of that political democracy have to be carefully built up. The most effective force, which will sustain a political democracy, is the simultaneous existence of an economic democracy. If the fundamental rights guarantee a political democracy in India, the Directive Principles ensure the economic democracy, which is necessary for the sustenance of the former.[14]

The Sapru Committee had recommended a division of fundamental rights into two classes: justiciable and non-justiciable.[15] They have got their origin even in the Government of India Act, 1935, Charter on United Nations and the Universal Human Rights Charter.

Article 36 to 51 embodied under Part IV of the Constitution under the title of Directive Principles of State Policy, cover a wide range of State activity embracing economic, social, legal, educational, administrative, cultural, environmental and international problems.

As far as the economic rights or policies are concerned some of the directives may require special attention. They are Article 39(a), (b), (c), (d), (e) and (f), 39-A, 41, 42, 43, 43-A, 45 and 46.

The main object behind the Directive Principles is to achieve the ideal of economic democracy. The economic rights that are enshrined under Part IV of the Constitution can be treated as the jural postulates propounded by Roscoe Pound. The jural postulates are for the Law but not of the Law. It is very clear from the later part of Art. 37 which reads as "...the principles therein laid down are nevertheless fundamental in the governance of the Country and it shall be the duty of the State to apply these principles in making Laws " means that these principles are for the Law but not of the Law.

The fundamental rights are no doubt important and valuable in a democracy, but there can be no real democracy without social and economic justice to the common man and to create socio-economic conditions in which there can be social and economic justice to everyone in the theme of directive principles.

The expression 'material resources' used in Art. 39 (b)[16] means all things, which are capable of producing wealth for the community. It covers not only natural or physical resources but also movable or immovable property such as land, buildings, workshops, vehicles etc.[17]

Art. 41[18]of the Indian Constitution, which is very much relevant to the three postulates propounded by Pound in 1942. The principle enshrined in Art. 41 read with Art. 45 provides that it is not only necessary but also desirable for the performance of the State's duty and responsibility to provide education to all its citizens.

Rights Based Approach

Western cultures are said to be 'rights' oriented and Eastern cultures are said to be 'duty' oriented. The human rights talk has western origin. The Common Law still bears the impression of individual rights. In the area of implementation of Directive

Principles, it becomes very much essential to discuss how far the directives, especially economic principles are implemented directly whenever they come into conflict with fundamental rights, or when it becomes necessary to read with or to bring under the umbrella of fundamental rights.[19]

Judicial behaviour is always regarded as national autobiography of any nation's civilization and culture. In twentieth century, the judicial behaviour not only in India but in other democratic countries also has undergone tremendous change. Instead of feeling content with their traditional role, perception as interpreter of Law, the judges have assumed the role of 'policy makers' not only for the government but for institutions also.[20] The economic goals must have priority over ideological ones on the ground that excellence comes only after existence.

Article 39(b) and (c) were implemented by the Supreme Court as they are for public purpose.[21] It has been observed that the judicial approach towards Directive Principles in the era of labour welfare has been more liberal than in case of economic reforms. Fixing of wage structure in different industries in India is justified to achieve the main objective of the welfare State.[22]

Certain policies or Directive Principles have been recognized as new or neo-rights wherein the directives were read into fundamental rights.[23] The following are some of such economic rights.

Right to Livelihood

The Supreme Court had recognized the right to livelihood into right to life under Article 21 for the first time in *Olga Tellis* v. *Bombay Municipal Corporation*[24] because "no person can live without the means of livelihood".

Right to Education

Education is the basic need of man with food, cloth and shelter. The Constitution makers were aware of the basic needs and hence incorporated the right to education as one of the Directive Principles.[25] The question of the fundamental right to education; its scope and limitation came up before the Court in *Mohini Jain* v. *State of Karnataka*[26]

The Court framed the general issue for consideration: is there a right to education guaranteed to the people of India under the Constitution? Justice Kuldip Singh, speaking for the Court, examined the 'right to education' mentioned under Art. 41 and observed:

> "The Directive Principles, which are fundamental in the governance of the country, cannot be isolated from the fundamental rights guaranteed under Part III. *The principles have to be read into the fundamental rights.* Both are supplementary to each other. The State is under a constitutional mandate to create conditions in which the fundamental rights guaranteed to the individuals under Part III could be enjoyed by all."

Thus, the learned judge advocated for inclusion of the right to education into fundamental right. This interpretation of a directive principle, which is non-justiciable, made it enforceable through the Court when the State could not realize that Constitutional obligation. Thus the Court, an organ of the State came forward to ensure this basic principle, when the other two organs of the State, i.e., legislature and executive failed to achieve those objectives.

Right to Status in Life

A man's wealth, his position in the society, social status, proprietary and personal rights constitute his status. The Supreme Court has given predominance to Art. 39(b) so that the material resources of the community are so distributed as best to subserve the common goal. Hence, under Art. 21 'right to life' included 'status in life'. Also, Art. 43 read into Art. 21 provides for the enjoyment of the fundamental right of decent standard of life.

Conclusion

The jural postulates propounded by Roscoe Pound, which are very important, are principles for law. They are the assumptions and these postulates are to be followed by Legislature and Judiciary. Under the Indian Constitution, the Directive Principles of State Policy enshrined under Part IV are recognized as jural postulates. They are fundamental in the governance of the country and it shall be the duty of the State applies these principles in making laws.

The economic justice embodied in the Preamble of the Constitution of India is enshrined in the Directive Principles of State Policy. In case of protecting the economic rights or principles, it has become difficult to the Supreme Court in view of the justiciability of the fundamental rights. Some of the economic principles might have been directly implemented.[27] But most of the directives in general and economic principles in particular have not been directly implemented because of the non-justiciable nature of the directive principles.

Under such circumstances the rights based approach has come for rescue. Poverty jurisprudence was at the core of the heart of the judiciary. The judiciary while protecting the interests of the poor[28] also recognized the fact that they get the right to livelihood. This judicial dynamism is well appreciated. Right to education, one of the important basic rights has been brought under Art. 21.

The role played by judiciary in the area of jural postulates has shown light to many poor who deserve education and this showed a path not only for individual development but also for nation's development. Now many States recognized the importance of right to education and trying to eradicate illiteracy and contesting for 100 per cent literacy award. It is clear that educating people will automatically result in a virtuous growth of standard of living of people, by creating opportunity for self-development for livelihood and it automatically gives chance for them to enjoy all economic and social rights enshrined in the Constitution of India.

References

1. Justice Satyabrata Sinha, "Human Rights: New Challenges in 2001", *Structural Adjustment and Implications of Human Rights,* Serials Publications, 2003, pp. 3-4.
2. *Universal Declaration of Human Rights.*
3. Art.1 of Universal Declaration of Human Rights, 1948.
4. Art. 3 of Universal Declaration of Human Rights, 1948.
5. Art. 17 of Universal Declaration of Human Rights, 1948.
6. Art. 21(2) of Universal Declaration of Human Rights, 1948.
7. Art. 22 of Universal Declaration of Human Rights, 1948.
8. Art. 23 of Universal Declaration of Human Rights, 1948.
9. Art. 25 of Universal Declaration of Human Rights, 1948.
10. Art. 26 of Universal Declaration of Human Rights, 1948.
11. Subs. by the Constitution (Forty-second Amendment) Act, 1976, Section 2, for "SOVEREIGN DEMOCRATIC REPUBLIC" (w.e.f. 3-1-1977).
12. Subs. by Section 2 for "Unity of the Nation" (w.e.f. 3.1.1977).
13. Preamble of the Constitution of India.
14. Wheare, K.C., *India's New Constitution,* C.W.N., p. 54.
15. Constitutional Proposals of the Sapru Committee, 1946.
16. Art. 39(b) provides that "The State shall, in particular, direct its policy towards securing - that the ownership and control of the material resources of the community are so distributed as best to subserve the common good".
17. Prof. Narendra Kumar, *Constitutional Law of India,* Allahabad Law Agency, 1997, p. 305.
18. Art. 41 provides that "The State shall, within the limits of its economic capacity and development, make effective provision for securing the right to work, to education and to public assistance in cases of unemployment, old age, sickness and disablement, and in other cases of undeserved want".
19. It is very evident from the former part of Art. 37, which reads "The provisions contained in this Part shall not be enforceable by any Court, but the principles therein laid down are nevertheless fundamental in the governance of the country and it shall be the duty of the State to apply these principles in making laws". Hence most of them are brought under Art. 21 through the judicial pronouncements.
20. Massey, "Legal Research Methodology for the study of Judicial Behaviour", *Gour Memorial Law Journal,* Vol. 1, 1987-88, p. 82.

21. *State of Bihar* v. *Kameswara Singh,* AIR 1952 SC 252.
22. *Crown Alluminium Works* v. *Their Workers;* AIR 1958 SC 30.
23. To secure to all its citizens, justice - social and economic.
24. AIR 1986 SC 180. The learned Judge in this case observed that the means of livelihood was found in Art. 39(a) and that principle must be regarded as equally fundamental in the understanding and interpretation of the meaning and content of fundamental rights.
25. Art. 41 provides that "The State shall, within the limits of its economic capacity and development, make effective provision for securing the right to work, to education and to public assistance in cases of unemployment, old age, sickness and disablement, and in other cases of undeserved want " and Art. 45 provides that "The State shall endeavour to provide, within a period of ten years from the commencement of this Constitution, for free and compulsory education for all children until they complete the age of fourteen years".
26. AIR 1992 SC 1858.
27. Land Ceiling Laws.
28. Freedom from Bonded Labour and Rehabilitation.

10

PUBLIC PROSECUTIONS IN INDIA
HUMAN RIGHTS OVERTONES

K.N. CHANDRASEKHARAN PILLAI

Many institutions and notions in the criminal justice administration system are being frequently interrogated and re-evaluated. The spurt of debates and discussions surrounding human rights jurisprudence has added impetus to the process of this interrogation and reevaluation. The international movements and the fall in standards of political activities in the developing nations have provided an environment conducive to the growth and development of changes in the basic notions of criminal justice system.

The institution of public prosecution emerged out of the growth of the modern State as the prime protector of the weaker in the society. It has been the duty of the State to maintain law and order affording protection of life and property of the citizenry. This institution was also the result of the realisation that private prosecutions may inundate the very institution of courts of justice apprehending the floodgates of vexatious litigation the court evolved and developed the doctrine of *locus standi,* which allowed the courts to filter the cases coming before them.

Today, it is interesting to note that both these—the institution of public prosecution and the doctrine of *locus standi*—are being questioned and revised in the context of criminal prosecution. Public prosecutions in India are being launched and at times withdrawn by the public prosecutor who is, generally speaking, appointed by the government concerned for a particular term. But the Additional Public Prosecutors are appointed by the government through a selection process by a committee in which the Collector of the District and the District Judge concerned are members. Additional Public Prosecutors form a cadre whereas Public Prosecutors do not have a cadre; they hold office till the Government that appointed them continue to govern.

The office of the Public Prosecutor is closely associated with politics. It is in fact an office, which is being distributed by the party in power among the lawyers owing allegiance to it. After the term of the Government the holders of this office go out of it on their own or on the persuasion of the party that takes over after the elections.

In India this situation had given rise to some problems. There have been some decisions dealing with appointment of Public Prosecutors. In *Kum. Srilekha Vidyarthi* v. *State of U.P.*[1], the question was whether the action of the State Government of U.P. in trying to remove the Public Prosecutors who were appointed by the former government was valid. The Supreme Court deprecated this trend and ruled that appointment to such important offices should not be allowed to be made by the spoil system by the political parties. But the situation has not changed. Even today public prosecutors are appointed by the government from among the sympathisers of the political party/parties. And they continue to side with the party/parties who sponsored them. It is, therefore, alleged that our public prosecutors are not independent or impartial.

In fact his office partakes judicial character. The Public Prosecutor though representing the State is not supposed to be a blind upholder of what all the State authorities do. Being a public functionary he is supposed to be independent and impartial. It is not for him to procure a conviction by hook or crook. It is also not for him to conceal information which may help the court to give the benefit of some defence like insanity to the accused in a criminal case. In short, it can be said that he is like the judicial officer whose function is to safeguard the society by punishing the offender in accordance with law.

In other democracies like UK and USA the office of the public prosecutor essentially retains this character.[2] However, there are some difference. In UK he is an official of the government—a functionary under the Director of Public Prosecutions. He is not to seek a conviction by hook or crook. He has to be impartial. The decision to prosecute is being taken by the prosecutor. In USA Public Prosecutors are sometimes elected by the public. They take the important decision to prosecute. They midwife plea bargaining. They resort to diversion of certain categories of offenders. Indeed, in effecting plea bargaining the court is also involved. These powers borderline with judicial powers.

In India the nature of powers of the Public Prosecutors does have similarities with judicial power. However, it seems that the office of the Public Prosecutor is considered an executive one. The statutory scheme establishing the prosecution system in India seems to signify this.

Sections 24 and 25 of Cr.P.C. provide for the appointment of Public Prosecutors and Asst. Public Prosecutors respectively. Ss. 301 and 302 speak about the appearance of the P.P. in the court to represent the State's case. While under S. 301(1) a P.P. or A.P.P. could appear and conduct the case without the permission of the court S. 301 (2) requires the pleader engaged by the private person to act only under the directions of the P.P. or A.P.P. with the permission of the Court. S. 302 allows the inquiring or trying magistrate to permit the prosecution to be conducted by any person other than a Police Officer not below the rank of inspector. No person other than the Advocate General or Government Advocate or a P.P. or A.P.P. shall be entitled to prosecute without such permission. While engaging a Police officer above the rank of Inspector it should be ensured that he did not participate in the investigation into the offence that is being tried. It is also laid down that the person prosecuting the offender could prosecute either by himself or by a pleader. Thus the pleader engaged by a private party including the victim of the crime could function only under the directions of the A.P.P/P.P. with the permission of the court.[3] The private prosecutor is subjected to two restrictions. Firstly he has to work under the directions of the P.P. Secondly, he has to seek the permission of the court to appear before the court for and on behalf of the victim—complainant.

The provision enabling the P.P. to withdraw prosecution also signifies that the P.P.'s prerogative is subjected to judicial scrutiny, S. 321 lays down:

> *"The Public Prosecutor or the Asst. Public Prosecutor in charge of a case may with consent of the court at any time before the judgment is pronounced, withdraw from the prosecution of any person either generally or in respect of anyone or more of the offences for which he is tried...."*

As mentioned earlier the decision to prosecute is taken by the prosecutor in USA. In India this decision is taken by the magistrate after appreciating the evidence collected by the police. The P.P. does not have any role in taking this decision. Thus both these decisions which require judicial appreciation of facts are not within the powers of the P.P. it could, therefore, be asserted that the P.P's office in India falls under the executive. However, as already discussed above bereft of the requirement of court's permission for withdrawal of prosecution the functions of the P.P. call for judicial approach. Unless the P.P. develops detachment and adopts neutrality in criminal prosecution, it can result in harassment and torture of accused. It can lead the system to disaster as the public may lose confidence in the efficiency of the system to contain crimes. It is, therefore, generally accepted that the P.P. should be independent and impartial. Even in cases of withdrawal of prosecutions the consistent stand of the judiciary, if case law is any guide, is that if the P.P. has taken the decision to withdraw the prosecution independently without being influenced by the State, the court may grant permission under S. 321.[4]

In this connection it is worthwhile to examine the reasoning of Justice Chettur Sankaran Nair of the Kerala High Court in *State of Kerala* v. *Balakrishna Pillai*.[5] His Lordship, himself a former Director of Public prosecutions after the examining the evolution and development of this offence observed thus :

> *"The Public Prosecutor exercises a power in the nature of a prerogative. In criminal law the State and its instrumentalities enjoy prerogatives, akin to Crown prerogatives in England. The power exercised by the Public Prosecutor under S. 321 of the Code of Criminal Procedure is in the nature of such a prerogative. The State may advise him in this regard, but he must exercise his mind independently, and he ought not to act under dictation. If he acts honestly, his act cannot be questioned. The limited role of the court is only supervisory, and not adjudicatory or appellate in character."*[6]

As regards the Court's role, it seems, he hit the nail on the head itself when he essayed thus :

> *"It is not for the court to decide whether withdrawal is justified on the facts, or whether the offence involved so serious as to merit punishment. These are matters for the Public Prosecutor to consider. As long as he acts in good faith in seeking withdrawal from prosecution, so long his action is not liable to be challenged. Every system must work on trust. The court even where it is required to act as a watch dog, is not required to act like a hound."*[7]

This approach signifies the point that the system requires P.P.—an executive functionary—to act judicially. And this situation has led to a conceptual confusion as to the nature of PP's powers. The confusion pervades the whole area of criminal justice system. There is thus confusion as to the role of the prosecutor in criminal trials. It is abundantly evident in the case law produced by the Courts. This confusion has been prevalent prior to *Balakrishna Pillai*[8] and it still continuous to pervade the case law.

The Kerala High Court in *Azeez* v. *State of Kerala*,[9] 1984 Cri. L.J. 1059 ruled thus :

> *"Every counsel appearing in a case before a court is expected to be fair and truthful. He must of course champion the cause of his client as efficiently and effectively as possible, but fairly and*

truthfully. He is not expected to be impartial, but only fair and truthful."[10]

In a different context[11] the same High Court distinguished the P.P. from a counsel of the private party thus:

"Public Prosecutors are really ministers of justice whose job is none other than assisting the State in the administration of justice. They are not representatives of any party. Their job is to assist the court by placing before the court all relevant aspects of the case. They are not there to use the innocents go to the gallows. They are also not there to see the culprits escape conviction. But the pleader engaged by a private person who is a de facto complainant cannot be expected to be impartial. Not only that, it will be his endeavour to get the conviction even if a conviction may not be possible."[12]

Thus though the office of the P.P. seems to have features of executive the judiciary does not seem to treat it as executive. It becomes clear when it disapproves Police officers as P.Ps. The Punjab and Haryana High Court in *Krishan Sigh Kundu* v. *Haryana*[13] has ruled that the idea of appointing a Police Officer as in charge of the prosecution agency is abhorrent to the letter and spirit of Ss. 24 and 25.[14]

It is interesting to note that the judiciary which does not want a Police Officer to be P.P. recognises that he should act as the counsel of the State with fairness. He need not be impartial but truthful and fair. He should assist the criminal justice system. It is not understood what the court stresses on. Does the court want the P.P. to be ethical as a lawyer in displaying his truthfulness and fairness in State prosecutions? Or is it asking for more than this as P.P.? It seems the court is not asking him to be simply lawyering because the Defence Attorney is also to be lawyering and the court can equally require him to be so since he is also bound by professional ethics; what the court asks for is, it seems, fairness and truthfulness. So the P.P. has to be additionally fair and truthful. He has to be at par with the judicial officer. This seems to be a reasonable conclusion as even in the context of withdrawal of prosecutions the courts have been reiterating the sanctity of P.P.'s independent decision to withdraw prosecution.

Irrespective of the question whether the office of the prosecutor is executive or judicial, it remains a fact that everyone expects this office to be independent, impartial and fair in its approach. But this expectation has often been belied.

In *Sunil Kumar* v. *Phota Sheikh*[15] the Supreme Court had to deal with a peculiar situation. The fact indicate how terrible it is if this office of the Public Prosecutor is dominated by politicians. In this case the public prosecutor who first appeared for the prosecution started appearing for the accused belonging to the ruling party in blatant violation of not only his position as P.P. but also as an advocate.

The Supreme Court expressed its anguish thus:

> *"It is difficult to understand how consistently with the ethics of the legal profession and fair play in the administration of justice the P.P. of Nadia could appear on behalf of respondents 1-9."*[16]

In the context of withdrawal of prosecution also we have had instances of prosecutional abuse of powers. In *State of Tamil Nadu* v. *Ganesan*[17] same office of the P.P. which got a criminal case withdrawn with the permission of the court, on change of government moved the court to launch retrospection. Fortunately the court did not permit and expressed its disappointment with the P.P. thus:

> *"I feel that the same office of the P.P. which acted for the State to withdraw the cases, cannot come forward to set aside the order permitting to withdraw the case, irrespective of the change in the ruling party as it will lead to uncertainty as to the finality of proceedings when the government, ruled by a particular party, withdraws the prosecution and successive governments, ruled by another party wanted to set aside that order, what will be the situation, if there were successive changes in the ruling parties and if this request is allowed,*

certainly it will be a havoc and prejudice to the accused persons, without knowing the destination of the prosecution apart from the embarrassment to the P.Ps. therefore I also feel that the office which moved for withdrawing the prosecution cannot seek to set aside the order of permission granting withdrawal of the prosecution. If a third party comes forward with such a prayer the position may be different".[18]

The erosion of values was not a phenomenon peculiar to the P.Ps in India. This was noticed with the Governments also. The judiciary responded to this situation harshly by lifting the embargo of *locus standi.* v. *Atchuthanandan* v. *P.R. Balakrishna Pillai* [19] is a classic example where the Supreme Court intervened and refused permission to withdraw the prosecution. This, was a departure from other court's earlier judgments like *Janata Dal* v. *H.S. Chaudhary*[20] probably because the decision to withdraw the case was not fair. However, the court has not adequately reasoned its decision to lift the embargo of *locus standi* of third parties.

This becomes clear when one examines the facts and decision of the High Court's judgment in *State of Kerala* vs. *Balakrishna Pillai.*[21] Though the Supreme Court did not elaborately deal with the question of *locus standi* of third parties in criminal cases, this aspect was very deeply gone into by the High Court. And it was categorically rule by it that third parties did have no jurisdiction to interfere in criminal cases:

"The view in Surjit Singh and Sheo Nandan finds reaffirmation in *Janata Dal* v. *A. S. Chaudhury* (1991) 3 SCC 756 *Simranjit Singh Mann* v. *Union of India* JT 1992 (5) 441 in second *Janata Dal* v. *A. S. Chaudhury* JT 1992 (5) SC 441, the Supreme Court held that even by invoking Art. 32 of the Constitution (which itself is a fundamental right), a third party cannot question the legality validity or correctness of an order of a criminal court. It was observed:

"Even if there are million questions of law to be deeply gone into and examined in a criminal case of this nature, registered

against specified accused persons, it is for them and them alone to raise all such questions and challenge the proceedings...and not for third parties under the garb of public interest litigation."[22]

His Lordship in his usual style depicted the resulting picture if third parties were allowed to have *locus standi*. He said:

"If the reasoning of the court below, or Shri Kallada Sukumaran is extended to its logical conclusion, a private party may bring witnesses at a trial, with the sole view of setting private scores and personal vendetta. Perjury and passions may prevail, polluting the clear stream of justice. The Criminal Justice system without its sense of objectivity will be 'Hamlet without the Prince of Denmark'.[23]

The exclusive power of the public prosecutor in conducting the prosecutions is reflected in the court's conceding the right of the P.P to engage a person to act on his behalf. The Kerala High Court in *Varghese John* v. *State of Kerala*[24] expressed its opinion on this question thus:

"The P.P. can require any person to act for and on behalf under his direction. If a person is so directed by the P.P., that person gets the status and power of the P.P. When a private party wants to take part in the inquiry, trial or appeal of a case and instructs a pleader to prosecute another in court, that pleader cannot act except under the direction of the P.P. or of the person who acts under the direction of the P.P. If the P.P. directs the pleader so instructed by the private person to prosecute the accused then such pleader will come under the ambit of the definition under S. 2(u) of the code and thereby can be treated as a P.P. This can happen only if the pleader instructed acts under the direction of the P.P.[25]

The court reinforced its argument by dwelling on the implications of S. 302(2) thus:

> *"Clause (2) of that section further states that any person conducting the prosecution may do so personally or by a pleader. It means that Advocate General, Government Advocate or P.P. or A.P.P. who is entitled to conduct the prosecution without the permission of the magistrate may conduct the prosecution by authorising another pleader".*[26]

Thus even if the office of P.P. is exclusively executive as discussed in *Shamsher Singh*[27] it definitely partakes judicial character and as such assumes a lot of importance particularly today when the human rights awareness is at a high pitch.

The misuse or abuse of power of the prosecutor the unprincipled politically motivated interference with criminal prosecution at every stage have made the public to clamour for a review of the arrangement. The court has also aided its anguish not only in prosecutions under the IPC but also in prosecutions under the new specialised laws having becoming on the economic heath of our nation. The observation of the Supreme Court in K.I. Pavunny[28] are instructive. The Court said :

> *"The Union of India should take care to entrust these sensitive cases of far reaching effort, in particular on question of law to caused who have experience and ability in that branch of law to defend their cases. Lest it is public justice that suffers and economy of the country put in jeopardy. Unfortunately the counsel did not make any effort to analyse the provisions of the Act nor did he make investigation into question of law from the decisions rendered by this court. At this juncture, it is further relevant to point out that when the Union of India has its panel of counsel, they should see to it that the work is assigned to the counsel who can competently argue the case in that behalf lest for lack of assistance, investigation and marshalling the questions of fact and law, public justice tends to suffer".*[29]

In our country in the new Criminal Procedure Code Amendment Bill provisions for the creation of a Directorate of Public Prosecutions has been envisaged. It is feared that the things will not improve if the quality of the personnel is not improved. It is, therefore, highly necessary that everyone in the system understands the importance of keeping this office above party–politics and appointments to key position are made accordingly.

Today the victims of crimes are without proper remedy if the prosecution gets derailed due to the lack of interests or negligence of the P.P. If the societal interest is not taken care of by the State governments as a measure of political expedience permitting of some individual to seek remedy from the court by way of lifting the time-tested embargo of *locus standi* is not the appropriate response. We would then be going back to the days of private prosecutions. Many prosecutions may be dropped or compounded due to undesirable influence brought to bear on the complainant-victims. Some people may launch vexatious prosecutions. Witnesses may be tampered with and many prosecutions may come to a standstill for want of evidence. Due to the inefficiency of the victims prosecution may not result in conviction. The cost of prosecution may be high and beyond the reach of the ordinary public.

There have been suggestions that we in India should associate the Public Prosecutor with criminal investigation to ensure efficiency in the latter. It is strongly felt that it would be oxymoronic to club prosecution and investigation. These suggestions may run counter to the basic philosophy of the institution of prosecution. It is gratifying to note that the Supreme Court in *R. Sarala* v. *T.S. Velu*[30] has deprecated this view. The Court observed:

> *"Investigation and prosecution are too different facets in the administration of criminal justice. The role of a P.P. is inside the court, whereas investigation is outside the court. Normally, the role of a P.P. commences after the investigating agency presents the case in the court on culmination of investigation. Its exception is that the P.P. may have to deal with bail applications moved by the parties concerned at any stage. Involving the P.P. in investigation is injudicious as well as pernicious in law. At any rate no investigating agency can be*

compelled to seek the opinion of a P.P. under the orders of the court."[31]

The Supreme Court reiterated this view in *Navin Chandra Majithia* v. *State of Meghalaya*[32] wherein the Court also set aside the order of the Sessions Judge as was approved by the High Court asking the complainant to finance criminal investigation on behalf of the State.

It is surprising that a High Court ordered a private party to arrange investigation which ought to be done by the State. It is indeed to protect the weak and the meek that we go for Public Prosecution preceded by investigation by way of a State agency. The fact that a High Court failed to appreciate the Human Rights implications of its orders is indicative of the insouciant attitude the legal fraternity has developed in relation to investigation and prosecution.

There is need for rethinking. Our reliance on the technical interpretation of statutory provisions without having regard for the basic philosophy underlying them might lead us to chaos and disaster. Understanding of the underlying values of the various provisions of the statute law is a difficult task. It could be achieved only by those who can reorient their thinking and act to suit the needs of the times and the people. Therefore, when one thinks of public prosecution in India, one should, first and foremost, emphasise on the quality of the personnel in terms erudition, integrity studiousness and commitment to protection of human rights.

We are now in a dilemma, the solution lies not in the creation of Directorate but in continued education of the personnel stressing the need for developing sympathetic detachment among the prosecutors. India cannot be oblivious of its international obligations to keep the system transparent and human rights—friendly as the UN agencies have been breathing life into the moribund statutory provisions in municipal laws of the member countries.[33] The P.P. of a developing country like India which swears by the name of human rights protection every minute should be aware of his country's obligations to its citizenry and to the world to prove that it is a free country where the human beings would be treated humanely even when they are accused of committing crimes.

References

1. (1991) S.C.C. 212.
2. See Kai Ambos, "The Status, Role and Accountability of Prosecutor of the International Criminal Court." A comparative overview on the basis of 33 National Reports, 8 European Journal of Crime, Criminal Law and Criminal Justice, (2000), 89.
3. The code does not empower a private party to file a revision petition against an order of acquittal passed in a case instituted on a police report. The prohibition against the victim's or private party's invoking jurisdiction is so strong that the Supreme Court ruled that a private party cannot claim *locus standi* by way of getting permission of public prosecutor in such a case. See *Krishan Swarup* v. *Govt. of N.C.J. Delhi* 1998, SCC (Cri.) 1587.
4. See discussion in *R.K. Jain* v. *State of Punjab*, AIR 1980 SC 1510, *Sheonandan Paswan* v. *State of Bihar*, (1987) 1 SCC 288 *Mohammed Mumtaz* v. *Nandini Satpathi* 1987 Cri. L.J. 778 (S.C.) *State of Punjab* v. *Union of India* 1987 Cri. L.J. 151 (SC) etc.
5. 1993 (1) KLT 473.
6. *Ibid.*, at 476.
7. *Id.*
8. Supra n. 3.
9. 1984 Cri. L.J. 1059.
10. *Ibid.* at 1060.
11. *Babu* v. *State of Kerala*, 1984 Cri. L.J. 502
12. *Id.*
13. 1989 Cri.L.J. 1309 (P & H).
14. See *S.B.Sahana* v. *State of Maharashtra*, 1995 SCC (Cri.) 787.
15. (1984)4 SCC 533.
16. *Ibid.* 537-538.
17. (1995) Cri.L.J. 3849 (Mad.) See also *R.M. Tervari* v. *State (Delhi)* 1996 SCC (Cri.) 361.
18. *Ibid.* at 3851.
19. (1994)4 SCC 299.
20. *Janata Dal* v. *H.S.Chaoudhari* (1992) 4 SCC 305
21. *Infra* n. 49.

22. *Ibid at 480.*
23. *Ibid* at 481.
24. 1995(1) KLT 374.
25. *Ibid.* at 377.
26. The court also relied on *Hamza* v. *A.P.P.* 1978 KLT 816.
27. (1974)2 SCC 831. Chief Justice Ray held in this case that the executive power is generally described as the residue which does not fall within the legislative or judicial power, but executive power also partakes of legislative judicial acts.
28. *K.L. Pavunny* v. *Asst. Collector, Customs.*
29. *K.L. Pavunny* v. *Asst. Collector, Customs,* 1997 SCC (Cri.) 444 and 456.
30. (2000)4 SCC 459.
31. *Ibid.* at 462.
32. 2000 SCC (Cri.) 1510.
33. Art. 2(3) International Covenant on Civil and Political Rights lays down among other things thus:

    Each State party to the present Government undertakes :

(a) To ensure that any person whose rights or freedoms as herein recognised are violated shall have in effective remedy, notwithstanding that the violation has been committed by person, acting in an official capacity;

(b) To ensure that any person claiming such a remedy shall have his right thereto determined by competent, judicial, administrative or legislative authorities, or by any other competent authority provided for by the legal system of the State and to develop the possibilities of judicial remedy;

(c) To ensure that the competent authorities shall enforce such remedies when granted.

11

PROTECTION OF HUMAN RIGHTS IN THE ADMINISTRATION OF CRIMINAL JUSTICE

K. RAMACHANDRA REDDY

In the ancient society the concept of human rights began with the fulfilment of the basic needs of food, clothing and shelter. But, in the modern society, this concept of human rights must cover the other needs of human beings, viz. education, environment and health, to live with basic human dignity, freedom from arbitrary arrest, detention and torture, elimination of all forms of discrimination against women etc.

The Constitution of India guarantees almost the entire gamut of civil and political rights. Civil and political rights are made fundamental and judicially enforceable according to Part III of the Constitution. Whereas the economic and social rights are made basic to the governance of the country through the Directive Principles of State Policy in order to establish an egalitarian society. Besides these constitutional rights, laid down in Part III and Part IV, some special legislations[1] have also been passed to protect the rights of women, children and downtrodden classes of the society. At the same time, in addition to this constitutional and statutory protection of human rights, Government of India has entered into various International Covenants[2] for the protection of human rights in India.

In addition to the regular courts, government has also established machinery for the promotion, protection and effective implementation of the human rights to all classes of people. In this connection, human rights commission has been established to protect the human rights provided under various legislations and the Constitution of India. Besides this, there are also other specialized agencies for the promotion and protection of human rights, viz. National Commission for Scheduled Castes and Scheduled Tribes, National Commission for Women and the Minority Commission. These commissions will review the socio-economic conditions of the concerned groups and related government policies and enactments.

In this chapter a modest attempt has been made to study the rights of the accused under the Constitution of India and the Criminal Procedure Code 1973, which is the only procedural Criminal Law of India and how the Supreme Court has conferred the new fundamental rights on the accused in the interpretation of Article 21 in the light of International Covenants on human rights.

Humanisation of Criminal Procedure Code, 1973

In the subject matter of Criminal Procedure Code (hereinafter called Cr.P.C.), human values are involved to a greater degree than in any other laws. Cr.P.C. 1973 provides several human rights to the arrested persons and also to the accused and the convicted persons in order to humanize the process of arrest and remand of the accused, and also investigation and trial of offences. Let us study the human rights provided under the Cr.P.C. to the accused in general and the special rights of women in particular.

Every police officer effecting the arrest shall communicate the grounds of arrest or the full particulars of the offence to the person to be arrested; and arrest in cases of bailable offences the police officer shall also inform the accused about his right to bail.[3] The person arrested shall not be subjected to more restraint than is necessary to prevent his escape.[4] Sec. 54 of the Cr.P.C. provides a right to medical examination to the arrested person by a registered medical practitioner. The arrested person has a right to be produced before a Magistrate having jurisdiction in the case without unnecessary delay.[5] The arrested person cannot be detained in police custody more than 24 hours without a special order from the Magistrate under Section 167.[6] The maximum period of detention before trial is specified under Section 167 Cr.P.C. After expiration of such detention, he will get a right to be released on bail.[7] Accused person has a right to obtain all documents relevant to the charges framed against him, with free of cost.[8] Section 300 of Cr.P.C. provides a rule of *'autre fois acquit'* and *'autre fois convict'*. Accused person has a right to counsel [9] and also the right to legal aid if he has not sufficient means to engage a pleader.[10] The Code provides the accused an opportunity to make representation against the punishment before it is imposed.[11] The code also prescribed period of limitation for taking cognizance of offences.[12] In addition to these general rights, women accused have some special rights.

Special Rights to Women Under Cr.P.C., 1973

According to Section 51(2) of Cr.P.C. whenever a person is arrested by a police officer and it is necessary to cause a search to be made and if such person is a female, the search shall be made by another female with strict regard to decency. When a person is arrested on a charge of committed an offence and there are reasonable grounds for believing that the medical examination of such person will afford evidence as to the commission of an offence or disapprove the commission of that offence, and if such person is female, such medical examination shall be made only by, under the supervision of a female registered medical practitioner.[13] As to the service of summons, when summoned person cannot be found the summons may be served by leaving one of the duplicates for him with some adult male member of his family residing with him.[14] Hence the code does not authorize the serving officer to serve the summons with the female members of the summoned person, in his absence. As regards the execution of search warrant also, special protection has been given to the women. If any person is reasonably suspected of concealing about his person any article for which search should be made such person may be searched and if such person is a woman, the search shall be made by another woman with strict regard to decency.[15] During the course of investigation also, no woman shall be required by a police officer to attend at any place other than the place in which such woman resides.[16]

With regard to granting bail, special consideration is shown towards women. When any person accused of the commission of any non-bailable offence is arrested, he may be released on bail, but (i) such person shall not be so released if there appears reasonable grounds for believing that he has been guilty of an offence punishable with death or imprisonment for life, (ii) such person shall not be so released if such offence is a cognizable offence and he had been previously convicted of an offence punishable with death, imprisonment for life, or imprisonment for seven years or more, or he had been previously convicted on two or more occasions of a non-bailable and cognizable offence: provided that the court may direct that a person referred to in Clause (i) and Clause (ii) be released on bail if such person is under the age of sixteen years or is a woman or sick or infirm.[17]

In order to eradicate dowry deaths a special procedure is also laid down under the code. When (i) the case involves suicide by a woman within seven years of her marriage; or (ii) the case relates to the death of a woman within seven years of her marriage in any circumstances raising a reasonable suspicion that some other person committed an offence in relation to such women; or (iii) the case relates to the death of a woman within seven years of her marriage and any relative of the woman has made a request in this behalf; or (iv) there is any doubt regarding the cause of death; or (v) the police officer for any other reason considers it expedient so to do; he shall forward the body to the nearest civil surgeon for medical examination.[18]

With regard to pregnant woman also, the code shows a sympathetic view. If a woman sentenced to death is found to be pregnant, the High Court shall order the execution of the sentence to be postponed, and may, if it thinks fit, commute the sentence to imprisonment for life.[19]

Supreme Court as a Sentinel of Human Rights

The constitutional rights in the context of Criminal Jurisprudence are contained in Articles 20, 21 and 22 of the Constitution. Article 20 prohibits *ex post facto* operation of Criminal law[20] and confers immunity against double jeopardy[21] and also provides protection against self-incrimination.[22] Article 21 guarantees that no person shall be deprived of his life or personal liberty except according to procedure established by law. Article 22 provides protection against arbitrary arrest and detention.

Clause (1) of Article 22 provides that no person who is arrested shall be detained in custody without being informed, as soon as may be, of the grounds for such arrest nor shall he be denied by a legal practitioner of his choice. Clause (2) provides that every person who is arrested and detained in custody shall be produced before the nearest Magistrate within a period of 24 hours of such arrest excluding the time necessary for the journey from the place of arrest to the court of the Magistrate and no such person shall be detained in custody beyond the said period without the authority of a Magistrate.

In the interpretation of the aforesaid fundamental rights and other statutory rights of the accused, the Supreme Court has been influenced by the Universal Declaration of Human Rights and the International Covenants on Civil and Political Rights and Economic, Social and Cultural rights. Supreme Court had developed more humanistic approach in the interpretation of Articles 20, 21 and 22 of the Constitution since Maneka Gandhi's case.[23] After Maneka Gandhi's decision, in the broad sweep and content of Article 21, the Supreme Court has elevated several human rights contained in the International Covenants to the status of the fundamental rights of the accused under Part III of the Constitution. In the light of Human Rights jurisprudence and the imported 'due process of law' the Supreme Court has changed the shape and content of Article 21 through its juristic activism and invented its new facets namely: Right against torture, cruel and inhuman treatment; Right to live with human dignity and socialize with members of the family and friends; Right to legal aid, speedy trial; Right to compensation etc. consequently, each of the components of this Article has reached to the status of international standards. Let us study various fundamental rights of the accused innovated by the Supreme Court in the interpretation of Article 21 of the Constitution.

Right against Torture and Custodial Violence

Torture has emerged as a world phenomena. State torture has become a fashion with a number of authoritarian governments. About fifty States have banned torture under their national constitutions.[24] In *Sunil Batra* v. *Delhi Administration,*[25] Krishna Iyer, J. delivering the majority judgement held that integrity of physical person and his mental personality is an important right of a prisoner, and must be protected from all kinds of atrocities. In *Kishore Singh* v. *State of Rajasthan,*[26] the Supreme Court held that the use of 'third degree' methods by police is violative of Article 21 of the Constitution and directed the government to take necessary steps to educate the police so as to inculcate a respect for the human person. Similarly torture and ill-treatment of women suspects in police lock-ups has been held to be violative of Article 21 of the Constitution.[27]

In *D.K. Basu* v. *State of West Bengal,*[28] the Supreme Court, through Dr.Justice Anand, held that[29] 'any form of torture or cruel, inhuman or degrading treatment, would fall within the inhibition of Article 21 of the Constitution whether it occurs during investigation, interrogation or otherwise.' Further his Lordship observed that[30] custodial torture is a naked violation of human dignity and degradation which destroys to a very large extent the individual personality. It is a calculated assault on human dignity and whenever human dignity is wounded civilization takes a step backward, flag of humanity must on each such occasion fly half-mast.

Right against Solitary Confinement and Bar Fetters

Solitary confinement is by itself a substantive punishment, which can be imposed by a court of law. It cannot be left to the whim and caprice of prison authorities[31]. In Sunil Batra case the Supreme Court, through D.A. Desai, J. held that [32] Bar fetters make a serious inroad as the limited personal liberty which a prisoner is left with and, therefore, before such erosion can be justified it must have the authority of law. The court further held[33] 'that the liberty to move, mix, mingle, talk, share company with co-prisoners, if sufficiently curtailed would be violative of Article 21, unless the curtailment has the backing of law.' The law must be right, just and fair and not arbitrary, fanciful or oppressive, as interpreted in Maneka Gandhi's case.

In *Kishore Singh* v. *State of Rajasthan,*[34] the apex court held that[35] the punishment of solitary confinement for a long period from 8 to 11 months and putting bar fetters as the prisoner in jail for several days on flimsy grounds like 'loitering in the prison', behaving insolently and in an uncivilized manner, 'tearing of his history ticket' must be regarded as barbarous and against human dignity and hence violative of Articles 21, 19 and 14 of the Constitution. In Sunil Batra (I) case,[36] Justice Krishna Iyer observed that fetters, especially bar fetters, shall be shunned as violative of human dignity within and without prisons.

Right against Handcuffing

In *Prem Shankar Shukla* v. *Delhi Administration,*[37] Krishna Iyer, J. held that handcuffing of a prisoner was unconstitutional, if there was any other reasonable way of preventing escape of the prisoner. Handcuffing should be resorted to only when there is clear and present danger of escape breaking out the police control and for this there must be clear material, not merely an assumption. His Lordship further observed.

> *"Handcuffing is prima facie inhuman and, therefore, unreasonable, is overharsh and at the first flush, arbitrary. Absent fair procedure and objective monitoring to inflict 'irons' is to resort to zoological strategies repugnant to Article 21...*

In *Sunil Gupta* v. *State of M.P.,*[38] the court directed the government to take appropriate action against erring escort party for having unjustly and unreasonably hand-cuffing the petitioners. In *State of Maharashtra* v. *Ravikant S. Patil,*[39] the Bombay High Court held that hand cuffing and parading of the petitioner was unwarranted and violative of Article 21 and directed the Inspector of Police who was responsible for this, to pay Rs. 10,000 by way of compensation. The Supreme Court upheld the judgement of the High Court directing payment of compensation but held that the Police Officer was not personally liable as he acted as an official.

In *Citizen for Democracy* v. *State of Assam,*[40] the Supreme Court expressed serious concern over the violation of the law laid down by that court in its earlier decisions against handcuffing of undertrial or convicted prisoners by police authorities. The court, therefore, laid down some directions for the strict implementation of the law against handcuffing . The court directed all ranks of police and the prison authorities to meticulously obey the directions given in this case. The court further held that any violation of any of the directions of this court in this case by any rank of police in the country or member of jail establishment shall be summarily punishable under the Contempt of Courts Act apart from other penal consequences under law.

Supreme Court through its dynamic and creative interpretation in Sunil Batra, Kishore Singh, Sheela Barse, Charles Sobraj, Prem Shankar Shukla, D.K. Basu etc. cases has elevated the human rights against torture, cruel, inhuman or degrading treatment or punishment provided under Article 5 of the Universal Declaration of Human Rights and Article 7 of the International Covenant on Civil and Political Rights to the Status of fundamental rights Under Article 21 of the Constitution. At the same time the court has given directions to the authorities concerned to implement these fundamental rights strictly during the period of custody/imprisonment of accused/convict, and also advised the Government to inculcate the police department officials with human rights jurisprudence. Thus, 'Article 21 stands like sentinel over human misery, degradation and oppression. Its voice is the voice of justice and fair play'.[41]

Right to Live with Human Dignity and Socialize with Members of the Family and Friends

Individual dignity is one of the cherished values of our Constitution.[42] Supreme Court also upheld the right to live with human dignity in *Francis Coralie Mullin* v. *Union Territory of Delhi.*[43] In this case, the court, speaking through justice Bhagwati, held that the right to life includes the right to live with human dignity. The court further held that the detenu's right to have interview with his lawyer and family members is part of his personal liberty guaranteed by Article 21 of the Constitution and cannot be interfered with except in accordance with reasonable, fair and just procedure established by law.

In the preamble of the Constitution, dignity of the individual has been assured to all the people. It is submitted that this preambulary value has been translated into fundamental right under Article 21 of the Constitution, so that the Supreme Court fulfilled the yearning of the people that to live with dignity.

Right to Separate Police Lock-up for Female Suspects

In *Sheela Barse* v. *State of Maharashtra,*[44] the Supreme Court held that female suspects should not be kept in a police lock-up in which male suspects are detained. The Court further held that interrogation of females should be carried out only in the presence of female police officers/constables. It is submitted that the Supreme Court has provided privacy, security and safety and also protected the dignity of the women in police lock-ups through this decision.

Right against Illegal Arrest and Detention

Article 22(1) and (2) provides protection to all persons against illegal arrest and detention. Article 21 assures a fair procedure to all persons to deprive the liberty of any individual. Therefore, the obligation to adopt a reasonable, fair and just procedure attaches at every stage from the moment of arrest of the accused till the last breath of his life.[45]

In *Jogendra Kumar* v. *State of U.P.*[46] the Supreme Court held that 'no arrest should be made without a reasonable satisfaction reached after some investigation about the genuinness and *bona fides* of a complaint and a reasonable belief both as to the person's complicity and even so as to need to effect arrest. Denying a person his liberty is a serious matter.' *N.D.K. Basu* v. *State of West Bengal,*[47] the Supreme Court issued guidelines to be followed in all cases of arrest or detention till legal provisions are made in that behalf as preventive measures. The court held that failure to comply with the requirements mentioned in this case shall apart from rendering the concerned officials liable for departmental action, also render his liable to be punished for contempt of court and the proceedings for contempt of court may be instituted in any High Court of the country, having territorial jurisdiction over the matter.

Right to Legal Aid

In *M.H. Hoskot* v. *State of Maharashtra,*[48] Supreme Court held that where the prisoner is disabled from engaging a lawyer, on reasonable grounds such as indigence or in communicado situation, the court shall if the circumstances of the case, the gravity of the sentence and the ends of justice so require, assign competent counsel for the prisoner's defence, provided the party does not object to that lawyer. In *Hussainara Khatoon* v. *State of Bihar,*[49] the court held that a procedure which does not make available legal services to an accused person who is too poor to afford a lawyer and who would have to go through the trial without legal assistance cannot possibly be regarded as reasonable, fair and just'. The right to free legal services is, therefore, clearly an essential ingredient of 'reasonable, fair and just procedure for a person accused of an offence and it must be held implicit in the guarantee of Article 21.

In Hoskot and Hussainara Khatoon cases, the Supreme Court conferred a fundamental right to legal aid on the accused persons because of its creative and dynamic interpretation of Articles 14, 21, 142 and 39A of the Constitution. In *Khatri* v. *State of Bihar,*[50] the Supreme Court moved a step forward to impose an obligation on the magistrates and sessions judges to inform the accused persons about their fundamental right to legal aid before the commencement of trial proceedings. In *Sheela Bose* v. *State of Maharashtra,*[51] the Supreme Court laid down certain guidelines for the strict implementation of legal aid to the poor. Legal aid, therefore, is very essential for the survival of healthy democracy, which is founded on the equality, dignity and worth of man as a live and valuable component of the society.[52]

Right to Speedy Trial

Speedy trial is the essence of criminal justice and there can be no doubt that delay in trial by itself constitutes denial of justice.[53] In *Hussainara Khatoon* v. *State of Bihar*[54] Justice Bhagwati observed:

> *"we think that even under our Constitution, though speedy trial is not specifically enumerated as a fundamental right, it is implicit in the broad sweep and content of Article 21 as interpreted in Maneka Gandhi* v. *Union of India."*

In *Sheela Barse* v. *Union of India*[55] the Supreme Court has drawn a deadline for completion of investigation and trial, as to the offences committed by juveniles.

In Hussainara Khatoon, the Supreme Court conferred a fundamental right to speedy trial on the accused person and in Sheela Barse the court provided a remedy to the juveniles for the violation of this fundamental right.

In *A.R. Anthulay* v. *R.S. Naik,*[56] the Supreme Court dealt with the scope of the right to speedy trial. The court held that the right to speedy trial encompasses all the stages namely stage of investigation, inquiry, trial, appeal, revision and retrial. In 'Common Cause' A Registered Society, (I [57] and II [58] cases) and Raj Deo Sharma (I[59] and II[60] cases), the Supreme Court has prescribed outer limit for certain type of offences and thereby given a shape to this right to speedy trial, finally.

Right to Compensation

It is now a well accepted proposition in most of the jurisdiction that monetary or pecuniary compensation is an appropriate and indeed an effective and sometimes perhaps the only suitable remedy for redressal of the established infringement of the fundamental right to life of a citizen by the public servants and the State is vicariously liable for their acts.[61]

In *Rudal Shah* v. *State of Bihar,*[62] the petitioner detained illegally in the prison for over fourteen years after his acquittal in a trial. The Supreme Court ordered the State to pay to the petitioner a total sum of Rs. 35,000. In *Bhim Singh* v. *State of J&K*[63] the court awarded compensation of Rs. 50,000 to the petitioner for his mischievous and malicious detention. In *Saheli* v. *Commissioner of Police,*[64] the court directed the Delhi Administration to pay Rs. 75,000 as exemplary compensation to the mother of a 9 years old child who died due to beating by the police officer. In *Nilabati Behera* v. *State of Orissa*[65] the court awarded Rs. 1,50,000 as compensation to the deceased mother, who died in police custody.

There is indeed no express provision in the Constitution of India for grant of compensation for violation of a fundamental right to life, nonetheless, the court has judicially evolved a right to compensation in cases of established unconstitutional deprivation of personal liberty or life.[66] It is submitted that by granting compensation for the established violation of the fundamental right to life and liberty guaranteed under Article 21 of the Constitution, the Supreme Court has elevated the human right laid down under Article 5(5) of European Convention for the protection of human rights and Fundamental Freedoms to the status of fundamental right under Article 32.

Conclusion

No doubt, the Supreme Court has elevated various human rights embodied in the International Covenants to the status of the fundamental rights of the accused, through its active and dynamic interpretation. However, it seems that these judicial pronouncements have less impact on the Executive, more particularly as the law enforcing machinery. Hence, it is submitted that the legislature shall bring out appropriate legislations or amendments to the Constitution and in the existing laws as quick as possible, giving effect to the decisions of the Supreme Court in human rights jurisprudence. Mere passing of laws is not sufficient to protect the rights of the people, at the same time men should fight for their laws as for the walls of their city.[67]

Suggestions

Apart from various suggestions already made by different quarters, the following suggestions with humble submission need to be considered for the effective implementation of the aforesaid human rights.

1. First of all, Police Department officials should be educated with human rights jurisprudence.
2. Arrest shall not be effected by the police for each and every offence in a routine manner. Only after making preliminary investigation, when police thinks that arrest and detention is necessary, then only with the prior permission of the court, accused shall be arrested by the police.
3. In order to avoid custodial violence/torture to the arrested persons, as for as possible courts shall remind the arrested persons to the judicial custody. Only in exceptional cases, the courts shall allow the police custody of the arrested persons. Even in such exceptional cases also the police custody shall be as less as possible.
4. While passing an order under Section 167 of Cr.P.C. to remand the arrestee for police custody, Magistrate shall direct the police to send him for medical examination before taking into custody. In such cases, it is easy to fix up the liability of the police, if any custodial violence happens.
5. Maximum period of remand under Section 309 Cr.P.C. shall be specified. So long as the maximum period of

remand is not specified under the section, the right to speedy trial shall remain as an empty vessel.

6. Human Rights Commission shall appoint adequate number of officials at grass-root level to discharge the functions effectively, specified under section 9 of the Protection of Human Rights Act, 1993 and also to investigate and inquire complaints expeditiously. Therefore, in order to achieve the goals of the Act, the Human Rights Commission shall penetrate into the grass-root level by appointing appropriate officials, as there is no machinery at present except Human Rights Court.
7. State shall appoint judicial police and attach them to the Human Rights Commission in order to investigate the complaints made to the Commission (H.R.C.) and submit the reports expeditiously. Statements recorded by the judicial police shall be made admissible before the Human Rights Courts.
8. In order to protect the rights of women, empowerment and enrichment of women is very essential. Therefore, 33 per cent women reservation shall be implemented strictly in police department. So that women accused may be arrested and interrogated by women police with decency and decorum.
9. Guidelines laid down by the Supreme Court in D.K. Basu case[68] shall be displayed in writing in all police stations so as to bring them to the knowledge of all the arrested persons. So that they can claim their rights against the police.

References

1. Suppression of Immoral Traffic in Women and Girls Act, 1956; Dowry Prohibition Act, 1961; Protection of Civil Rights Act, 1976; Bonded Labour System (Abolition)Act, 1976; Scheduled Castes and Scheduled Tribes (Prevention of Atrocities) Act, 1089; Juvenile Justice Act, 1986, etc.
2. Universal Declaration of Human Rights, 1948; International Covenants on Civil and Political Rights, 1966, and International Covenant on Economic, Social and Cultural Rights, 1966.

3. Sections 50 and 75 of Cr.P.C.
4. Sec. 49 of Cr.P.C.
5. Sec. 56 of Cr.P.C.
6. Sec. 57 and 76 of Cr.P.C.
7. Sec. 167 of Cr.P.C.
8. Sec. 207 and 208 of Cr.P.C.
9. Sec. 303 of Cr.P.C.
10. Sec. 304 of Cr.P.C.
11. Sec. 235(2) and 248(2) of Cr.P.C.
12. Secs. 467 and 473 of Cr.P.C.
13. Secs. 53 and 54 of Cr.P.C.
14. Sec. 64 of Cr.P.C.
15. Sec. 100(3) of Cr.P.C.
16. Sec. 160 of Cr.P.C.
17. Sec. 437 of Cr.P.C.
18. Sec. 174(3) of Cr.P.C.
19. Sec. 416 of Cr.P.C.
20. Clause (1) of Article 20.
21. Clause (2) of Article 20.
22. Clause (3) of Article 20.
23. A.I.R. 1978 SC 597.
24. *Jitendra Pandey* and *R.K. Dubey*, 1992 Civil Liberty under Indian Constitution, Deep and Deep Publications (p. 180).
25. A.I.R. 1980 SC 1597.
26. A.I.R. 1981 SC 625.
27. *Sheela Barse* v. *State of Maharashtra* (1983) 2 SCC 96.
28. A.I.R. 1997 SC 610.
29. *Ibid.* p. 618.
30. *Ibid.* p. 615.
31. *Sunil Batra* v. *Delhi Administration*, AIR 1978 SC 1675 (1728).
32. *Ibid.* p. 1733.
33. *Ibid.* p. 1732.
34. A.I.R. 1981 SC 625.
35. *Ibid.* p. 628.
36. A.I.R. 1978 SC 1675 (1723).
37. A.I.R. 1980 SC 1535.
38. (1990) 3 SCC 119.
39. (1991) 2 SCC 373.

40. A.I.R. 1996 SC 2193
41. Sher Singh v. State of Punjab (1983) 2 SCC 344 (354)
42. See the Preamble of the Constitution
43. A.I.R. 1981 SC 746.
44. (1983) 2 SC 96.
45. D.D. Basu, *Human Rights in Constitutional Law,* p. 379, Prentice Hall of India (Pvt) Ltd. (1994).
46. (1994) 4 SCC 260.
47. A.I.R. 1997 SC 610.
48. A.I.R. 1978 SC 1548.
49. A.I.R. 1979 SC 1369.
50. A.I.R. 1981 SC 928 see also *Suk Das* v. *Union Territory of Arunachal Pradesh,* A.I.R. 1986, SC 991.
51. (1983) 2 SCC 96.
52. *Peoples Union for Democratic Rights* v. *Union of India,* A.I.R. 1982 SC 1473.
53. *Hussainara Khatoon* v. *State of Bihar,* A.I.R. 1979 SC 1360 (1365).
54. *Ibid.,* p. 1365.
55. A.I.R. 1986 SC 1773.
56. A.I.R. 1992 SC 1701.
57. A.I.R. 1996 SC 1619.
58. A.I.R. 1997 SC 1539.
59. A.I.R. 1998 SC 3281.
60. A.I.R. 1999 (8) SC 237.
61. *D.K. Basu* v. *State of West Bengal,* A.I.R. 1997 SC 610 (628).
62. A.I.R. 1983 SC 1086.
63. A.I.R. 1986 SC 494.
64. A.I.R. 1990 SC 513.
65. (1993) 2 SCC 746.
66. *D.K. Basu* v. *State of West Bengal,* A.I.R. 1997 SC 610 (625).
67. Roscoe Pound, 1998, *An Introduction to Philosophy of Law,* Universal Law Publishing Co. Pvt. Ltd. p. 35.
68. A.I.R. 1997 SC 610.

12

RIGHT TO COMPENSATION

D.S.N. Somayajulu

Compensation means monetary damages payable by the wrongdoer to the injured. The question then is how far the government can be made liable to pay compensation to an individual for the wrongs committed by its servants? Compensation differs from judicial review. In the case of judicial review *status quo ante* is restored by quashing the administrative action. While in the case of compensation an injured party gets monetary damages from the administration for the injury done to him by an action of the administration.[1] The law relating to the liability of public authority to compensate is in a state of flux and is in the process of judicial development. The question for consideration is whether the principle of vicarious liability be extended to the government to hold it liable to compensate the injured person for the wrongs committed by its servants.

Prior to the passing of Crown Proceedings Act of 1947 in England, the Crown enjoyed immunity from tortuous liability because of the principle of "King can do no wrong", which means that neither any wrong can be imputed to the Crown nor could it authorize any wrong.[2] Another reason appears to be that " the doctrine of immunity was regarded as an attribute of sovereignty " and that a State cannot be sued in its courts without its consent. However, by passage of time, this rule has become outdated because of vast changes taking place in and around the State. The British Parliament enacted the Crown Proceedings Act 1947 and made the Crown in principle liable to the same extent as a private person of full age and capacity subject to exceptions like defence of realm, maintenance of armed forces and postal services.

The Crown thus became vicariously liable to a very large extent for the torts committed by its servants. The Act has revolutionized the law in England.[3]

Functions of the modern State are highly complex. State acts through its officials. This being the case the interaction between the State and its subjects is on the increase. These interactions often may give rise to legal problems and call for solutions based upon application of various provisions and doctrines. In such cases where relief is desired through civil courts, the law of torts figures. By definition "a Tort is a civil wrong (not being a breach of contract or breach of trust or other wrong for which the remedy is unliquidated damages".[4] Considering the importance of law of torts, and the increased interaction of State in modern times, it is necessary to ascertain the liability of State in Tort. The law on this subject in India is still unsatisfactory and chaotic. Even after fifty seven years of the working of the Constitution no attempt has been made so far either by the Parliament or the State legislatures to bring forward a law containing principles governing liability of the State for the torts committed by its agencies which should not only be just in substance, but also be reasonably certain in form and predictable in its working.[5]

It is necessary to delve into the pages of history to understand better the present state of law and steps to be taken for remedying the situation.

Pre-Constitutional Position

India was governed by the East India Company till the passage of the Government of India Act 1858. The British Parliament has enacted the Charter Act of 1833 and entrusted the governance of India to the East India Company. The East India Company was asked to hold "the territories in trust for His Majesty, his heirs and successors". Finally as a result of the

Sepoy Mutiny or First War of Indian Independence in 1857, the British Crown took over the governance of India from the hands of East India Company by enacting the Government of India Act 1858. Section 65 of the Act sets out the liability of the Crown for acts committed by its servants. The Section reads as follows:

> *"The Secretary of State in Council shall and may sue and be sued as well as in India as in England by the name of the Secretary of State in Council as a body corporate; and all persons and bodies politic shall and may have and take the same suits, remedies and proceedings legal and equitable, against the Secretary of State in Council of India, as they could have done against the said company; and the property and effects hereby vested in Her Majesty for the purpose of the Government of India, or acquired for the said purposes, shall be subject and liable to the same judgments and executions as they would, while vested in the said company, have been liable, to in respect of debts and liabilities lawfully contracted and incurred by the said company."*

This very position was again reiterated by section 32 of the Government of India Act, 1915 which reads as :

> "(1)The Secretary of India in Council may sue and be sued by the name of the Secretary of State in Council, as a body corporate.
>
> (2) Every person shall have the same remedies against the Secretary of State in council as he might have had against the East India Company if the Government of India Act, 1858, and this Act had not been passed."

Section 176 (1) of the Government of India Act, 1935 continued the same legal position. It reads as follows:

> *"The Federation may sue and be sued by the name of the Federation of India and a Provincial Government may sue or be sued by the name of the Province, and without prejudice to the*

> *subsequent provisions of this chapter, may, subject to any provisions which may be made by an Act of the Federal or a Provincial Legislature enacted by virtue of powers conferred on that Legislature by this Act, sue or be sued in relation to their respective affairs in the like cases as the Secretary of State in Council might have sued or been sued if this Act had not been passed."*

Constitutional Position

India attained independence on 15th August, 1947. The Constituent Assembly drafted a new Constitution for India, which came into force from 26th January, 1950. Clause (1) of Article 300 of Constitution now provides

> *"First, that the Government of India may sue or be sued by the name of the Union of India and the Government of a State may sue or be sued by the name of the State, secondly, that the Government of India or the Government of a State may sue or be sued in relation to their respective affairs in the like cases as the Dominion of India and the corresponding Provinces or the corresponding Indian States might have sued or be sued, "if this Constitution had not been enacted, "and thirdly, that the second mentioned rule shall be subject to any provisions which may be made by an Act of Parliament or of the Legislature of such State, enacted by virtue of powers conferred by the Constitution."*

From a plain reading of the above provision, it is clear that the Parliament, or the State Legislatures are empowered to bring forward legislation making its servants liable for the torts committed. Till then the governments would be liable only if under similar circumstances the erstwhile Governments were liable under the predecessor Government of India Acts. It is disheartening to state that till today, neither the Parliament nor the State Legislatures made an attempt to bring forward a law on the lines of the Crown Proceedings Act, 1947 passed in England. This being the case a good amount of confusion created by Article 300 still subsists. Even the decisions of the Supreme Court have not been uniform for clearing the prevailing confusion.

The question of State liability in Torts came up for consideration before the Supreme Court of Calcutta in *Peninsular & Oriental Steam Navigation Company* vs. *Secretary of State for India in Council.*[6] Some workers belonging to Government Kidderpore Dockyard were carrying a piece of iron funnel casing from one part of the dockyard to another part for loading it on a steamer under repair. While they were on a public highway running through the dockyard, the plaintiff's horse drawn carriage encountered the iron. Due to the negligence of the workers one of the horses was injured. The plaintiffs sued the Secretary of State for the damage caused by the said accident. Sir Barnes Peacock C.J. observed that the doctrine of "King can do no wrong" has no application to the East India Company. He held that Section 65 of the Government of India Act 1858 equated the liability of the Secretary of the State and traced it with that of the East India Company.[7]

However, Peacock C.J., made some *obiter* observations in the case regarding sovereign and non-sovereign functions of the East India Company, which in later years had a far reaching effect on shaping of the law in India. He observed, that mere fact that the company exercised sovereign powers as a delegate of the Crown did not make it sovereign. Therefore, the Crown immunity could not extend to it.[8] The Court stated that no action could be taken against the Company where an act was done in exercise of sovereign powers. If the company were allowed for the purpose of government, to engage in undertakings such as bullock train and the conveyance of goods and passengers for hire, it was only reasonable that they would do so, subject to the same liabilities as individuals. This is aptly stated as follows[9] :

> *" There is a great and clear distinction between acts done in the exercise of what are usually termed as sovereign powers, and acts done in the conduct of undertakings which might be carried on by private individuals without having such power delegated to them."*

Sovereign powers were defined as "powers which cannot be lawfully exercised except by a sovereign, or private individual delegated by a sovereign to exercise them". Following this reasoning, the company was held liable for the negligence of its servants in repairing the steamer or in doing any acts in connection with that work. Thus the Secretary of State was held liable. From this decision two principles emerge:[10]

1. That apart from special statutory provisions suits could have been brought against the East India Company, and, consequently against the Secretary of State as successor to the company, in respect of acts done in the conduct of undertakings which might be carried on by private individuals without sovereign powers.
2. That Secretary of State was not liable for anything done in the exercise of sovereign powers.

The Calcutta High Court reiterated the principle of sovereign functions enunciated in P& O case in *Nobin Chander Dev* v. *Secretary of State*".[11] The plaintiff contended that the government had made a contract with him for the sale of ganja and committed a breach of the contract. The High Court held that[12]

1. On evidence, no breach of contract had been proved, and
2. Even if there was a contract, the act was done in exercise of sovereign power, and, therefore it was not actionable.

The Madras High Court considered the P & O Case in *Secretary of State* vs. *Hari Bhanji*.[13] During the course of transit of salt from Bombay to Madras port, the rate of duty on salt was enhanced and the merchant was called upon to pay the difference at the port of destination. The merchant paid the duty under protest and sued the State for its recovery. The Court held that the immunity of East India Company extended only to ' acts of State' strictly so called and that the distinction based on sovereign and non-sovereign functions of the East

India Company was not well founded. This line of reasoning found support in some later cases.[14]

The principle laid down in Hari Bhanji was reiterated by the Madras High Court in *Ross* v. *Secretary of State,*[15] and by the Allahabad High Court, in *Krishan Chand* v. *Secretary of State.*[16] The liberal approach of Hari Bhanji was modified in *Secretary of State* v. *Cockraft,*[17] where the Court held, that making or repairing a military road was held to be a sovereign function and the government was not liable for the negligence of its servants in the stacking of gravel on road resulting in a carriage accident injuring the plaintiff. The position in regard to the liability of the government would have been entirely different in India had the principle laid down in Hari Bhanji been followed in later cases.[18]

Following this trend, collection of land revenue[19] wrongful confinement of plaintiff by the Police,[20] maintenance of public path,[21] maintaining a hospital for the benefit of public at the expense of public revenues,[22] purchase of munitions for the purpose of war and commandering of stores,[23] and running a treasury[24] were held to be sovereign functions.

The question of tortious liability of the government came up for re-examination before the Supreme Court in *State of Rajasthan* v. *Vidhyawati.*[25] Here in this case, a driver of a Jeep, owned and maintained by the State for the official use of the collector fatally injured a pedestrian, while it was on its way back from the workshop to the residence of the collector after repairs. The State pleaded immunity on the ground that the jeep was being maintained "in exercise of sovereign powers." Rejecting that plea, the Supreme Court held, that the State was vicariously liable for the negligence of the driver. The tortious act had been committed " in circumstances wholly disassociated from the exercise of sovereign powers." approving the ruling of the High Court, it held that:[26]

> *"The State is in no better position in so far as it supplies cars, and keeps drivers for its civil service. It may be clarified that we are not considering the case of drivers employed by the State for driving vehicles which are utilized for military or public service."*

The government is not immune from the tortious acts of its servant whether committed in exercise of sovereign or non-sovereign functions. This view though not clearly articulated can be inferred from the following observation.[27]

> *"Viewing the case from the point of view of first principles, there should be no difficulty in holding that the State should be as much liable for tort in respect of a tortious act committed by its servant within the scope of his employment and functions as such, as any other employer. The immunity of the Crown in the United Kingdom is based on the old feudalistic notions of justice, namely, that the King was incapable of doing a wrong and, therefore, of authorizing or instigating one, and that he could not be sued in his own courts... Now that we have, by our Constitution, established a Republican form of Government, and one of its objectives is to establish a Socialistic State with its varied industrial and other activities, employing a large army of servants there is no justification, in principle, or in public interest, that the State should not be held liable vicariously for the tortious acts of its servants."*

From this, it is clear, that the Supreme Court did not accept the view that "the maintenance of a car for the collector, in the discharge of his official duties is a sovereign function.

This new trend visible in the area of State liability and the efficacy of the view expressed in Vidhyawati is short-lived and whittled down by the Supreme Court in *Kasturilal Ralia Ram Jain* v. *State of Uttar Pradesh.*[28] In this case police arrested one Ralia Ram and seized some gold from him on suspicion that it was a stolen property. The gold kept in government *malkhana* was misappropriated by the chief constable in charge who fled to Pakistan. Ralia Ram on acquittal of the charge of possessing stolen goods, sued the State for the return of his gold or in the alternative damages for the loss suffered by him. The Supreme Court affirmed the distinction made in *P & Co* case between sovereign and non-sovereign functions as[29]:

This case (P & O case) recognizes a material distinction between acts committed by the servants employed by the State where such acts are referable to the exercise of sovereign powers delegated to the Public servants, and acts committed by public servants which are not referable to the delegation of any sovereign powers."

The Supreme Court further pointed out that[30]:

"If a tortious act is committed by a public servant and it gives rise to a claim for damages, the question to ask is: was the tortious act committed by the public servant in discharge of statutory functions which are referable to, and ultimately based on, the delegation of sovereign powers of the State to such public servant. If the answer is in the affirmative, the action for damages for loss caused by such act will not lie. On the other hand, if the tortious act has been committed by the public servant in discharge of duties assigned to him not by virtue of the delegation of Sovereign power, an action for damages would lie."

Referring to Vidhyawati's Case, the Court held[31] "the employment of a driver to drive the jeep car for the use of a civil servant is itself an activity which is not connected in any manner with the sovereign power of the State at all." On the other hand the power to arrest a person, to search him and to seize property found on him" are powers which can properly be characterized as sovereign powers." In this case, since the act of negligence was committed by the police in exercise of their statutory power of seizing the property no claim of damages can be allowed against the State. The reason for this inference is that maintaining police is a Sovereign function.

The Court expressed its unhappiness at the prevailing state of tort law in India. To mitigate this hardship, the Court made a suggestion to the government to bring forward a law on the lines of the Crown Proceedings Act 1947. It observed[32]:

"The thought that a citizen whose property was seized by law, has to be told, when he seeks a remedy in a court of law on the ground that his property has not been returned to him, that he can make no claim against the State.... The remedy to cure the position, however, lies in the hands of the legislature".

Law Commission Recommendations

The Law Commission of India in its First Report (Liability of State in Tort) submitted in 1956 recommended the relaxation of the governmental immunity and doing away with the distinction between sovereign and non-sovereign functions.

The Commission in its report suggested[33]:

"In the context of a welfare State it is necessary to establish a just relation between the rights of the individual and the responsibilities of the State. While the responsibilities of the State have increased, the increase in its activities has led to greater impact on the citizen ....." There is no convincing reason why the government should not place itself in the same position as a private employer subject to the same rights and duties as imposed by statute."

The Commission did not want the law to remain stagnant and at the same time it was also not in favour of leaving it to the courts to develop the law according to the views of the judges.[34] The Commission opined that[35]:

"It is necessary that the law should, as far as possible, be made certain and definite... The citizen must be in a position to know the law definitely..."

The Commission in its report pointed at the difficulty involved in defining the liability of State for the tortuous acts in following words[36]:

"It involves, undoubtedly, a nice balancing of considerations so as not to unduly restrict the sphere of activities of the State and at the same time to afford sufficient protection to the citizen."

Government (Liability in Tort) Bill modelled on Law Commissions recommendation was introduced in the Parliament in 1965, but nothing has materialized. Again the Bill was reintroduced in 1967. This Bill was referred to the Joint Select Committee of Parliament, which suggested certain modifications in 1969. The fact remains that till today no headway was made in getting the law being passed.

Post Kasturilal Scenario

This being the fact, the Courts still maintained the old distinction between "sovereign" and "non-sovereign" function in theory for the purpose of governmental liability. In practice the Courts have given restrictive meaning to the concept of sovereign functions to mitigate the hardship faced by the aggrieved persons who came for relief. Judicial creativeness went a long way in adjusting old law to the changing new situations.[37]

Construction of reservoir,[38] embezzlement of money deposited by sub-treasury officials,[39] negligence of State officials in not providing life saving devices resulting in the death of person travelling on boat in river Kosi,[40] negligence of drivers of State transport,[41] were held to be not sovereign functions and damages were awarded.

Arrest and detention according to traditional classification were considered as sovereign functions. The Covenant on Civil and Political Rights under Article 9 para 5 laid down that

> *"Any one who has been the victim of unlawful arrest or detention shall have enforceable right to compensation."*

The right to compensation is not specifically guaranteed under the Indian Constitution. At the time of ratifying the Covenant, India expressed its reservation stating that under our legal system, there is no enforceable right to compensation for persons claiming to be victims of unlawful arrest or detention against the State.[42] However, this reservation lost its significance in view of the apex court giving a broad and liberal interpretation to the expression "life and personal liberty" in *Maneka Gandhi's Case.*[43] This innovation has led to giving a new content and thrust to the development of human rights jurisprudence in post Maneka Gandhi era. The Court has maintained that the State has no right to take any action which may deprive the citizen of the enjoyment of his basic fundamental rights except in accordance with a law which is reasonable, fair and just.[44] It is heartening to state that the apex court did not allow the legal technicalities to come in its way for granting relief to the victims of State terrorism or of State lawlessness, otherwise it would have amounted to surrendering to State lawlessness, or showing cold indifference to the personal liberty of the individual or its immense indifference to sufferings not contemplated by the Constitution.

The apex court considered the question of giving compensation to a person who has unduly suffered detention and bodily harm. In *Khatri* v. *State of Bihar (Bhagalpur Blinding Case)*,[45] the question was whether the State was liable to pay compensation for the alleged blinding of certain prisoners by the police. Dealing with the question of granting relief to the person who has suffered deprivation of his life or liberty guaranteed under the Article 21 Bhagawati J. held[46]:

> *"Why should the court not be prepared to forge new tools and devise new remedies for the purpose of vindicating the most precious of the precious fundamental right to life and personal liberty."*

Addressing the leading question, i.e "Would the State be liable to pay compensation for acts of its servants outside the scope of their power and authority affecting life or personal liberty of a person and thus infringing Article 21?" Answering in affirmative, the Court held that[47]:

> *"If it were not so, Article 21 would be reduced to a nullity, a mere rope of sand, for in this view, if the officer is acting according to law there would be no breach of Article 21 and if he is acting without the authority of law, the State would be able to contend that it is not responsible for his action and therefore there is no violation of Article 21."*

Rudul Sah exposed "a sordid and disturbing state of affairs" for which the responsibility was squarely on the administration. Petitioner was acquitted by Muzaffarpur Sessions Court on June 3rd 1968, but he was released on 16th October 1982 on a *habeas corpus* petition. The question before the court was whether it could grant some compensation under Article 32 for his wrongful detention. The Court held that[48]:

> *"It is true that Article 32 cannot be used as a substitute for enforcement of rights and obligations which can be enforced efficaciously through the ordinary process of courts civil and criminal..."*

Referring to the fact, that the petitioner was detained illegally in the prison for over 14 years after his acquittal in full dressed trial, the Court felt that[49]:

> *" If it refused to pass an order of compensation in favour of the petitioner, it will be doing merely lip service to the fundamental right to liberty which the State government has so grossly violated. It would denude their right to life and liberty under Art. 21 of its significant content if the power of the court was limited merely to passing orders of release from illegal detention."*

Further, it observed[50]:

> *" One of the telling ways to which the violation of that right can reasonably be prevented and due compliance with the mandate of Art. 21 secured, is to mulct its violators in the payment of monetary compensation. Administrative sclerosis leading to flagrant infringements of fundamental rights cannot be corrected by any other method open to the judiciary to adopt. The right to compensation is some palliative for the unlawful acts of instrumentalities which act in the name of public interest and which present for their protection the powers of the State as a shield...."*

Compensation was awarded by the Supreme Court in *Sebastian M. Hongray* v. *Union of India.*[51] Two persons were taken to the military camp by the jawans of the army. On an *habeas corpus* petition filed against the State by the wives of the detenues the State expressed its inability to produce them. The Court being not satisfied by the explanation given by the State, took into account the torture, agony and mental oppression suffered by the wives of the detenues in awarding compensation.

The State was held liable to the torts committed by its servants in *Saheli* (a women's rescue centre) v. *Commissioner of Police, Delhi*[52] In this case Kamlesh Kumari was living with her children in one room tenement in the ground floor. She obtained a stay order from the court against eviction by the landlord. The landlord on her refusal to vacate, took the law into his own hands and in the presence of S.H.O. tore her clothes and molested her. Her son Naresh, who was nine years old became scared clung to his mother. The boy was dragged forcibly, and thrown on the floor. The S.H.O. also took part in beating her. Kamlesh Kumari was arrested and sent to jail and later released on bail next day. Meanwhile her son, Naresh had fever and finally died in the hospital due to pneumonitis. Seeing her plight in the newspapers *Saheli,* a women's rescue Centre espoused her cause. The Supreme Court in this case not only awarded compensation to the victim but it also asked the State to recover the amount from the salaries of the erring officials.[53]

Nilabati Behara v. *State of Orissa,* [54] was a case of custodial or lockup death. There was a theft in a locality. The Police called one Suman Behera aged 22 for investigation at 8.A.M. on 1st December 1987. On next day at about 2 p.m. mother of the accused came to know that her son's body with multiple injuries was lying on a nearby railway track. The circumstances indicated that the death was an unnatural one. State contended, that the accused has escaped from police custody in the late hours of night in pitch of darkness and he was run over by a passing train. Hence the presence of multiple injuries. However, the post-mortem report discounted the State's version, and the conclusion was that the injuries were caused by hard or blunt object. The injuries on the face and left temporal region were post-mortem while the rest were ante-mortem. Medical evidence of the doctor testifies that the cause of the death was not run over by passing train but possibly by severe lathi blows.

The Supreme Court held that the doctrine of Sovereign immunity has no application when a person invokes public law remedy for violation of his fundamental rights. This principle is succinctly laid down in following words that[55]:

> " A claim in public law for compensation for contravention of human rights, and fundamental freedom, the protection of which is guaranteed in the Constitution, is an acknowledged remedy for enforcement and protection of such rights, and such a claim based on strict liability made by resorting to a Constitutional remedy provided for the enforcement of a fundamental right is "distinct from, and in addition to the remedy in private law for damages for the tort resulting from the contravention of the fundamental right. The defence of sovereign immunity being inapplicable, and alien to the concept of guarantee fundamental rights, there can be no question of such a defence being available in the Constitutional remedy. It was this principle which justifies award of monetary compensation for contravention of fundamental rights guaranteed by the Constitution."

The distinction between sovereign and non-sovereign functions were again reviewed at length in *N. Nagendra Rao* v. *State of Andhra Pradesh.*[56] From a reading of the judgment following principles emerge

(a) Non-Existence of the Distinction[57]

> "In the modern sense, the distinction between sovereign and non-sovereign power thus does not exist... it is in (the) public interest that for acts performed by the State,

either in its legislative or executive capacity, it should not be answerable in torts. That would be illogical and impracticable. It would be in conflict, with even modern notions of sovereignty.

(b) Non-Liability for Political Acts[58]

" One of the tests to determine if the legislative or executive function is sovereign in nature is, whether the State is answerable for such actions in courts of law e.g. defence, foreign affairs, etc."

(c) Immunity Ends with Political Acts[59]

" No legal or political system today can place the State above (the law) as it is unjust and unfair for a citizen to be deprived of his property illegally by negligent act of officers of the State without any remedy.... The modern social thinking of progressive societies and the judicial approach is to do away with archaic State protection and place the State or the Government on a par with any other juristic legal entity. Any watertight compartmentalization of the functions of the State as "sovereign and non-sovereign" or Governmental or nongovernmental is not sound. It is contrary to modern jurisprudential thinking". From this follows that statutory power is to be viewed as statutory duty.

(d) Primary and Inalienable Functions[60]

"The demarcating line between sovereign and non-sovereign powers, for which no rational basis survives, has largely disappeared. Therefore, barring functions such as administration of justice, maintenance of law and order, and repression of crime etc., which are among the primary and inalienable functions of a Constitutional government, the State cannot claim any immunity."

(e) Misfeasance Doctrine[61]

"Vicarious liability of the State is linked with the negligence of officers. The law of misfeasance in discharge of public duty having marched, there is no rationale for the proposition that even if the officer is liable, the State cannot be sued."

(f) Kasturilal Case—Inalienable Functions[62]

"Kasturilal case related to powers of arrest, search etc. The power to search and apprehend a suspect under the Criminal Procedure is one of the inalienable powers of the State. Distinguishing Kasturilal, the court held, that when similar powers are conferred under the other statute as incidental or ancillary power to carry out the purpose and objective of the Act, then, it being an exercise of such State function which is not primary or inalienable, an officer acting negligently is liable personally and the State vicariously..."

Commenting on the uncertainty of the prevailing law of torts, Constitutional Review Committee opined that on review of Nagendra Rao and other cases on the subject, that definiteness of the precise contours and certainty of principles of universal application are lacking[63]. Further the distinction between sovereign and non-sovereign functions has become academic in the present day welfare State. The Supreme Court again affirmed and accepted the theory of "primary and inalienable functions" in Nagendra Rao's Case. Nagendra Rao's case was decided by a bench of two judges, while Vidhyawati and Kasturilal's cases were decided by a bench of five judges. This exposes the reason for continued confusion in the existing state of law.

Right to life is one of the basic human rights protected under the Constitution. A prisoner whether a convict or under trial or a detenue does not cease to be a human being even when he is lodged in the jail. On conviction he is deprived of his liberty of movement in accordance with the procedure established by law. He has all other residue of Constitutional rights, which form part of the right to life. *State of Andhra Pradesh* v. *Challa Ramakrishna Reddy,*[64] exposes the utter failure of the State in providing protection to an inmate of the jail, inspite of his representation fearing threat to his life on the fateful day to the Police. Challa Chinnappa Reddy and his son Challa Ramakrishna Reddy were lodged in cell No.7 of the Koilakuntla subjail, Kurnool District. Apprehending that a conspiracy is being hatched to kill them in jail, they made written representations to the Circle Inspector, Collector and Home Minister seeking protection for their life. Inspite of their apprehension of fear, no extraprotection was provided by the police. Instead on the fateful day, there is reduction in security guards than the usual number. During the late night on 5th May 1977 a bomb was hurled into the cell No. 7. As a result of explosion, both the prisoners suffered injuries and Chinnappa Reddy died in the hospital.

Supreme Court rejected the claim of State immunity holding that,[65]

> *"The fundamental rights, which are also basic human rights are available to a prisoner and those rights cannot be defeated by pleading the old and archaic defence of immunity in respect of sovereign acts, which has been rejected several times.*

Further, the court held that plethora of cases indicated that[66]:

> *"Where so far as fundamental right and human rights are concerned, the law has marched ahead like a Pegasus but the government attitude continues to be conservative and it tries to defend its action or the tortious action of its officer by raising the plea of immunity for sovereign acts or acts of State, which must fail."*

There is no wrong without a remedy. The law wills that in every case where a man is wronged and endamaged, he must have a remedy. A mere declaration of invalidity of an action or finding of custodial violence of death in lock-up, does not by itself provide any meaningful remedy to a person whose fundamental right to life has been infringed. Much more needs to be done.[67]

Article 9(5) of the International Convention on Civil and Political Rights 1966 (ICCPR) provides that "any one who has been a victim of unlawful arrest or detention shall have enforceable right to compensation". Of course, the Government of India at the time of its ratification (of ICCPR) in 1979 had made a specific reservation to the effect that the Indian legal system does not recognize a right to compensation for victim of unlawful arrest or detention. That reservation, however has now lost it relevance in view of the law laid down by the court in a number of cases awarding compensation for the infringement of the fundamental right to life.[68]

There is indeed, no express provision in the Constitution of India for grant of compensation for violation of a fundamental right to life, nonetheless, this court has judicially evolved a right to compensation in cases of established unconstitutional deprivation of personal liberty or life.[69] The claim in public law for compensation for unconstitutional deprivation of fundamental right to life and liberty, the protection of which is guaranteed under the Constitution, is a claim based on strict liability and is in addition to the claim available in private law for damages for tortious acts of the public servants. Award of compensation for established infringement of the indefeasible right guaranteed under Article 21 of the Constitution is a remedy available in public law. Since the purpose of public law is not only to civilise public power but also to assure the citizens that they live under a legal system wherein their rights and interests shall be protected and preserved. Grant of compensation is for penalizing the wrong doer and fixing the liability for the public wrong on the State which has failed in the discharge of its public duty to protect the fundamental rights of the citizens.[70]

Monetary compensation for redressal by the court finding the infringement of the indefeasible right to life of the citizens is, therefore, useful and at times perhaps, the only effective remedy.[71] Quoting extensively from the above case, the Supreme Court granted compensation of one lakh each to the families of the two villages who were killed by Manipur Police in a fake encounter.[72]

The National Commission on Review of the working of the Constitution expressed its unhappiness over the prevailing state of confusion in the area of Governmental liability for the torts committed by its servants. The committee observed in their report that the distinction between Sovereign and non-Sovereign: functions is outdated and archaic and does not stand to scrutiny in view of the changed concept of functions of the State. The Commission in its summary of recommendations listed under chapter 11 suggested amendment of Article 21 of the Constitution. It suggested renumbering the existing article as clause 1 and to insert two new clauses thereafter. The proposed new clause 2 relates to "torture or cruel" and clause 3 relates to "Compensation". The new clause 3 reads as:

> *"Every person who has been allegedly deprived of his right to life or liberty has an enforceable right of compensation."*

The amendment if carried through by the Parliament will go a long way in giving relief to helpless victims of State terrorism or State lawlessness. It is high time that Parliament should make a move in the right direction in defining governmental liability in torts committed by its servants. In the absence of such a law, and any further delay in making a law will lead to the people losing faith in the functioning of the system of the Government. Law should allow a person to seek redress from a court for any wrong done to him by the State or its officers. The State or its officers should not be allowed to escape their liability on the pretext of sovereign immunity. Sovereign immunity has no place in a democracy.

References

1. M.P. Jain and S.N. Jain *Principles of Administrative Law*, p. 762 fourth Edition, 1986 N.M. Tripathi Pvt. Ltd. Bombay.
2. Tamlin V. Hannaford (1951) 1 K.B. 18 – To mitigate the injustice arising out of the immunity rule, the government would pay compensation in proper cases to the injured persons. But this is a matter of grace and not as of right.

3. *Supra* Note 1 as p. 762-763 - Granville Williams "Crown Proceedings" (1974); "Street Governmental Liability (1953); Hogg " The Liability of the Crown. (1971).
4. Salmond & Heuston, *Law of Torts,* 20th Edition (1993).
5. Report of the National Commission on the Review of the Working of the Constitution, Volume II, Book I, page 673.
6. 5 Bom. H.C.R. App.1.
7. *Ibid.*
8. *Ibid.,* p. 13.
9. *Ibid.,* p. 15.
10. *Supra* note 1, 765.
11. (1873) *I.L.R.I.,* Cal. 1.
12. *Ibid.*
13. (1882) 5 *I.L.R.* Mad. 273.
14. *Forrester* v. *Secretary of State for India* I.A. Supp. Vol. 55; *P.V. Rao* v. *Khushaldas* A.I.R. 1949 Bom. 277 on appeal *Province of Bombay* v. *Khushaldas Advani* A.I.R. 1950 S.C. 222 (Mukerjea J).
15. A.I.R. 1915 Mad. 434.
16. (1881) I.L.R. 2 AU 829.
17. A.I.R. 1915 Mad. 993.
18. *Supra* note. 1, p. 765.
19. *State of Andhra Pradesh* v. *Ankanna* A.I.R. 1967, A.P. 41.
20. *Gurucharan Kaur* v. *Madras Province,* A.I.R. 1942, Mad. 539.
21. *Mc Inerny* v. *Secretary of State,* (1911), 38 I.L.R., Cal 797.
22. *Etti* v. *Secretary of State,* A.I.R. 1939, Mad. 663.
23. *Kesssoram Poddar & Co.* v. *Secretary of State* (1927), 54 I.L.R., 909, *Purnenda Deb* v. *India,* A.I.R. 1936, Cal. 66.
24. *District Board Bhagalpur* v. *Bihar,* A.I.R. 1954, Pat. 259.
25. A.I.R. 1962, S.C. 933.
26. *Ibid.,* p. 935.
27. *Ibid.,* p. 940.
28. A.I.R. 1965, S.C. 1039.
29. *Ibid.*
30. *Ibid.,* p. 1046.
31. *Ibid.,* p. 1048.
32. *Ibid.*
33. Law Commission of India, First Report Liability of State (in Tort) 36 (1956)
34. *Supra* note 1, p. 783.

35. *Supra* note 32, p. 37.
36. *Ibid.*, p. 36.
37. *Supra* note 1, 784.
38. *State of Mysore* v. *Ramachandra*, A.I.R. 1972, Bom. 73.
39. *State of Uttar Pradesh* v. *Hindustan Lever*, A.I.R. 1972, All. 486.
40. *State of Bihar* v. *S.K. Mukerji*, A.I.R. 1976, Pat. 24.
41. *Amulya Patnaik* v. *State of Orissa*, A.I.R. 1967, Ori. 116—Accident due to negligence of a driver of police vehicle; *State of Madhya Pradesh* v. *Ram Pratap*, A.I.R. 1972 M.P. 219 Negligence of driver of Truck belonging to P.W.D; *Shyam Sundar* v. *State of Rajasthan*, A.I.R. 1974 S.C. 890-Negligence of a government driver engaged in famine relief work; *Indian Insurance Co. ASS, Pool* v. *Radhabai*, A.I.R. 1976 M.P.-164—Motor Vehicle allotted to Primary Health Centre; *State of Andhra Pradesh* v. *K. Padmarani*, A.I.R. 1976 A.P. 122, Tipper engaged in Srisailam Dam work.
42. Dr. H.O. Agarwal, *Human Rights*, p. 192, Fifth Edition 2002, Central Law Publications, Allahabad.
43. *Maneka Gandhi* v. *Union of India*, A.I.R. 1978, S.C. 597.
44. *Ibid.*
45. A.I.R. 1981 S.C. 928.
46. *Ibid.*, 930.
47. *Khatri* v. *State of Bihar*, A.I.R. 1981 S.C. 1068, at p. 1074.
48. *Rudul Shah* v. *State of Bihar*, A.I.R. 1983 S.C. 1089.
49. *Ibid.*
50. *Ibid.*
51. A.I.R. 1984 S.C. 1026.
52. A.I.R. 1990 S.C. 513.
53. *Ibid.*, p. 514.
54. A.I.R. 1993 S.C. 1960.
55. *Ibid.*, p. 1969, see also opinion of Dr.Anand Jar, p. 1972.
56. A.I.R. 1994 S.C. 2663.
57. *Ibid.*, p. 2682.
58. *Ibid.*
59. *Ibid.*, p. 2683.
60. *Ibid.*
61. *Ibid.*
62. *Ibid.*, p. 2684.
63. *Supra* note 5, p. 685.
64. A.I.R. 2000 S.C. 2083.

65. *Ibid.*, p. 2089.
66. *Ibid.*, p. 2090-91.
67. Per Anand J. in *D.K. Basu* v. *State of West Bengal* (1997), I SCC 416. at p. 437 Para 40.
68. *Ibid.*, p. 438, para 42.
69. *Ibid.*
70. *Ibid.*, p. 439, para 44.
71. *Ibid.*, p. 439, para 45.
72. *Peoples Union for Civil Liberties* v. *Union of India* (1997) 3 SCC 433.

13

THE RIGHT TO CLAIM COMPENSATION AS A HUMAN RIGHT

N. Balu

The right to bring to claim for a violation of internationally recognized human rights is well established under international law. Article 8 of the Universal Declaration of Human Rights says that "Everyone has the right to an *effective remedy* by the competent national tribunals for acts violating the fundamental rights granted him by the Constitution or by law. Similarly, Article 2(3)(a) of the International Covenant on Civil and Political Rights, which has been ratified by more than 140 countries also guarantees the right to compensation and imposes a duty on the State to protect it through constitutional or legal means.

Compensation for Violation of Art. 21

In a judgment of far reaching importance in *Rudal Shah* v. *State of Bihar*[1] the Supreme Court has held the Court has power to award monetary compensation in appropriate cases where there has been violation of constitutional right of citizens. In the present case the Supreme Court directed Bihar Government to pay "compensation" of Rs. 30,000 to Rudal Shah who had to remain in the jail for 14 years because of the irresponsible behaviour of the State Government officers even after his acquittal. He was acquitted by the Sessions Court on June 30,

1968 but was released from jail only on October 16, 1982 when the Court intervened. Describing this state of affairs as '*sordid and disturbing*" the court asked the Patna High Court to find out if there were any other detainees suffering a fate similar to Rudal Shah. Thus, it is clear from this ruling that the Court can order payment of compensation to victims of state violence. Similarly, in *Bhim Singh* v. *State of J&K*[2] the court awarded a sum of Rs. 50,000 to the petitioner as compensation for the violation of his constitutional right of personal liberty under Art. 21 of the Constitution. The petitioner a MLA was arrested and detained in police custody and deliberately prevented from attending session of the Legislative Assembly. The police officers acted deliberately and *mala fide* and magistrate and the Sub-Judge aided them either by colluding with them or by their casual attitude. When the constitutional right of personal liberty is invaded the invasion is not washed away by his being set free. In appropriate cases the Supreme Court has jurisdiction to award monetary compensation by way of exemplary costs or otherwise. In *Peoples Union for Democratic Rights* v. *Police Commissioner, Delhi Headquarters*[3] a labourer was taken to the police station for doing some work. He was severely beaten when he demanded wages and ultimately succumbed to the injuries. It was held that the State was liable to pay compensation and accordingly directed to the Government to pay Rs. 75,000 as compensation to the family of the deceased . Similarly, in *Saheli* v.*Commr. of Police*[4] the Supreme Court directed the Delhi Administration to pay Rs.75000 as exemplary compensation to the mother of a 9 years old child who died due to beating by the Police officer.

In *State of Maharashtra* v. *Ravikant S. Patil*[5] an under trial prisoner was handcuffed and paraded on streets. He was suspected to be involved in a murder case. A local newspaper carried a news item that he would be taken in a procession from Police Station through the main streets of the city for the purpose of investigation. The Bombay High Court held that handcuffing and parading of the petitioner was unwarranted and violative of Art. 21 and directed the Inspector of Police who was responsible for this, to pay Rs. 10,000 by way of compensation. It also directed that this act of violation of Art. 21 should also be entered in his service record. The Supreme Court upheld the judgment of the High Court directing payment of compensation but held the police officer was not personally liable as he acted as an official.

In *Chiranjit Kaur* v. *Union of India*[6] an Army Officer died in service due to negligence of army officers resulting in great mental agony and physical and financial hardship to the widow of the deceased and two minor children. The court awarded the widow of the deceased a compensation of Rs. 6 lakhs as well as Special Family Pension and Children allowances.

In *Shakuntala Devi* v. *Delhi Electric Supply Undertaking*[7] the petitioner's husband died when he came into contact with the live electric wire while returning from the place of his employment and got electrocuted. The live electricity wire was lying open in the field in a rainy season and was not repaired inspite of many complaints. The court held the Delhi Electricity Supply Undertaking liable for the negligence and awarded compensation of *ex-gratia* amount to the widow and her minor children.

In *Kewalpati* v. *State of Uttar Pradesh*[8] the Court has awarded compensation to the widow of the convict who was killed in jail by a co-accused while serving his sentence under section 302 IPC as it resulted in deprivation of his life contrary to law and in violation of Art. 21. A prisoner does not cease to have constitutional right except to the extent he has been deprived of it in accordance with law. His death was caused due to the failure of jail authorities to protect him. Accordingly, the Court directed the Government to pay a compensation of Rs. 1,00,000 to the widow and children of the deceased.

In *People's Union for Civil Liberties* v. *Union of India* the petitioner Peoples Union for Civil Liberties, filed a writ petition under Art. 32 of the Constitution for issuing appropriate direction for instituting a judicial inquiry into the fake encounter by Imphal Police in which two persons were killed, to direct appropriate action to be taken against the erring officials and to award compensation to the members of the family of deceased. The police authorities denied the allegation of "fake encounter". The Supreme Court held that killing of two persons in fake encounter by the police was clear violation of the right to life guaranteed in Art. 21 of the Constitution and the defence of sovereign immunity does not apply in such case. The court awarded Rs. 1,00,000 as compensation to each deceased. Following *Nilbati Behera* v. *State of Orissa,* the court held that the provisions of Art. 9 (5) of the International Covenant on Civil and Political Rights, 1966 which says "anyone who has been a victim of unlawful arrest or detention shall have an enforceable right to compensation for enforcing fundamental rights.

Compensation to Rape Victims

In *Delhi Domestic Working Women's Forum* v. *Union of India*[9] the petitioner Women's Forum through public interest litigation brought the pathetic condition of four domestic women servants who were raped by seven army personnel in a running train while travelling by the Muri Express from Ranchi to Delhi. The victims were helpless tribal women belonging to the State of Bihar. Notwithstanding the occurrence of such barbaric assault on the person and dignity of women neither the Union Government nor the State Government has bestowed any serious attention as to the need for rehabilitating and the court expressed serious concern about the increase of crimes against women in recent times and suggested that the defects in criminal laws be removed soon. The Court observed as follows :

> *"The defects in the present system are firstly, complaints are handled roughly and are not giving such attention as is warranted. The victims, more often than not, are humiliated by the police. The victims have invariable found rape trials a traumatic experience. The experience of giving evidence in Court has been negative and destructive. The victims often say, they considered the ordeal to be even worse than the rape itself. Undoubtedly the Court proceedings added to and prolonged the psychological stress they had to suffer as a result of rape itself."*

In view of this, the Court laid down the following guidelines for trial of rape cases:

1. The complainants of sexual assaults cases should be provided with legal representation, such a person must be well acquainted with criminal justice. The victims advocate's role should not be only to explain her the nature of proceedings, to prepare her for the case and to assist her in the police station and in court but to provide her with guidance as to how she might obtain help of a different nature from other agencies, for example, mind consulting or medical assistance. It is important to secure continuity of assistance by ensuring that the same person who looked after the complainant's interests in the police station represents her till the end of the case.
2. Legal assistance will have to be provided at the police station since the victim of sexual assault might very well be in a distress at the police station the guidance and support of a lawyer at this stage would be of great help to her.
3. The police should be under a duty to inform the victim of her right to representation before any questions were asked of her and the police report should state that the victims was so informed.
4. A list of advocates willing to act in these cases should be kept at the police station for victims who did not have any particular lawyer in mind, or whose own lawyer was unavailable.
5. The advocate shall be appointed by the court on application by the police at the earliest convenient movement, but in order to ensure that victims were questioned without undue delay Advocates would be authorized to act at the police station before leave of the Court was sought or obtained.
6. In all rape trials anonymity, (name not be disclosed), of the victim must be maintained, as far as necessary.

7. It is necessary, having regard to the directive principles contained under Art. 38 (1) of the Constitution to set a Criminal Injuries Compensation Board to protect rape victims who frequently incur substantial loss, some, for example, are too terrorized to continue in employment.
8. Compensation for victims shall be awarded by the Court on conviction of the offender and by the Criminal Injuries Compensation Board whether or not a conviction has taken place. The Board will take into account pain, suffering and shock as well as the loss of earnings due to pregnancy and childbirth if this accrued as a result of rape.

The National Commission for Women is asked to frame schemes for compensation and rehabilitation to ensure justice to victims of such crimes. The Union of India shall then examine and take necessary steps to implement them at the earliest.

Interim Compensation to Rape Victim

In a landmark case of *Bodhisathwa Gautam* v. *Subhra Chakraorty*[10] the Supreme Court awarded an interim compensation of Rs. 1000 per month to the victim of rape until her charges of rape are decided by the trial court. The complainant Subhra Chakraborty was a student of the Baptist College Kohima and the accused Sri Bodhisathwa was a lecturer in that college. According to the FIR filed by the complainant, the accused not only induced the complainant and cohabited with her, giving her a false assurance of marriage but also fraudulently gave through a certain marriage ceremony with knowledge and thereby dishonestly made the complainant to believe that she was a lawfully married wife of the accused. Bodhisathwa married the complainant before the God he worshipped by putting her vermilion on her forehead and accepted her as his wife but later refused to recognize her as his life partner. The said ceremony made the complainant to believe that she was a lawfully married wife of the accused.

Referring to the pitiable condition of women in society Mr. Justice Saghir Ahmad observed that *"unfortunately, a woman in our country, belongs to a class or group of society who are in a disadvantaged position on account of cultural social barriers and impediments and have, therefore, been victim of tyranny at the hands of men with whom they, unfortunately, under the Constitution enjoy equal status' ".*

Women also have the right to life and liberty; they also have the right to be respected and treated as equal citizens. Their honour and dignity cannot be touched or violated. They also have the right to lead an honourable and peaceful life.

Rape is a crime against basic human rights and is also violation of the victim's most cherished fundamental rights, normally, the right to life contained in Article 21.

In a landmark judgement[11] the court awarded the compensation for the death of housewife who met in a fire accident. The court further calculated the services rendered by her to the house and made an estimation to Rs. 3000 per month in case of the house wife is between 34-59 years of age and for elderly house wife of 62-72 years age group, the value of services to the house would be Rs. 20,000 per annum. The court upheld the compensation to the victim due to the accident.

In another important case,[12] the court awarded the compensation to the victims of riots following the assassination of Prime Minister Indira Gandhi. The Delhi High Court issued direction to pay compensation of Rs. 2 lakhs with interest. The Supreme Court further directed High Courts of Delhi, Rajasthan, Orissa , Punjab and Haryana, Himachal Pradesh, Patna, MP, Allahabad and Bombay to treat petition filed in Supreme Court as a petition filed in High Court and deal with the matter in respect of claims arising in their respective jurisdiction.

The right to compensation for violation of Human Rights has been accepted as one of the cardinal principles of Human Rights Jurisprudence. In addition, the Indian Parliament in the latest Prevention of Terrorism Act, 2002 has included in section 58 a provision for punishment and compensation for malicious action. Section 58 states:

1. Any police officer who exercises powers corruptly or maliciously, knowing that there are no reasonable grounds for proceeding under this Act, shall be punishable with imprisonment which may extend to two years, or with fine, or with both.
2. If the special court is of the opinion that any person has been corruptly or maliciously proceeded against under this Act, the court may award such compensation as it deems fit to the person, so proceeded against and it shall be paid by the officer, person, authority or Government, as may be specified in the order.

The recognition of the right to compensation by the Parliament is a significant step in the protection of Human Rights.

References

1. (1983) 4 SCC 141. See also *Sebastian M. Hongray* v. *Union of India.* AIR 1984 SC 1026.
2. (1985) 4 SCC 677.
3. (1989) 4 SCC 730.
4. AIR 1990 SC 513.
5. (1991) 2 SCC 373.
6. (1994) 2 SCC 1.
7. (1995)2 SCC 369.
8. (1995) 3 SCC 600.
9. (1995) 1 SCC 14.
10. (1996) 1SCC 490.
11. AIR 2001 Sc 3218.
12. AIR 2001SC 1309:2001AIR SCW 1130.

14

GLOBALISATION, MYTH AND REALITY OF HUMAN RIGHTS IN INDIA

Ranbir Singh

Globalisation though a catchword of new millennium, what is especially disturbing is the discovery of a dangerous trend in the inequality; the increasing hiatus between the urban and rural areas. In fact, the bank report on 'attacking poverty' quotes *National Account Statistics* (NAS) to argue that the signs of rising inequality is mainly due to rising average consumption in the urban areas but not in the rural areas. This surely provides credibility to the argument that modern development has led to the emergence of two Indias: the rural *versus* the urban, the poor *versus* the rich. The Kisan leader Sharad Joshi had aptly described it as Bharat *versus* India. The one time rhetoric has today uncomfortably been proved true. What are then the lessons to be learnt from such a revelation? First, with two-thirds of the population still continuing to eke out a living from agriculture even after half a century of independence and given a slower rate of poverty reduction in the rural areas, the task of poverty alleviation is surely gigantic. We need to go on a war footing to tackle endemic poverty in the rural areas.

The fact that a rising trend in economic growth, in the short-term, leads to increasing inequality, is an old hat. After all, it is common knowledge that a boom in the markets generates wealth, not equity and redistribution. Attempting to achieve greater equality even in classical political economy was supposed to be a function of State intervention. What is, however, surprising is that today even the marketfriendly World Bank admits it. The World Bank's development report 2000-2001, notes that while India's gross domestic product (GDP) grew in the 1990s by 6.1 per cent, the decline in poverty levels has been rather sluggish. In fact, the bank recommends a comprehensive and direct approach involving 'opportunity, empowerment and security'. This would certainly come as a big blow for those who still continue to believe in the wonders of 'trickel-down economics'.

As a necessary fallout of trend of globalisation and liberal economic policies, India too has moved from its 'socialistic pattern' stance to the 'free market economy' with a distant shift in the role of the State in the emerging economic order. India's new economic policy is based on the notion that economic growth is possible only if the internal entrepreneurs are liberated from State controls so that foreign investors in India help this goal the government is promising attractive returns for the investment from Indian and foreign businessmen. For instance, the government has introduced or likely to introduce cuts in governmental expenditure on development as well as mass welfare schemes such as basic health care, education, subsidies on fertilizers and other welfare measures. On the other hand, various concessions and incentives are being offered to enlarge the capacities of private and foreign enterprises to invest in India on soft terms with very few or no regrates strings at all.

The developing countries, like India are likely to face new challenges for the world trading system after coming into force of World Trade Organization (WTO). Insistence of some developed countries on making environmental and labour standards as a precondition to market access and free trade would have a far reaching consequences for developing economies. The million dollar question is, Will the developing economies be able to claim an equitable share of the new world over. How to cope with the adverse effect of preferential trading arrangements and growing regionalism despite WTO's guiding principle of non-discrimination? What strategic laws and policies should be evolved to meet the challenge of the new world trade over?

It is worth pondering that the enforcement of labour standards will include the entire gamut of worker's rights such as freedom of association, acceptable standards of work, the rights of the migrants and immigrants and enforcement of ban on child labour, bonded labour and prison labour. Can these standards be truly enforced in our country with a liberal foreign investment regime? It is true that free market forces will further reduce the overwhelming majority of the rural poor into agrarian serfs, bonded and child labour, unemployed citizens and marginal farmers? By and large, the experience of countries that have gone through the process of restructuring the privatizing their economies has been a negative one. This is true that this economic model has contributed to increased inequalities, dismantling of social services with adverse effects on the poor and restrictions on trade union rights? The development projects have negative impact on the local population, particularly indigenous people. India, which has launched the liberalization process will be an interesting case-study to watch, whether the system would be able to protect human rights or sacrifice them for the sake of the new economic model. India forces an uphill task and a great challenge in the fiscal reform regime. One may ask: Will India's economy continue to remain stuck-up in the mess of stagflation? Who will be the ultimate beneficiary of economic growth? We also need to analyse the economic management policies with structural adjustment so as to analyse the economic management policies with structural adjustments so as to evolve a paradigm of 'socially responsible market economy'. This would require proposals for reform in existing legal and economic institutions and also an examination of the social meaning of various judicial decisions creating a new regime of human rights. In other words, the glib talk among vested interests and official propagandists promising economic growth through free market economy has to be judged in terms not merely economic but social particularly when the preamble to the Constitution ensures justice, social, economic and political to 'We the people of India'.

Second, a precondition for a successful democracy, according to the noted political sociologist Barrington Moore, has been a successful alliance between the urban middle classes and the rural peasantry. This cannot come about if the few cities continue to prosper while the millions of villages suffer. Finally, if poverty reduction became sluggish during the 1990s were the reform years, such a discovery would immediately lead those against reforms to argue: 'I told you so'. But on careful consideration it will be abundantly clear that one cannot blame the reforms for the slow process of poverty alleviation, especially in the rural areas. The markets have indeed performed. Consider the following: today the World Bank admits that India is the fourth largest economy in the world going by purchasing power parity estimates. But why does India continue to house the world's largest poor? The State is the real culprit. Instead of investing in education, public health and empowering the poor by rebuilding their entitlements, the State continued to regulate and throttle the markets for the first four decades. Today, instead of planning out the strategies of long term poverty alleviation, it has even abandoned the basics of governance. (*The Indian Express*, September 13, 2000).

India with the freedom history of 54 years behind is a peculiar story. Today India is free. Indian's are not. Ours is a story of Republican India betrayed, promises unkept, unfulfilled and the Indian Democracy hijacked. The manifesto of the people of India provided in the Preamble of the Constitution, Justice, Social, economic, political still remains a distant dream. The big question is what we have achieved provided in the preamble. The answer is a big no. Why this has happened? Answer is not very difficult to find, in more than five decades of freedom. India is not one India. It is two Indias. One is ' We the People of India' that is those people who are rich, wealthy and powerful and the other category is ' We the Other People of India' those who are poor, downtrodden, *dalits*, Harijans, have-nots, disadvantaged etc., etc., sections of society. Frankly speaking the fourth World within the third world. Why this has happened when the present day India has covered a long journey of freedom things has not changed much. Instead of White Britishers we have bred White Indians. The petty Indian, the have-nots, have not only remained invisible to affluent eye but also feel distanced from the democratic agenda of the Indian Republic. This has happened not without a reason in all these years though the Britishers have gone, the masters have changed in place of Britishers we have Indian masters but the system remains the same, it has not changed. It would be everybody's wish in the free India in the twenty-first century to at least if not achieved, aspire to have some fruits of what is provided in the preamble of India which in human rights terms we call 'first generation of human rights'. The fundamental rights provided in the Constitution of India and the promises of human rights would mean something real to all Indians if the system would respond positively to the demands of the needy, the neglected, the hapless women and the bonded child etc. The problem is not that we do not have enough laws or we are not aware of the human rights. The problem is because of the insensitivity of the people those who matter in the system. The difficulty is also of the right attitude towards the problems. Of the 80 per cent India agriculturally based dependent on labour living in the countryside mostly without enjoying any facilities worthy name may it be proper food, shelter, clothing, health care or even education. The myth of the human rights comes more apparently visible in India and threatens to pose a much bigger problem in the new millennium. The starvation deaths are still a reality not only in Kalahandi (Orissa) but in various parts of the country. The suicides of farmers have become common feature. The situation is really grim and explosive. It is not that we do not have enough, we have enough but not to share. I quote:

> *'The fields are fruitful, and starving men moved on the roads. The granaries were full and the children of the poor grew up rachitic, and pustules of pellagra swelled on their side. The great companies did not know that the line between hunger and anger is a thin line'.*

If the implementation of the human rights in India have to be properly effectuated and implemented the reality of violation of human rights has to be faced with a much more sense of sincerity and honesty towards the other people of India. Otherwise what is engraved in the Constitution in the chapters thereon fundamental rights and directive principles will always remain a distant dream to achieve. Law would become a teasing illusion and in a state of suspended animation. One may ask how long. No body knows except the power that be. But the time to face the problem squarely is today not tomorrow. Because tomorrow may be too late. I conclude by a conversation between Tagore and Gandhi.

> Once Gurudev Rabindranath Tagore asked Gandhiji, 'Gandhiji are you so unromantic? When in the early dawn, the morning sun rises, does it not fill your heart with joy to see its reddish glow? When the birds sing does not your heart thrill with its divine music? When the rose opens its petals and blooms in the garden does its sight not bring cheer to your heart?'
> The Mahatma Gandhi replied,'Gurudev, I am not dumb or insensitive, as not to be moved by the beauty of the rose or the morning rays of the sun or the divine music of the birds. But what can I do? My one desire, my one anxiety, my one ambition is when shall I see the red tint of the rose on the cheeks of hungry naked millions of the people? When shall I hear the sweet and melodious song of the birds in place of their agonizing sights? When will such music come out their soul and when will that day come when the light of the morning sun will illumine the heart of the common man of India? When will I see its lustre and brightness on his face?'

We have miles to go before we sleep to realize the dream of Gandhiji. It should not be forgotten that the people of India and their human rights must have a priority in twenty-first century if the system has to survive the shock.

15

HUMAN RIGHTS JURISPRUDENCE
PROBLEMS AND PROSPECTS

D. Surya Prakasa Rao

The history of the Human Rights is the history of natural law. Natural is nothing but a participation of eternal law in a rational creature. Its origin dates back even before Christ. There is not one theory; many versions have evolved throughout this enormous span of time. Thus Natural Law thinking by and large should offer indirect help with two contemporary problems, namely the abuse of power and the abuse of liberty. The human rights jurisprudence in the modern context deals with the problems of abuse of power and abuse of liberty.

Human Rights through Constitutional Culture— Indian Perspective

The Constitution confers on the individual certain basic rights enforceable against the State. It can perhaps best he described as a document which, while upholding and protecting individual interest in the form of fundamental rights guaranteed against the State, envisages a positive role for it in ensuring realization of these basic rights by every individual. In other words the fact that an individual has a right would mean the State has a duty not to interfere with it. This can be best explained in terms of Rawl's First principle of justice that each person is to have equal right to the most extensive, total system of equal basic liberties compatible with a similar system of liberties for all.

The Constitution aims at the creation of new legal norms social philosophy and economic values which are to be effected by striking synthesis, harmony and fundamental adjustment between individual rights and social interests to achieve the desired community goals.

In India we adopted a parliamentary democracy with constitutional supremacy to achieve a casteless and classless egalitarian society, and socio-economic justice as the ultimate goal. After 50 years of experience in post-independence era, now we are rethinking about means to reach this end. We are liberalizing every thing so as to minimize the State interference. In the process we are moving from collectivism to individualism, of course for the collective good. How far it is good or bad in the interest of the society will be proved in near future.

As Justice Krishna Iyer rightly pointed out we live in an age wherein a new world legal order is blossoming, the Universal Declaration of Human Rights, the Great Covenants, the many conventions and other United Nations resolutions have woven a garment of human rights, social justice, defence of dignity and cultural development, not merely for individuals but also for homogeneous groups, communities and minorities. Alas, alongside of these advancing frontiers of humanist jurisprudence is the massive invasion, even annihilation of those very rights and claims to economic and social justice. State terrorism is a growing menace. Mini-wars and neo-imperialist maneuvers are proliferating.

No doubt the recent teleological approach of Indian Supreme Court towards fundamental rights particularly in post Maneka Scenario gave impetus to contemporary international human rights and constitutional protection of individual liberty. The protection extended from abuse of official power to official neglect is well demonstrated in the expansion of constitutional remedies i.e., the compensation through writs, public interest litigation and the dynamics of the concept of State. The Judicial Activism in India reaches its high peak in protecting the constitutional spirit.

Human Rights and Civil Society

In the Greek political thought, as seen in the writings of Plato and Aristotle, there was not much of a difference between State and society and hence there was no antagonism between the two; probably due to smallness of the State and the emphasis on moral authority. Accordingly State then was an organized society. But there is change of perception as witnessed in the Roman Empire and biblical statements, according to which society and State were two distinct groups. Gradually, civil society came into prominence and it could successfully defeat armed rebellions, the examples of which are French Revolution and American Revolution.

Civil society, in simple terms, could be termed as set of diverse non-governmental groups or associations that influence the rest of the society. The Marxist reinterpretation of society from the capitalist mode of production has revived the concept of civil society. In the classless society, as envisioned by Marx, individual has little power as powers rest with the entire society. Accordingly importance is given not to the State but only to the civil society.

Globalization may be artificially promoting civil society as seen in the rise of multinationals. Anthony Giddens talks about the crisis of identity and capitalism. Private appropriates public property, because what is called public now is privately managed and what is called private is anyway privately managed.

Civil Society can also be explained in the context of human rights. In the Human Development Report, Amartya Sen emphasizes rights and also duties. Over a period of time, civil society will stand for a balanced development and it has a role to play to boost the State. Civil society should play and active role in protecting the rights of children, parents handicapped etc. In the fundamental rights, we have positive as well as negative rights. The positive rights such as right to property, equality, freedom of speech, etc., could be the responsibility of the State and negative right such as the State shall not discriminate on the basis of sex, religion, caste, race, etc., could be the task of civil society and it should play an active role in protecting the rights of the individuals.

Human Rights of Poor

Human Rights are the rights of a human being and without those basic inalienable sacrosanct human values there is no meaning of human life. All the civilized countries recognized this basic human rights jurisprudence. The Universal Declaration of Human Rights is the culmination of human rights movement in the world. The process of enforcing the human rights by the States as well as civil societies is always a debatable issue.

Those who advocate universality assert that human rights must be same everywhere. Those who believe that human rights are relative to particular history and culture contend this. They contend that notions of rights differ since they are based on culture, which is diverse. The relativists include women movements, Christianity *versus* Islam, and Asian values debate (North-South divide). Universalistic concepts from existing international standards ratified by various governments, certain values shared universally since they arise out of shared sufferings and hopes of all humanity, ensuring cultural legitimacy of human rights, cross cultural approach identifying the intolerable and the involvement of the civil society are the major approaches towards the effective implementation of human rights throughout the world. Human rights of the poor include all these aspects.

Human Rights in the Asian Context

Regarding Asia, Yash Ghai identifies the following aspects that characterize the Asian context and mediate human rights. First, the intent of human rights discourse differs in Asia and the West. The West is devoid of radically opposed political models. As a result human rights are non-controversial and strengthens existing administrative and judicial structures. On the contrary, Asia is characterized by conflicts arising from the unequal distribution of power and wealth, political corruption, the rapaciousness of domestic and international capital and authoritarianism. In which case, human rights in Asia are a weapon for fighting injustice and oppression. It becomes an agenda item of those working for the transformation of society. "Human rights are, therefore, a terrain for struggle for power and the conceptions of good society." Asian ruling elite challenges the compatibility of human rights with so called Asian values in order to engage their own citizens in a debate rather than with the West.

Secondly, the gross violations of human rights in Asia encompass civil, political, social, economic and cultural rights. The State is a major violator of these rights. However, violations also occur in and throughout civil society. These violations, range from ethnic conflict, contemporary forms of slavery such as debt bondage and gender and caste based discrimination and violence.

Thirdly, despite serious human rights violations, consciousness of human rights is not wide enough to counter such violations. Ethnic divisions and ethnicity legitimize the oppression of others and may contribute to inadequate appreciation of human rights. Another possible factor is widespread poverty which "destroys the capacity to challenge the system of oppression."

Finally, in Asia most often the human rights of groups and not individuals are violated. Therefore, the strategies to be adopted in Asia are vastly different from those adopted in Western countries. For example, court strategies may not be as effective in Asia. On the other hand, the concretization and mobilization of the oppressed based on an understanding of their oppression and the violation of their rights is more effective. In conclusion Ghai states that, "Fruitful Asian perspectives on human rights must, therefore, transcend obfuscation of culture, locate human rights in the contingencies of their political economy, and urge struggle domestically as well as globally."

The Impact of Intellectual Property Rights on the Poor

We have now accepted the rights and obligations of an internationally accepted patent protection regime and respect for intellectual property rights as part of our commitment to WTO and the economy is now increasingly focusing itself on productivity and competitiveness. The international economy represents a highly competitive arena where only the productive and efficient will survive and grow.

But as a matter of fact, most of the poverty in developing countries is due to a history of colonial exploitation and continuing feudal structures which are both exploitative and a hindrance to economic and social development. Culture, custom, law and the dominant public opinion legitimize the roots of poverty and its consequences. Whatever development takes place bypasses the poor relatively, if not absolutely. The relative neglect of agriculture, corruption comes in the way of benefits going to the poor. No doubt the incidence of poverty has declined significantly over the last three decades, but still every third Indian is below the poverty line.

India is a mega bio diverse region of the world. In India like any other developing or relatively poor country, the poor depend directly on the natural resource environment for their livelihood. Agriculture, Forestry, Fisheries and Mining has a fairly good share of Gross Domestic Product (GDP) in India.

How can we withstand and give competition in world market with poverty? Laws on I.P.R are about providing a framework for protection to the creator of the intellectual property. The total process of the regulation is complex and far from the reach of rural masses. Here the danger of violating the Human Rights of the poor is pertinent. The Human face of I.P.R needs to be strengthened to overcome this danger. As most of the poor people live on agriculture, it should be protected. The antidumping laws are to be implemented to save the domestic products. Some have apprehensions that India's agreement with WTO on agriculture would severely affect agriculture and pave the way for the import of rice, vegetables, fruits and so on. It will play havoc with our economy.

All is not well with the science and technology sector with even a decline in the expenditure on research and development over the past decade in India. Food security and livelihood concern are the core areas to be protected from the impact of globalization. In trade related intellectual property rights protection of the traditional knowledge and extension of the protection for geographical indications to additional products such as Basmati rice and Darjeeling tea are to be effectively ensured.

The inequalities between developed and developing countries must be meaningfully addressed to protect the human rights of the poor. Reorienting India's labour laws in the wake of decline in the employment growth in organization sector and simultaneous increase in casual work in the past decade is an important pointer to what economic restructuring to the labour market in a labour surplus economy. Enforceable fundamental rights must be made available to citizens against private firms and individuals in view of privatization and the role of the State being receded and reduced and a mere facilitator.

W.T.O was no doubt designed to protect the developed countries economic interest in general and Multinational Corporations interest in particular. MNC's interests are protected and promoted through W.T.O, which is an instrument for globalization for individual benefit, but the need of the hour is, it should be individual effort for Global village. Now W.T.O is emerging more powerful than I.M.F and World Bank. There is accordingly a strong need to make it more democratic. Even though Indian voice is not that much powerful before W.T.O. we can keep on making the noise in protecting our economic interest.

However we should not forget that in order to make our voice more powerful before W.T.O. we should create a new national order first in which growth of the recourses, raising standard of living, economic progress, and increase in G.N.P. are to be achieved. World history proves that progress and prosperity are not the monopoly of any part of the globe. A real attempt to reshape the world order is to be made towards a more equitable, more cooperative and more progressive system.

Curbing Challenges to Constitutional Fundamentals—The Real Test for the Effective Implementation of Human Rights

The constitution of a country is the expression of the will of the people to govern them. It reflects the people's aspirations. In any country the constitution is the fundamental law of the land. It is a live law. The Constitution of India being a mid-twentieth century document, the Constitution makers had the advantage of consulting various constitutions, human rights documents and prepared the best document in maintaining balance between human rights and duties, which is tested through times. Even though the challenges were there to the very existence of the Constitution in the past, it was proved successful in facing the challenges. But new challenges are developing often and some challenges posed a problem even for the survival of the country and the Constitution. Five decades of working experience with the Constitution provides us an opportunity to understand these challenges in the past and present as impediment to achieve the constitutional goals. How for the goals were achieved even against the challenges and what are the possible solutions to make the present constitutional system more effective are to be examined.

Some have the opinion that the Constitution of India is a great failure in curbing the challenges. But it is not true. If at all any failure is there; it is the failure of the people who are called to work upon the Constitution. May be the Legislators, Judges Executive or the people at large in cultivating the true democratic spirit?

The dialectics of law and society in India has been determined by the historical experience during the passage from colonialism to nationalism. In this process both legal and social systems have evolved. Indian experience can be viewed as a conflict resulting from a search for a balance between the use of law by elite for purposes of domination and the use of law to moderate elite domination by providing avenues of participation for the disadvantaged.

What is the reality during the last 50 years? The country has seen the execution of various five-year plans involving huge expenditure by the government for various nation-building activities. The corrupt officers, businessmen and contractors never had it so good. No doubt the country did made some progress but the white-collar criminals pocketed big chunk of money earmarked for developmental projects.

In the words of Justice Krishna Iyer, "xenophobic mentality is controlling even development and simian conception of corporate greed has displaced the basic needs of the voiceless masses. Recolonialism, criminalism, communalism above all corruptions deadened democracy, paralyzed development negative every socio-economic value in the National Charter."

For the last 50 years no doubt development is there. But the creamy class of the society only enjoyed the benefits. Some new classes are emerged due to implementation of some positive measures like reservations, constructing irrigation projects, green revolution etc. Due to negative factors like scams, corruption, windfalls due to uncertain, directionless economic policies, criminalization of politics etc., also cause the emergence of class-caste convergence with yawning gap between haves and have-nots. All these human problems are the subject matter of human rights jurisprudence. The development of a society can be assessed only on the basis of the effective implementation of human rights.

Thus the concept of human rights is so complex and dynamic which remains the goal of contemporary and even of future communities—a just man, a just law, and a just government. Harmony is the quality of human rights which can be a achieved by reason and wisdom by giving equal access to all who seek human rights as of right according to the just Law. To sum up like the story of god, the story of human rights is a continuous and a never-ending exercise for it brings the foundation of moral-cum-legal and social ordering.

16

AFFIRMATIVE ACTION TO CURB SALE AND TRAFFICKING OF GIRLS

SADIQ A. JILANI SYED

"We cannot waste our precious children. Not another one, not another day. It is long past time for us to act on their behalf." – Nelson Mandela and Graça Machel

The Constitution of India guarantees wide range of rights for the protection and proper upbringing of children in general and girl children in particular. It empowers the State to take protective measures for the redressal of the cumulative disadvantages on account of the stranglehold of archaic traditions and beliefs. Prior to the adoption of the Constitution there were few legislations, which dealt with the child marriages, child labour and the other issues relevant to the children. The implementation of these legislations was not up to the expectations and almost failed to achieve their purpose. The protection and empowerment of girl children is a positive concept and requires State action in support of those who are to be empowered. The Constitution envisages State intervention on behalf of the girl children.[1]

The sale and sexual victimisation of girl children through trafficking has been in existence throughout the history of mankind and across cultures. It is not confined to a particular country rather a worldwide phenomenon. The protection and empowerment of girls from trafficking and sale has become an issue of global concern in the recent times with the increasing number of incidents reported. The issues such as sale, trafficking, genital mutilation, foeticide and infanticide and sexual abuse of girls are increasing in the horrifying dimensions. The United Nations and its various agencies joined by the national governments have expressed grave concern since decades towards the elimination of worst practices including violence against the girl children and called upon the national governments to take legislative and other initiatives for the protection and empowerment of children and girl children in particular. It is no exaggeration to state that every day thousands of girls are brought from various States within the country and also trafficked from other countries to force them into sex trade, bondage, or for sale within and outside India.

The Preamble to the Constitution of India states that "We, the people of India, having solemnly resolved to constitute India into a SOVEREIGN SOCIALIST SECULAR DEMOCRATIC REPUBLIC and to secure to all its citizens: among others Justice, Social, Economic and Political, Liberty, Equality and Fraternity. In the words of Cardozo, `a written constitution states or intended to state not rules for the passing hour but principles for an expanding future'.[2] The Supreme Court of India in its various pronouncements had reiterated its stand that the Preamble, thus, contains the ideals and aspirations[3] or the objects which Constitution makers intended to be realised.[4]

The Court in *Gita Hariharan's case*[5] held that "Normal rules of interpretation shall have to bow down to the requirement of the Constitution since the Constitution is supreme and the statute shall have to be in accordance therewith and not *de hors* the same".

The Court in the recent past gave a new impetus to the concept of 'Social Justice'. In *Sadhuram's case*[6] held that "*Social justice is the recognition of greater good to a larger number without deprivation or accrual of legal rights of anybody. If such a thing can be done, then social justice must prevail over any technical rule. As between two parties if a deal is made with one party without serious detriment to the other, then the Court would lean in favour of the weaker section of the society"*. Further the Constitution under various chapters guarantees to its citizens various rights in the form of *'Fundamental Rights'* and *'Directive Principles of State Policy'*.

The Constitution of India under Part III guarantees Fundamental Rights to the citizens. These rights represent the values cherished by the people and are meant to safeguard the dignity of the individual and also helps in creating conditions in which human beings can develop their personality to the fullest extent. The Constitution of India guarantees equality of laws to all the persons. The concept of equality is applied mainly to criminal laws and procedures. While several civil laws are also equally applicable to all the sexes some of the personal laws not only treat women and girls unequally but even where legal recourse is warranted, they are unable to obtain justice from the law enforcing and dispensing machineries.

Article 14 of the Constitution states that "the State shall not deny to any person equality before the law or the equal protection of the laws within the territory of India". Article 14 though guarantees equality it does not prevent the State from introducing a reform towards the betterment. Article 14 is a general provision and has to be read subject to the other provisions included within the Part on Fundamental Rights. Hence any law making special provisions for women (or children) under Article 15(3) cannot be challenged on the ground of contravention of Article 14.[7]

Article 14 of the Constitution prohibits class legislation and not reasonable classification for the purpose of legislation. *'If the Legislature takes care to reasonably classify persons for legislative purposes and if it deals equally with all persons belonging to a 'well-defined class', it is not open to the charge of denial of equal protection on the ground that the law does not apply to other persons'.*[8]

Article 15 is an instance of the right of equality which is

generally stated in Article 14. While Article 14 is available to all persons, Article 15 is available to citizens only.[9] This Article enables the State to make special provisions for various sections of the society. In this context Article 15(3) of the Constitution states that 'Nothing in this Article shall prevent the State from making special provision for women and children'. Further, a discrimination against a man or a woman, only on the ground of sex would be violative of Art. 15(1).[10] An exception to this general rule is engrafted in Clause (3) of Article 15 saving measures protective of or beneficial to women and children. This clause is an exception to the rule against discrimination provided by clause (1) as well as (2).[11] Thus the Courts validated the '*provision of maternity relief for women workers*[12] *and held that this will not be a contravention of the prohibition against discrimination under Clause (1) of the present Article: nor will be the provision of free education for children*[13] *or measures for provision against their exploitation.*[14] *The provision for separate accommodation, entrances, etc., for women and children at places of public resort will not be a violation of Cl. (2) of the present Article.* The Legislative provisions which are discriminatory in favour of women and children have been declared to be *valid,* in view of the special provisions enunciated under Article 15(3).

Article 17 of the Constitution of India prohibits untouchability. The Article as such does not define the word 'Untouchability' under the Constitution. A single judge of the Mysore High Court[15] held that 'untouchability' in the Act refers to the social disabilities historically imposed on certain classes of people by reason of their birth in certain castes and would not include an instigation of social boycott by reason of the conduct of certain persons. Further the Constitution under Article 19(1)(a) guarantees right to freedom of speech and expression, but the rights guaranteed under Article 19(1) are subject to the power of the State to impose restrictions on the exercise of those rights. The Article was thus intended to protect these rights against *State action* other than in the legitimate exercise of its power to regulate private rights in the public interest.[16]

Article 21 of the Constitution of India states that "No

person shall be deprived of his life or personal liberty except according to procedure established by law". The Supreme Court of India in as early as in 1968 in *Indo Afghan Agencies case*[17] held that "The object of Article 21 is to prevent encroachment upon personal liberty by the executive save in accordance with law and in conformity with the provisions thereof". Keeping in view the needs of the society the Supreme Court has widened the scope of Article 21 from time to time to include, among others, right to live with human dignity,[18] the right of a person not to be subjected to bonded labour [19] or to unfair conditions of labour,[20] the right of a bonded labourer to rehabilitation after release,[21] right to a decent environment,[22] and also an obligation on the State to preserve the life of every person by offering immediate medical aid to every patient, regardless of the question whether he is an innocent or a guilty person. The criminal law shall operate after the life of the injured is saved.[23] The Court in *Chandrabhan's case* has opened up a new dimension and held that "*Right to life enshrined in Article 21 means something more than survival or animal existence*".[24]

The Supreme Court while taking note of the increasing child labour and corresponding illiteracy in the country gave new impetus to the directives principles enshrined under the Constitution and brought them to a highest pedestal. While recognising the importance of education the Supreme Court in *Mohini Jain case*[25] observed "'Right to life' is the compendious expression for all those rights which the courts must enforce because they are basic to the dignified enjoyment of life. It extends to the full range of conduct, which the individual is free to pursue. The right to education flows directly from right to life. The right to life under Article 21 and the dignity of an individual cannot be assured unless it is accompanied by the right to education. The State Government is under an obligation to make endeavour to provide educational facilities at all levels to its citizens."

The Court in *Unnikrishnan's case* further clarified that "The right to education further means that a citizen has a right to call upon the State to provide educational facilities to him within the limits of its economic capacity and development. By saying so we are not transferring Article 45 from Part IV to Part III, we are merely relying upon Article 45 to illustrate the content of the right of education flowing from Article 21.[26]

The Constitution of India prohibits traffic in human beings and beggar and other similar forms of forced labour and any contravention of this provision shall be an offence punishable in accordance with law.[27] The Supreme Court in *Raj Bahadur's case*[28] held that *"traffic in human beings includes traffic in women and children"*. The Court while dealing with the aspect of the Constitutionality of the validity of the law under Art 19(1)(g) which guarantees to the citizens *'right to practice any profession, or to carry on any occupation, trade or business'* held that *"a law for the suppression of such traffic would be valid and intra-vires the Constitution of India.*

The Supreme Court in *People's Union case*[29] held that *"'forced labour' is a wide expression, which would be attracted whenever a person is compelled to give his labour or service, even though remuneration be paid for it. The same would be the result where the labourer is obliged to work at wages less than the minimum wage"*. Further the Court while going a step ahead gave directions to the State for the identification and rehabilitation of bounded labourers. In this content the court in *Bandhu Mukti Morcha case*[30] held that *"Article 23 has to be read with the Directives in Arts. 39(c), 41, 42. So read, the State should not only identify bonded labourers but also provide for their rehabilitation"*.

The Constitutional makers while keeping in view the magnitude of child labour force in the country and also to protect the childhood from exploitation have made appropriate provisions prohibiting the employment of children in factories and other hazardous employment. In this context the Constitution states that, *"No child below the age of 14 years shall be employed to work in any factory or mine or engaged in any other hazardous employment"*.[31] The Supreme Court in *People's Union case*[32] while making the applicability of the Act to various other establishments held that *"The expression 'hazardous employment' is wide enough to include construction industry"*. It also held that *"the right of a child is enforceable even in the absence of implementing legislation, and in a 'public interest' proceeding"*. Further, the

Supreme Court in *M.C. Mehta's (Child Labour Matter) case* observed that *"while Article 24 of the Constitution has been a fundamental right since inception, Article 45 too has been raised to a high pedestal; by Unnikrishnan.* Though other Articles are part of directive principles, they are fundamental in the governance of our country and it is the duty of all the organs of the State (Article 37) to apply these principles. Judiciary, being also one of the three principal organs of the State, has to keep the same in mind when called upon to decide matters of great public importance. Abolition of child labour is definitely a matter of great public concern and significance".[33]

The Constitution of India under Article 32 provides, the right to move the Supreme Court by appropriate proceedings for the enforcement of the rights conferred and guaranteed, under the Constitution.[34] To this end any effected person whose rights have been infringed can move the Supreme Court. The Court in the recent past has relaxed the concept of *locus standi* in public interest. While defining the objective of Article 32 the Supreme Court in *Gopal Das's case* held that, "*The sole object* of Art. 32 is the enforcement of the fundamental rights guaranteed by the Constitution. Whatever other remedies may be open to a person aggrieved, he has no right to complain under Art. 32 where no 'fundamental' right has been infringed".[35]

In the recent past the Supreme Court has liberalised the traditional private law rule that only a person who has suffered injury by reason of violation of his legal right or interest is entitled to seek judicial redress. The Supreme Court has enlarged the rights of the citizens under this Article for the purposes of dealing with public law. The Court in *Fertiliser Corporation case*[36] held that *"The concept of a 'person aggrieved', to include any public spirited individual or association"*. The Court further clarified by saying that, 'provided only he acts *bona fide* to vindicate the cause of justice and is not actuated by political motive or other oblique considerations, or he is not a mere busybody or interloper'.[37]

The Directive Principles of State Policy enunciated under the Constitution unlike fundamental rights are not enforceable by the Courts. But in the recent years the Judiciary has broadened the concept of the Directive Principles and gave a wider definition to it. The Court by applying the concept of doctrine of '*harmonious construction*'[38] has applied the Directive Principles to adjust the ambit of the Fundamental Rights.[39] Under the Directives it is provided that the State shall ensure that the health and strength of workers, men and women, and the tender age of children are not abused, and that citizens are not forced by economic necessity to enter avocations unsuited to their age; or strength.[40] The Court in *Bandhua case* interpreted Article 21 in such a way to include the right to live with human dignity, free from exploitation, in the light of the directives contained in Arts. 39(e)-(f), 41 and 42 of the Constitution.[41] In *M.C. Mehta's case* it directed that children should not be employed in hazardous jobs in factories for manufacture of match boxes and fire works, and positive steps should be taken for the welfare of such children as well as for improving the quality of their life.[42]

The Supreme Court while dealing with a matter under Arts. 32, 24, 39(f) and 45 of the Constitution of India in *M. C. Mehta's case*[43] held that "spirit of the Constitution is that children should not be employed in factories as childhood is the formative period and they instead should be subjected to free and compulsory education until they complete the age of 14 years." That children are given opportunities and facilities to develop in a healthy manner and in conditions of freedom and dignity and that childhood and youth are protected against exploitation and against moral and material abandonment. Further while coming to the rescue of the children in prostitution in *Vishaljeet's case*[44] the Supreme Court gave directions to the Government for framing a national policy to rescue and rehabilitate such children.

The illiteracy and the dropout rates among girl children is a matter of concern for the last few decades. By keeping in view the deteriorating conditions and the state of education in the country the Constitution makers have made appropriate provisions in the Constitution of India. Article 45 of the Constitution states that, ' The State shall endeavour to provide, within a period of ten years from the commencement of this Constitution, free and compulsory education for all children until they complete the age of 14 years'. Further Article 15(3) enables the State to make special provisions for women and children. It may be noted that, even after 50 years of Independence there is no substantial progress in the state of education in the country. The Supreme Court in its various judgements had stressed the need to provide free and compulsory primary education to all the children in the country. The Court in *Unnikrishnan's case* held that 'Though right to education is not stated expressly as a fundamental right, it is implicit in and flows from the right to life guaranteed under Article 21 having regard to the broad and expansive interpretation given by the Court. .... Without education being provided to the citizens of this country, the objectives set forth in the Preamble to the Constitution cannot be achieved. The Constitution would fail'[45] To realize the constitutional resolve, the directives by the Supreme Court and the nation's commitments at the International sphere[46] the Government finally recognised 'right to education' as a fundamental right and inserted a new clause (A) to Article 21 through Eighty-sixth amendment to the Constitution in the year 2002.

Most significantly the Constitution says that, it shall be the duty of every citizen of India, to renounce practices derogatory to the dignity of women.[47] A deep study of the various provisions of the Constitution reveals that the Constitution recognizes and protects the rights of the girl children. Further the Constitutional makers have made some of the rights related to girl child implicit such as the phrases 'women' and 'children' includes a girl child. These rights have been well recognized and made explicit due to the activist role played by the concerted individual and the organizations in the recent past. Most importantly the judicial craftsmanship and commitment towards the cause of children's rights by the judges of the Supreme Court to greater extent contributed to the improving of standards of girl children in the society. Thus the Constitution of India has contributed to the recognition of new rights and it also helped the judiciary in fixing the responsibility on the States for taking measures for the welfare of girl children.

The exploitation of girl children for sexual abuse is not a new phenomenon and exists since time immemorial. Girl child prostitution has remained an integral part of the institution of prostitution due to preference of young girls by the customers. There is growing evidence that large number of children, mostly girls in the age group of 6-18 years, are being forced into prostitution in the major Indian cities, and that many of the adult women working as prostitutes were forced into it against their will when they were minors. Precise figures are not known, but the several studies that have been conducted, provide evidence to support the view that the sexual exploitation and trafficking of children is a significant problem, and one, which is growing. The sale of children from villages of India and neighbouring countries, particularly Nepal and Bangladesh, is a lucrative business for a network of procurers, pimps and brothel owners. Researchers claim that there are at least 10,00,000 children in prostitution in Asia. It is unacceptable to the countries where child prostitution occurs, and it is unacceptable to the many other countries whose citizens are among those creating the demand for children as sexual partners.

In a survey conducted by Central Social Welfare Board on prostitution in six cities (Delhi, Bombay, Calcutta, Hyderabad, Madras and Bangalore) in 1991-92, it is found that the total number of prostitutes in these cities was likely to be between 70,000-100,000 and out of these 30 per cent were below the age of 20 and 40 per cent of them became prostitutes when they were children (18 or under), 86 per cent of the prostitutes came from 6 States (Andhra Pradesh, Karnataka, Tamil Nadu, West Bengal, Maharashtra and Uttar Pradesh) out of them, 94.6 per cent were Indians, 2.6 per cent were Nepalis and 2.7 per cent were Bangladeshis, 84.6 per cent were Hindus; 10.95 per cent Muslims, 3.5 per cent Christians, 36 per cent were from scheduled castes and tribes; 24 per cent from other backward castes and 40 per cent others. Out of these 71 per cent were illiterate, 4 per cent were literate and 24 per cent had some formal schooling, 66 per cent of prostitutes came from families who are very poor - (less than Rs. 5000 per annum),

60 per cent of prostitutes earned less than Rs. 3000 per month, of which 50 per cent had to be given to the brothel keeper. Prostitutes would have to pay further charges for their lodgings and food, as well as providing for their families (either living with them or back in their villages). They therefore had very little money to spare, and would frequently fall into debt. Brothel keepers share their income with pimps, procurers, local goondas and allegedly with the police, thus creating a network of vested interests in the continuance of the trade.[48]

The above figures exemplify that there are thousands of children who were forced into prostitution. Even it is estimated that in Mumbai red light area alone there are nearly 5,000 Nepali girls in prostitution. These figures on the increasing number of exchange of girls between various countries in the SAARC region had encouraged the respective governments to join together for the enactment of a convention to combat transborder trafficking and the rehabilitation of the rescued women and girl children.

Adding to this in India in few of the communities the girls were dedicated in the form of *'devadasi' yellamma* and *'jogins'*. The *devadasi* system clearly demonstrates the conflux of economic and social forces that robs young girls of any control over their lives and forces them into a lifetime of prostitution. Historically, *devadasis* served a god to which they were ritually "married" by dancing and singing in the temple of that god. They became prostitutes at the instigation of the priests, who were trying to attract additional income to the temple. Today, although some *devadasi* dedications are motivated by genuine religious devotion, the majority are the result of a variety of economic motivations. The system exists in Andhra Pradesh, Maharashtra and Karnataka and the sites of the most intense *Devadasi* activity are located in a belt on either side of the Karnataka/Maharashtra border: Belgaum, Dharwar, Bijapur and Gulbarga in Karnataka and Tagnagiri, Satara, Kolhapur, Sholapur and Osmanabad in Maharashtra. Estimates as to the numbers of *devadasis* vary widely. The newspaper reports clearly shows that in spite of the legislations prohibiting these practices, these practices are still followed in our country. In June, 1999 four young girls were dedicated as *devadasis* in the

State of Andhra Pradesh.[49] Keeping in view the India's commitments at the International sphere and also the condition of the girl child sexual abuse in the society there is an imminent need to overhaul the existing system, so as to protect the girl children from exploitation.

Another major area of concern for the activists and other organizations in the recent years is the protection and welfare of the children of women in prostitution. It is being felt by the social activists that the children of prostitutes are often being neglected due to various reasons. Further there is a possibility that these children are bound to imbibe the undesirable atmosphere of the brothels. More significantly, a study conducted by the Central Social Welfare Board, it is found that, the prostitutes want to have a child because they preceive a child as something of their own and the only one in their harsh and doomed existence with whom they share a truly loving and trusting relationship. Further Prof. Mukherjee in his extensive study stated the degree of women in prostitution to have a child in her words as "Man may come and go after using us, but it is my child who will be my only support. I shall, therefore, not mind doing anything for proper upbringing of my child even if it means to stay away from him or her for his or her better mind". The Indian Medical Association has recommended for treating child prostitution equivalent to rape and should be made a punishable crime under section 412 of the Cr.P.C. It also stressed the need to train the police official in preventing the growing menace.[50] The Supreme Court in *Gaurav Jain's case*[51] issued directions to the Government for the formulation of various schemes and programmes for the rehabilitation and empowerment of children of women in prostitution. Further the National Commission for Women has recommended for strengthening the existing laws. In this context the National Law School of India University has done an extensive study of the laws concerning women and girls in prostitution and prepared alternative draft bills for the consideration of the government. Further the National Commission for Women has also recommended for the reservation of seats for the children of prostitutes in Navodaya Vidyalayas and other residential schools.

The United Nations Development Fund for Women (UNIFEM) reported that 70 per cent of the world's 1.3 billion people living in poverty are women. And, despite the pledges made by governments at Beijing, the situation for women is getting worse in certain areas. For example, the number of rural women living in absolute poverty, i.e. life-threatening poverty has risen by 50 per cent over the last two decades as opposed to 30 per cent for men. UNIFEM further reported that although women work two-thirds of all hours worked, they earn one-tenth of all income and own less than one-tenth of the world's property. The UN Secretary-General Kofi Annan at the World Education Forum in Dakar, Senegal, noted with concern that two-thirds of the 130 million children who are not receiving education are girls. As per the ILO EPEC there are 25,00,00,000 children between the age of 5-14 years working in various establishments worldwide. Out of which 12,00,00,000 are working on fulltime basis.

The women and girls are not only discriminated lot in the society but also subjected to violence and sexual abuse. Every year, approximately two million girls are mutilated by the traditional practice of female genital mutilation. No religion in the world provides for mutilation, however it is practiced traditionally in many societies with a blind belief that such a practice would preserve virginity and chastity so as to ensure marriageability. The preference for male sons is another force directed against women, particularly in Asia. This many a time results in female foeticide, infanticide and unsafe abortions. In recent times, the technological advancements have made it possible to use genetic planning to prevent the female from ever being conceived, much less being born. As rightly observed by the Beijing document "the girl-child is discriminated against from the earliest stages of life, through her childhood and into adulthood. In some areas of the world, men outnumber women by 5 in every 100. The reasons for this discrepancy include harmful attitudes and practices, such as female genital mutilation, son preference . . . early marriage ...violence against women, sexual exploitation, sexual abuse, discrimination against girls in food allocation and other practices related to health and well-being. As a result, fewer girls than boys survive into adulthood."[52]

The sale of girls is considered as the third most lucrative organised crime in the world. This practice is one of the worst violations of the Convention on the Rights of the Child. This practice must be eliminated because it violates every principle of human rights. Over the years at the international as well as national levels through some affirmative action by the United Nations emphasis was being laid on safeguarding the rights of girl children with specific reference to their protection from sale, sexual abuse. This chapter addresses some of the issues having bearing on trafficking and sale of girls in the light of international and national legal provisions and practical realities at the ground level.

International Legal Framework

The history of sale of girls or forcing women and girls into prostitution has its roots in the age-old traditions and customary practices. This has been practiced under various names in different regions. To address this issue as early as in 1926 the League of Nations adopted the Slavery Convention.[53] This may be said as a milestone in the history of mankind, which set international human rights standards to combat slavery and trafficking. The Supplementary Slavery Convention of 1956 widened the understanding of slavery-like practices by explicitly prohibiting debt-bondage, serfdom, servile marriage and child labour. Article 1 of the 1956 Convention specifically condemns incidents of child labour when children are 'delivered' by a parent or guardian in order that their labour can be exploited by someone else. It also denounces the practices whereby women are promised, for any kind of payment, without a right of refusal, for marriage or other purposes to another person or group.[54]

The United Nations which came into existence on October 24, 1945 reaffirms its faith in securing, *inter alia,* "...fundamental human rights, in the dignity and worth of the human person, in the equal rights of men and women and of nations large and small, and to establish conditions under which justice and respect for the obligations arising from treaties and other sources of international law can be maintained, and to promote social progress and better standards of life in larger freedom."[55] Since its inception the UN is making a relentless crusade for the protection of human rights of all the human beings around the world. Within three years of its functioning the UN General Assembly put in place the *Universal Declaration of Human Rights*[56], with an aim to set 'common standard of rights for all people'. This was followed by the two international Covenants i.e., *Covenant on Economic, Social and Cultural Rights*[57] and the *Covenant on Civil and Political Rights.*[58] The Universal Declaration, together with the two international Covenants and their optional protocols, comprise the 'International Bill of Human Rights'.

Followed by these early human rights instruments recognising general rights of individuals there came into being specific Conventions for addressing various issues of concern to the society. The Convention for the Suppression of the Traffic in Persons and of the Exploitation of the Prostitution of Others adopted by the UN in 1949 is considered as the first attempt by the international community to address the issue. Though the Convention addressed the issue of trafficking of girls it mainly emphasized on the elimination of prostitution. It calls for the eradication of 'traffic in persons' and makes clear that this term is to be equated solely with recruitment into prostitution and not with any other kind of 'traffic in persons' or trafficking for any other type of sexual exploitation. The fact that it also prohibits the 'exploitation of prostitution' by others even with the consent of the person involved, substantiate its real focus of the abolition of prostitution.

In 1989, the United Nations adopted the first global document recognising the right to survival, protection and development of every child, regardless of sex. The Convention on the Rights of the Child (CRC) was most rapidly accepted human rights treaty in history, with highest ratifications.[59] The CRC was ratified unequivocally by all the nations except the US and Somalia. The CRC defines a child as a person under 18 years old, "unless under the law applicable to the child, majority is attained earlier".[60] The specific human rights concerns arising from the trafficking of children have been given normative status by the Convention on the Rights of the Child.[61] It calls upon State Parties to take 'all appropriate national, bilateral and multilateral measures to prevent the abduction, sale of or traffic in children for any purpose or in any form'.[62] It also contains important safeguards against illegal adoption and transfer of children from their parents and particularly stresses that international adoption must not involve 'improper financial gain'.[63] Most importantly, the Convention puts the interests of the child at the centre of any debate of his or her rights.[64]

The Trafficking in Persons Protocol

Since the adoption of the Convention for the Suppression of the Traffic in Persons and of the Exploitation of the Prostitution of Others in 1949, new dimensions of trafficking of women and girls came to be recognized. Most worrying is the fact that the child sexual exploitation has grown exponentially in all countries around the world. Though there are no exact statistics available as to the magnitude of sale or trafficking of girls around the world, as per the United Nations estimates trafficking is a 5-7 billion U.S. dollar operation annually, with 4 million persons moved from one country to another and within countries. When compared with drug and arms trafficking, the punishment provided for human trafficking are lower in many countries.

Keeping in view the increasing number of offences committed against children and the demands by the international community collectively for taking effective measures to curb trafficking of women and girls, the Commission on Crime Prevention and Criminal Justice and the Economic and Social Council, in 1998 recommended for constituting a inter-governmental *ad hoc* committee for the purpose of drafting a comprehensive international Convention against transnational organized crime and three supplementary protocols by December 2000.[65] The Committee held 11 sessions in Vienna from January 1999 through October 2000, with over

120 countries in attendance, which include, among others, Argentina, India Mexico, Venezuela, Columbia, China, Bangladesh, Pakistan, Egypt, the United Arab Emirates, Syria, Algeria, at various meetings, along with a number of international NGOs who played a key role in the consultation process. The *Ad Hoc* Committee finalized the text of the mother convention and two of its supplementary protocols in October 2000.

The two-year long consistent efforts by the inter-governmental *ad hoc* committee resulted in adoption of a *Protocol to Prevent, Suppress and Punish Trafficking in Persons, Especially Women and Children,* which is a wide-ranging international agreement to address the crime of trafficking in persons, especially women and children, on a transnational level.[66] The *Protocol* comprises of 20 Articles, which addresses the human rights dimensions necessary for the protection of victims of trafficking. The Protocol recognizes the need for a combined approach that integrates the protection of human rights and assistance to victims with effective prevention, prosecution and judicial cooperation. The Protocol specifically addresses the trade in human beings for purposes of the exploitation of prostitution and other forms of sexual exploitation, forced labour or services, slavery or practices similar to slavery, servitude and the removal of organs. With the adoption of the Protocol the trafficked persons, especially women and girls in prostitution and child labourers, are no longer viewed as criminals but as victims of a crime. It also advocates addressing the issue of trafficking at the global level through affirmative action to fight against the powerful traffickers, smugglers, pimps, brothel keepers, forced labour lords, enforcers, and gangs and to this end calls for more cooperative action between police, immigration authorities, social service agencies and NGOs.[67] Irrespective of the fact of consent by a victim of trafficking,[68] it assures protection not only to those who prove force but also to all the victims.[69] Keeping in view the increasing modes of trafficking of children it provides a wider definition for taking to task the culprits. To this end it defines trafficking to mean "the recruitment, transportation, transfer, harbouring or receipt of persons, by means of the threat or use of force or other forms of coercion, of abduction, of fraud, of deception, of the abuse of power or of a position of vulnerability or of the giving or receiving of payments or benefits to achieve the consent of a person having control over another person, for the purpose of exploitation".[70] The UN Protocol is first of its kind to address the demand, which results in women and children being trafficked, calling upon countries to take or strengthen legislative or other measures to discourage this demand that fosters all forms of exploitation of women and children.[71]

The *Protocol to Prevent, Suppress and Punish Trafficking in Persons, Especially Women and Children* is a progressive one which anticipates accomplishing what national legislation cannot do on its own. It is also intended to jumpstart national laws and to harmonize regional legislation against the trafficking in women and children. Though it does not address specifically the growing incidence of sale of children in the guise of adoption the progressive interpretation of the provisions would help in addressing the issue.

Besides the above Conventions there exist other Conventions and Declarations, which emphasize with force on the need to eliminate, trafficking of women and girls. The Convention on the Elimination of All Forms of Discrimination Against Women (1979)[72] specifically mandates the States Parties to "take appropriate measures, including legislation, to suppress all forms of traffic in women and exploitation of prostitution of women."[73] The Vienna Declaration and Programme of Action (1993) highlighted the human rights abuses, which push woman into trafficking and called for concerted action by State Parties.[74] The Programme of Action also provided for the appointment of a Special Rapporteur on Violence Against Women.[75] The Stockholm Declaration and Agenda for Action adopted by the World Congress against Sexual Exploitation of Children (1996) provides policy guidelines for government action. The Beijing Declaration and Platform for Action at the Fourth World Conference on Women (1995) has as one of its strategic objectives the elimination of trafficking in women and the assistance of victims of violence due to prostitution and trafficking by counties of origin, transit and destination. It also widened the scope of trafficking and exploitation to include forced marriage and forced labour. One of the most striking developments in the recent times (2000) is the conducting of special sessions of the UN General Assembly for the Beijing + 5 Review (Beijing + 5) and the CEDAW + 5 to assess progress in improving women's status—was how actively some governments were willing to work to thwart recent gains in protecting women's human rights.[76] Besides, the Statute of the International Criminal Court also recognized trafficking in women as a crime against humanity.[77]

Role of ILO in Protecting Women and Children

The International Labour Organisation (ILO)[78] plays an important role in setting standards and guiding the nations in taking measures for the improvement of working conditions for all the human beings in general and protection of children in particular. In furtherance of the objectives of its Constitution the ILO formulates international labour principles in the form of Conventions and Recommendations,[79] set minimum standards to be followed by the member-nations. Over the years it has contributed substantially towards the protection of basic labour rights in various fields, among others, equality of treatment[80] child labour[81], migrant labourers, women workers[82], indigent workers[83], freedom of association[84], the right to organize, collective bargaining, abolition of forced labour[85], equality of opportunity and treatment, and other work related issues. The International Labour Organisation's (ILO) Forced Labour Conventions [86] strengthened the prohibition of it. Article 2(1) of the 1930 Convention, defines forced or compulsory labour as, 'all work or service which is exacted from any person under the menace of any penalty and from which the said person has not offered himself voluntarily'.

The ILO views that the countries have, however, taken action to eliminate child prostitution, an activity the ILO report characterizes as "a serious human rights violation and an intolerable form of child labour." Child prostitution risks growing as poverty and unemployment strain family income and contribute to the expanding ranks of street children who are an increasingly common sight on the streets of cities worldwide.[87] A new International Labour Organisation (ILO) Convention and Recommendation on "the Prohibition and Immediate Action for the Elimination of the Worst Forms of Child Labour" went into force and achieved the fastest rate of ratification in ILO history.[88] The Convention, targeted practices such as child slavery, sexual exploitation, debt bondage, and trafficking as priority areas and called upon the States to take immediate measures for elimination of these practices.[89] Besides, over the years the ILO has adopted several Conventions aimed at economic empowerment of workers both in organized and unorganised sectors in the form of social security.[90] These initiatives though didn't address specifically the issues concerning sale and trafficking of women and girls but they do contribute in elimination of poverty and the corresponding sale of children.

The Special Rapporteur on the Sale, Prostitution and Child Pornography

The Special Rapporteur on the Sale of Children, Child Prostitution and Child Pornography was appointed in 1990 with a mandate to "consider matters" related to the sale of children, child prostitution, and child pornography, including causes and effects. The Convention on the Rights of the Child (CRC) is the primary legal framework for the Special Rapporteur's activities. The special rapporteur has submitted a report in 1999 highlighting the steps to be taken to prevent the growing menace.[91]

The Special Rapporteur defines the sale of children as "the transfer of parental authority over and/or custody of a child on a more or less permanent basis in exchange for financial or other reward or consideration." This includes sale for purposes of: (i) trafficking into prostitution or other sexual exploitation; (ii) commercial adoption; (iii) prostitution; (iv) pornography; (v) child labour; (vi) the use of children in armed conflicts; or (vii) organ transplantation. This definition applies to the sale of girls for marriage.[92]

Child prostitution is currently defined by the Special Rapporteur as "the act of engaging or offering the services of a child to perform sexual acts for money or other consideration with that person or any other person." Child pornography is defined by the Special Rapporteur includes the following types of material intended for the sexual gratification of the user: visual depictions of a child engaged in explicit sexual activity; visual depictions involving the lewd exhibition of a child's genitals; and audio pornography. The production and distribution of such material, as well as its use, falls within this definition.

In recent reports, the Special Rapporteur has focused on commercial sexual exploitation of children. She identified the justice system, education, and the media as key tools, or catalysts, for prevention and intervention. In recommendations concerning the justice system, she addressed law enforcement procedures and criminal procedures in the courts, with emphasis on the protection of victims and the need to ensure that criminal justice responses do not further victimize the child.[93]

Despite the international and national legal protection and widespread acceptance of the children's needs and rights, large numbers of children continue to be malnourished, sold, prostituted, abused, exploited and murdered. The girl child especially in the developing world suffers the double bind of age and gender discrimination, regarded as inferior in all societies, encumber to be sold off as a commodity in the open market, or aborted before she is even born and thousands of girls are killed by force or due to neglect after their birth.

Initiatives at the Regional Level

For the protection and realisation of the rights of the child as enunciated under the Convention on the Rights of the Child it is necessary to adopt a multi-pronged strategy including the ratification of related Conventions and Protocols at the international levels, take legislative initiatives in conformity with these Conventions and most importantly to enact regional Conventions including creation of regional mechanisms for effective monitoring. To this end it is pertinent to mention herein that in mid 90's an attempt has been made by the South Asian Association for Regional Co-operation (SAARC) nations comprising of India, Maldives, Pakistan, Bangladesh, Sri Lanka, Bhutan and Nepal to address the issue of trans-border trafficking by adopting a regional Convention during the SAARC decade of Girl Child (1991-2000). India hosted an expert group meeting to negotiate the *SAARC Regional Convention on Combating Trafficking in Women and Children for Prostitution* drafted by it, in New Delhi on June 18-19, 1998. The draft as approved at the expert group meeting was further deliberated at the XIII meeting of the SAARC Technical committee on Women in Development at Kathmandu (Nepal) from 28-30 June, 1998. The Regional Draft Convention has been endorsed by the SAARC Council of Ministers meeting held at XX SAARC summit at Colombo (Sri Lanka) from July 29-31, 1998 for adoption by the SAARC countries.[94] The convention would seek to take measures to prevent trans-border trafficking through proper international governmental coordination as well as harmonizing of various laws and legal provisions relating to trafficking and rehabilitation of rescued victims.

Trafficking and Sale of Girls: The Case of India

India is a founder member of the United Nations and has ratified various international Conventions promising to secure the rights of all the individuals in general and various groups in particular. Over the years the legislature and judiciary have played a commendable role in upholding the Constitutional principles and also to put in place an effective mechanism for the protection of rights of women and children. The enactment of specific legislations such as the Immoral Traffic Prevention Act, 1986, the National Commission for Women Act, 1990, the Juvenile Justice (Care and Protection) Act, 2000, etc., are steps in the right direction. Most worrying is the fact that in spite of the existence of long list of legislations and the plethora of institutions for the protection of rights and person of women and children the offences especially the sale and trafficking of women and girls go unabated. The following field experiences exemplify the way in which girls are trafficked and sold in the open market for few pennies.

In India the legal definition of 'child' varies with purpose.[95] The Census of India treats persons below the age of fourteen as "children". According to the SAARC year of the Girl Child the accepted age of a girl child is 0-20 years. While making use of standard demographic data, social scientists include females in the age group of 15-19 years under the category of the "girl child".[96]

Forcing Girls into Prostitution

Though there is no authentic data to show the number of children trafficked and sold in the country, over the years' social scientists, judiciary and legislators have expressed grave concern over the increasing incidents of exploitation of children. As per the ILO report in India, some 100,000 Nepalese women work as prostitutes, with an additional 5,000 Nepalese trafficked to the country each year. An estimated 200,000 women from Bangladesh have been trafficked to Pakistan over the past decade and thousands more to India.[97] In a survey conducted by *Central Social Welfare Board* on prostitution in six cities (Delhi, Bombay, Calcutta, Hyderabad, Madras and Bangalore) it was found that the total number of prostitutes in these cities was likely to be between 70,000-100,000 and out of these 30 per cent were below the age of 20 and 40 per cent of them became prostitutes when they were children (18 or under), 86 per cent of the prostitutes came from 6 States (Andhra Pradesh, Karnataka, Tamilnadu, West Bengal, Maharashtra and Uttar Pradesh) out of them, 94.6 per cent were Indians, 2.6 per cent were Nepalis and 2.7 per cent were Bangladeshis, 84.6 per cent were Hindus; 10.95 per cent Muslims, 3.5 per cent Christians, 36 per cent were from scheduled castes and tribes; 24 per cent from other backward castes and 40 per cent others. Out of these 71 per cent were illiterate, 4 per cent were literate and 24 per cent had some formal schooling, 66 per cent of prostitutes came from families who are very poor—(less than Rs. 5000 per annum), 60 per cent of prostitutes earned less that Rs. 3000 per month, of which 50 per cent had to be given to the brothel keeper. Prostitutes have to pay further charges for their lodgings and food, as well as providing for their families (either living with them or back in their villages). They, therefore, had very little money to spare, and would frequently fall into debt. Brothel keepers share their income with pimps, procurers, local goondas and allegedly with the police, thus creating a network of vested interests in the continuance of the trade.[98]

The legal provisions in India prohibit persons from having sex with minor children below the age of 16 years and provide stringent punishment to the perpetrators. In this context the Indian Penal Code 1860 clearly states "a man is said to commit rape with or without her consent when she is sixteen years of age".[99] The Court reiterated its stand in number of cases by rejecting the plea of 'consent' taken by the accused and convicted them of the offence. The Court in *Narasimha's case*[100] where the victim was aged 16 years held that the consent was of no help. Similarly the Court in *Bhupendra's case*[101] held that 'although the prosecutrix was a consenting party to the sexual intercourse, she being minor question of consent is wholly irrelevant.' In spite of the legal provisions very few cases reach the portals of courts for justice due to various reasons.

The above startling revelations make it clear that poverty and illiteracy have lot of bearing on growing numbers in sex trade. Cases are not lacking wherein parents have sold their children to brothels for paltry sums. During the field studies and also interviews with the women in prostitution it was revealed that no women is willing to prepare their daughters enter the sex trade. They have narrated their problems and the way in which the society segregates their children thereby restricting their school and social life.

Prevalence of Devdasi System

As per the reports, in spite of the legislations prohibiting the practice of Devdasi system[102] it still continues to thrive in various parts of the nation. A number of girls from poor families are forced into the flesh trade every year in the guise of marriage to gods. The issue came to lime light when four young girls two of them below the age of 10 years, having been dedicated as *devdasis* in Andhra Pradesh.[103] The Supreme Court of India way back in 1990 in *Vishaljeet's case*[104] while keeping in view the deteriorating conditions of girls in the country observed that "in-spite of stringent and rehabilitative provisions under the various Acts, desired result yet to be achieved. Both Central and State Governments having obligation to safeguard interest and welfare of children and girls, must evaluate various measures and implement them in the right direction. Severe and speedy legal action against erring persons such as pimps, brokers and brothel keepers suggested. Direction for conducting CBI enquiry throughout the country not practicable. However certain directions issued, *inter alia,* for setting up a separate Advisory Committee, for taking steps for those providing rehabilitative homes for delving into *devdasi* system and *jogin* tradition etc.

Use of Girls for Making Yellow Films

Quite apart from the age old unethical and illegal practices of use of girls for sale, bondage, prostitution, paedophilia, dancing etc., a new trend has come to light with the passage of time i.e., the use of minor girls for making "Yellow Films". The 'Yellow Films' are quite similar to the 'Blue Films' but the basic difference is in 'blue films' the sex between human beings and human beings or between animals is shown, whereas in 'Yellow Films' the girls are forced to have sex with animals in most cases trained dogs. Poor and innocent girls usually fall into the hands of perverts who subject them to sexual perversions such as masochism and making them sleep with dogs while they watch.

Starvation and Sale of Girls in India: A Case for Retrospection

If we look into the historical background, the sale of girls in India and other parts of the world is not a new phenomenon and it has been practiced since ages. In olden days the purpose of sale was confined mainly to slavery or prostitution. Keeping in view at the international level slavery and trafficking conventions and at the national level special provisions were incorporated under the Indian Penal Code, 1860[105] to curb these kinds of practices. But now with the passage of time there is a dramatic change and the women and girl children have been exploited in various ways such as incest, sale to foreigners through marriage and adoption, forced into begging, slavery, prostitution, paedophilia etc., and many of these acts are not in the reach of law.

The issue of sale of girls has been coming to the fore time and again in various parts of the country due to diverse reasons. The startling revelations made in 2001 by the 14 years old girl Fareeda about the ordeal of her sale and subsequent rescue by police. Fareeda who was given to middle women by her poor parents for getting her married to an Arab national has managed to return from Mumbai and lodged a complaint to the police in Hyderabad about the sale of girls to Arabs on the pretext of marriage. This incident reminds us of the many other similar incidents reported in the past such as Ameena, Sanju and many more girls in the Lambada Tandas in Andhra Pradesh. Earlier, in 1993 Ameena aged 13 years was given in marriage to a Shaikh from Saudia aged 60 years for a meagre *Meher* of Rs. 6,000 and attempted to bundle off her to Dubai. Fortunately for young Ameena the plane landed at Delhi and a resourceful and helping Air Hostess, Amrita Ahluwalia rescued her from the clutches of the Shaikh and arranged to send her to Nari Niketan. Similarly poverty drove the parents of the girl Sanju aged 8 years to mortgage her for a simple deal of two bagfuls of grain, and Rs. 150, in a village in Bolangir District in Orissa. Recently the Supreme Court of India in *People's Union for Civil Liberties* v. *Union of India & Ors.*[106] after taking into consideration the starvation deaths in various States observed that:

> What is of utmost importance is to see that food is provided to the aged, infirm, disabled, destitute women, destitute men who are in danger of starvation, pregnant and lactating women and destitute children, especially in cases where they or

members of their family do not have sufficient funds to provide food for them. Plenty of food is available, but distribution of the same amongst the very poor and the destitute is scarce and non-existent leading to mal-nourishment, starvation and other related problems. Accordingly the Court directed the States to see that all the PDS shops, if closed, are re-opened and start functioning within one week and regular supplies made.

Sale of Girls in the Guise of Adoption: Ground Realities

Due to lacunae in the existing laws and the demand for buying minor girls at cheaper rates by the foreigners and others had led to increasing number of girls being sold in the open market. The issue of sale of girls has once again become a smouldering issue with the increasing cases of sale of girls by *Tandas* in Andhra Pradesh as reported in the newspapers. The National Commission for Women (NCW), Government of India, on receiving a complaint and also upon reading the reports published in the newspapers about the alleged sale of girls in Nalgonda and other Districts in the State of Andhra Pradesh,[107] in pursuance of the powers conferred on it under Sections 8 and 10 of the National Commission for Women Act, 1990 set up a two-member Committee comprising K. Santha Reddy, Member, NCW and the author to enquire into the matter.

Sale of Girls by *Tandas*

In Telugu dialect the word *Tanda* connotes 'a group' of people. Since these tribal people many of them evacuates of Nagarjuna Sagar Project moved with their families in groups and settled in various parts of Andhra Pradesh they are called as *Tandas.* They are poor tribal people who are deprived of the privileges and have been doomed for generations to live in oblivion. Out of a total of 9 *lakh.* population in the Miryalaguda revenue division 3 *lakh* are *Tandas.* Added to their unrecognised status, they become vulnerable to all kinds of exploitation. In Devarakonda during our meetings with the district administration and also the NGOs. The officials briefed us with their statistics of sale of girls in the region according to which there were 46 cases of sale of girls which had been identified[108] but NGOs working in this area puts this figure to around 200 and much more. As members of the enquiry committee we wanted to have first hand knowledge about the facts and the reasons for the sale of girls so as to enable us to assess the situation and also suggest remedial measures to the Government and hence we had decided to cover as many villages as possible.

During our visit to Bridge Tanda (one of the tribal hamlets) the villagers said that one Lakshmi had sold her daughter for Rs. 1500. Bichini who is aged nearly 65 years, mother-in-law of Lakshmi said that due to acute poverty and dowry related problems they are resorting to selling their children. She recollected the good old days where there existed a system in their tribe of giving *Hooli* (a form of *Kanyasulkam* or gift from boy's side) in the form of goats, sheep, marriage expenses etc., from boy's side to the girl's side in marriage. But now the system had totally changed with the passage of time, resultantly the boy's side is demanding huge amounts in the form of dowry, she said.

In yet another hamlet (Moda Tanda) one Ambali said that she had 4 children 1 daughter and 3 sons. Due to acute poverty she had given away her daughter to a person with the help of middlemen i.e., Ramkoti, Ramulu and Dharma. She could not able to see the person to whom she gave her daughter. 'I was taken to a dark place in the night and was asked to leave my daughter, that's all I did, she said'. Likewise we could cover few of the tribal villages and witness the poor lifestyles of tribal population leading to neglect and killing of girl children in few families and selling of children in few others. The reasons for sale of children is almost similar in all the cases i.e., acute poverty, larger families, lack of basic amenities, unemployment, barren lands and ignorance about new techniques of water preservation and farming, demand for buying children by giving false hopes of better future of children etc.

Ignorance about Family Planning Methods

The slogan "Health Care for All" is unknown to these villagers since they are totally dependent on Quacks or *Dais* for their regular health care including deliveries. The villagers said that the hospitals are not in their reach due to lack of proper roads and transportation facilities they take recourse to approaching Quacks and *Dais.* Due to traditional modes of deliveries in the hands of *Dais* or Quacks only few of the children could see the light of the world and among these many of the children were born underweight due to tender age of mother or large families or otherwise lack of nutritious food during pregnancy and lacks post-natal care. Though the Miryalaguda division is drought prone and the people are living below poverty line (BPL) many of them are not in possession of ration cards, which entail them to various benefits including identity.

Most worrying is the fact that in all these hamlets we found women having 5-6 children on an average and few of them had more than 6 children. Women though interested are reluctant to undergo family planning operations due to fear of losing their livelihood. The *Anganwadi* workers and *dais* have failed to sensitise them about the alternate methods of family planning. The method of vasectomy is entirely unknown to these villagers. Although we informed the local administration about our visit to these villages we couldn't able to find many of the *Anganwadi* workers and *ANM's* in these villages. Upon enquiry it has come to light that due to the meagre wages paid to *Anganwadi* workers (Rs. 500 p.m.) and *dais* (Rs. 400 p.m.) they were unable to fulfil their job responsibilities and the lack of infrastructure and transport facilities make them practically immobile. Due to fear of losing daily earnings the women are reluctant to undergo family planning operations and the *Anganwadi* and other workers seems to possess meagre knowledge about other alternate methods of family planning except distribution of condoms which are of no use to these villagers who lose their conscience as the sun dips by becoming slaves to country made liquor.

Thus during our field visits to the tribal villages we found that poverty and gender discrimination coupled with dowry demands drove these tribals sell their daughters for a meagre amount as low as Rs. 1500. Some of the families even went to the extent of stating that they prefer to give their daughters freely if some good families approach them. It is also learnt that prior to the entering of the middlemen for buying the girls in these villages they used to kill girl children with the help of a grain or by giving poisonous liquid. Now they feel it better to hand over the child to others and take benefit out of that. There is a direct link between the abusive exploitation of girls and the prevalent low economic and social status of families. For many poor families, the girl child is property, whose only redeeming quality is her selling price. For many men, the only question is the buying price.

Role of NGOs in Sale of Children

Further from the Government and police officials' versions it is made clear that the *Tandas* are selling or giving away their girl children. Once it is confirmed our next task has been to enquire as to who is buying these children and for what purpose. No one is revealing the identity of the buyer excepting the persons who were caught red handed with the child. Majority of them say that they went to a secluded dark place and left their child and few others say they handed over their child to a person who came to the weekly market. A report submitted by the local police officials reveals that seven children were allegedly sold for Rs. 5,000 to 10,000 per infant to a home being run in Hyderabad, which is duly recognised by the Central Adoption Resource Agency (CARA). During the visits to this along with other homes in Hyderabad and other orphanages it was confirmed that the records are not proper and majority of the children are given in inter-country adoptions. In another case the police have arrested four persons (two women and two men) who were caught red handed along with the child in a bus on their way to Hyderabad. An FIR[109] was registered under Section 372 of the IPC and all the four accused were sent to judicial custody.

The adoption of children by persons belonging to Hindu community are governed by the Hindu Adoptions and

Maintenance Act, 1956 and persons other than Hindus can adopt children under the Guardian and Wards Act, 1890 but they will be appointed only as 'guardians'. Foreign citizens desirous of adopting children are required to give an undertaking to Indian Courts, that they would legally adopt their wards as per the law of their country, within a stipulated period of time.

The issue of sale of children to foreigners in the name of adoptions is not a new phenomenon. Keeping in view the alarming conditions and the state of affairs in the country the Supreme Court of India in *L.K. Pandey* v. *Union of India* case since 1984 has given series of directives dated September 19, 1986, August 14, 1991, October 29, 1991, November 14, 1991, November 20, 1991 and also in 1999 for regulation of inter-country adoptions. In pursuance of the Supreme Court judgement, the Union Government has issued revised guidelines through its notification dated May 29, 1995 to regulate the matter relating to adoption of Indian children. In this context the Ministry of Social Justice and Empowerment has formulated detailed guidelines to be followed by CARA and other agencies and has also assigned various responsibilities to different agencies. In accordance with its guidelines the CARA has granted recognition to 5 NGOs in the State of Andhra Pradesh for undertaking adoption related activities. It has also granted licence to one NGO by the name of Voluntary Adoptions Coordinating Agency (VCA) with the powers *inter alia* to monitor these organisations and to issue adoption clearance certificates after due verification.

The guidelines issued by the Government of India also imposes an obligation on the State Governments to issue special licences to the organisations to do in-country adoptions and also undertake periodical inspection to ensure that (1) adoption activity is being pursued by the organisation as a welfare measure in the interest of the children and not as a commercial activity, and (2) that proper records are maintained and children admitted are provided with basic minimum facilities, qualified social workers are employed, proper adoption follow-up are done, and the accounts of the organisation are being maintained and audited annually.

Besides the State Government is also empowered under the Orphanages and other Charitable Homes (Supervision and Control) Act, 1960, to levy penalties and initiate legal proceedings for those who run orphanages and other children's homes without following the prescribed norms.

After visiting the tribal villages and inspecting few of the orphanages in Hyderabad we had visited Tandur for inspecting an orphanage being run by John Abraham Bethelaham Home the next day. Unlike the Devarakonda Revenue Divison roads, which are broken and seems to be temporary the Tandur roads are well maintained. On our way we could find big farmhouses, residential colleges, schools etc. We reached Tandur at around 3.30 p.m., to inspect John Abraham Memorial Bethany Home, (R.R. District) accompanied by the police officials, RDO, NGOs and other officials. There we were shocked to see the deplorable conditions prevailing in the orphanage. We came to know from the police that all the members of the Managing Body had run away and were not traceable for the last few days. We found that all the children of the orphanage were left without any care. Adding to this the state of health of children is worse and we found many of the children under total neglect and five others severely ill. Besides, during the inspection of some of the files we found astonishing facts even to the extent of issuing of adoption clearance certificates by the VCA after death of the children. Out of nearly 30 available files of case history of children inspected, we were surprised to read that 16 infants were died during the year 2000 alone.

The situation being so grave, our immediate priority shifted from investigation to the care of the children. We have, therefore, instructed the RDO, Vikarabad, to give immediate medical aid to the children and to post two *Anganwadi* workers with the orphanage on a 24-hours basis and also two police officials for security of children and also guarding the seized files and other documents. We have further instructed that the *Anganwadi* workers should start taking care of the children with whatever feeding material was immediately available in the stocks. However, the stocks are found to be sufficient only for about 4-5 days. Therefore, we sent SOS letters to the Chief Minister of Andhra Pradesh and other concerned officials at the Centre and also State recommending them to take over the charge of the orphanage at Tandur and also institution of an enquiry against all the organisations undertaking adoption activities in the State. The Government of AP which has granted equal property rights to women and set up a State Commission for Women is striving hard to empower women in various spheres has taken a serious note of the incidence of sale of girls in the State and the role being played by some of the agencies in the process. In pursuance of the reports received by it the Government has ordered for a probe by the State C.I.D. on the alleged involvement of some of the NGOs in sale of children to foreigners.

Issuance of Clearance Certificates in the Names of Dead Children By VCA

During our visits to various orphanages engaged in in-country and inter-country adoptions we found deplorable conditions prevailing in these homes. The records are not properly maintained and there is a conflict between the figures submitted to us by the organisations and the figures available with the VCA. During the inspection of some of the files at the John Abraham Bethany Home at Tandur in Ranga Reddy District we found astonishing facts even to the extent of issuance of adoption clearance certificates by the VCA after the death of children. Out of nearly 30 available files of history of children inspected, we found that 16 infants were died during the year 2000 alone in this home. Whereas the Secretary, VCA during his depositions before us said there is only one death in this home during the year 2000. With regard to issuance of clearance certificates in the names of dead children the Secretary, VCA admitted his fault and said it is mainly the fault on the part of the organisation, which sent false reports to the VCA. The Secretary also gave an assurance to take up this issue with CARA against the errant organisation.

With the creation of CARA at the Centre and VCA in the State majority of the officials are feeling that it is the responsibility of the CARA and VCA to monitor these agencies. They went to the extent of saying that these agencies submit their records periodically to the VCA/CARA and the CARA depending on their performance renews their licence for every three years. The police officials also say that no legislation grants them powers to inspect the files in a home without a formal complaint.

After experiencing the arduous things and hearing the statements of the responsible officials several questions galore in our minds. Whether the government should leave the most important task of issuing clearance certificates to an NGO such as VCA in which majority of the members are representatives of various adoption agencies? What is the role of the Department of Women and Child Development? Is it compulsory on the part of the orphanages and other homes to register the births and deaths Act, 1969? Is there any accountability of the organisation for the death of innumerable number of children in a year? The other mysterious question, which strikes our mind, is what is the motive behind issuing or obtaining clearance certificates in the names of those children who are already dead?

In the light of the above facts one thing is clear that is a serious fault lies somewhere. The CARA has assigned the great responsibility of monitoring and issuance of clearance certificates to an NGO, which comprised in majority the representatives of the adoption agencies. This undoubtedly results into domination of VCA thereby making the VCA virtually ineffective. There is lot of need on the part of the Government to review the CARA guidelines and the power of issuing clearance certificates should be vested with the Government or its agency comprising a responsible officer not below the rank of Secretary to the Government of India. Since the registration of births and deaths taking place in the home is the responsibility of the homes detailed guidelines should be issued in this behalf and the violators should be prosecuted under the appropriate legislations. The government should initiate a joint enquiry with the coordination of Ministry of Home Affairs, External Affairs, Ministry of Social Justice & Empowerment, Department of Women and Child Development and other agencies of the State about the clearance certificates obtained in the name of dead children. The Devarakonda,

Tandur and Hyderabad incidents sets an example of the blatant violation of the basic rights of the child to survival and protection and reminds us of the need to have a powerful separate commission for children in the country.

The Government should not leave the total responsibility of monitoring of these agencies to the VCA. Besides VCA, the Department of Women and Child Development and other agencies should make periodic visits to these homes and have an effective check on the number of children admitted, number of children given in adoption, health care of children including the number of children died and the quality of treatment given by the doctors, etc.

The incidents of children in the State of Andhra Pradesh has led to lot of criticism from juristic circles, media, academicians, NGOs etc. Keeping in view the increasing incidents reported in the newspapers the Government of Andhra Pradesh has resorted to concrete action which if implemented would go a long way in curbing the growing menace. The State officials during their raids to various institutions have recovered 34 babies from a fake child adoption agency. They have also taken custody of all the children kept in the orphanage run in Tandur. In pursuance of the reports the Government has ordered for a probe by the State C.I.D. on the alleged involvement of some of the NGOs in sale of children to foreigners.

Besides, to put together the things clear and to make the officials responsible the Government has formulated the Orphanage Rules 2001, which *inter alia* empowers the Department to inspect any institution and to cancel the licence and recognition granted to the children's home, and transfer the children to another home if deemed fit. As per the new Rules the Government has now prohibited relinquishment of children by biological parents and making it mandatory to all the hospitals and nursing homes to give full details of abandoned children to the Project Director, Women and Child Development. The Rules also provide for setting up of special courts and also an adoption cell in the Department of Women and Child Development with the sole authority for issuing the licences and recognition and for monitoring the activities of the institutions in future.

The 'AP Sale of Children Scandal' should be taken as an example by other States especially by the CARA and necessary steps should be taken to check and curb the growing menace. Keeping in view the failure on the part of VCA in performance of its statutory obligations including commission of wrongful acts such as the issuance of Clearance Certificates in the names of 'Dead' children, the licence of the VCA should be immediately suspended and an enquiry should be conducted against the VCA. If possible the Government should assign the responsibility of issuing clearance certificates to an officer not below the rank of Secretary to the Government of India by making appropriate amendments under the CARA guidelines. Besides, in view of the experiences the Ministry of Social Justice and Empowerment may take up the task of review of CARA guidelines so as to achieve the objectives of the Supreme Court judgement. The composition of the VCA should be changed by making appropriate amendments to the CARA Rules. The VCA should comprise of a senior official of Department of WCD, senior police officer, a retired judge, member of the State Commission for Women, representative of the Social Welfare Department, NGOs etc. This is all the more necessary in view of the increasing number of inter-country adoptions taking place in the country. Table 15.1 gives a description of the number of children given in in-country and inter-country adoption in India:

Table 15.1 : Country-wise number of NOC(s) issued for Inter Country Adoption[110]

Name of the Country	*No. of Adoption in 2000*	*No. of Adoption up to 31st Aug. 2001*	*Total*
Australia	22	19	41
Austria	32	14	46
Bahrain	0	1	1
Belgium	21	8	29
Canada	17	13	30

Table 15.1 (*contd.*)

Name of the Country	*No. of Adoption in 2000*	*No. of Adoption up to 31st Aug. 2001*	*Total*
Denmark	152	71	223
France	31	21	52
Germany	39		
Indonesia	0		
Ireland	0	1	1
Italy	78	59	137
Kuwait	0	0	0
Mauritius	2		
Netherlands	62	25	87
New Zealand	1		
Norway	36	24	60
Singapore	11		
Spain	118	57	175
Special needs Children	19	11	30
Sweden	36	21	57
Switzerland			

Indian Adoption Agency-wise Data on Children given in In-country and Inter-Country Adoptions during January 1999 to December 1999[111]

State	*Name of Agency*	*City*	*In-Country*	*Inter-Country*
Delhi	Delhi Council for Child Welfare	Delhi	63	77
Delhi	Welfare Home for Children	New Delhi	30	25
Goa	Cartias Goa	Panji	4	3
Gujarat	Mahipatram Rupram Ashram	Ahmedabad	23	19
Haryana	Haryana State Council for Child Welfare	Chandigarh	4	4

State	*Name of agency*	*City*	*In-Country*	*Inter-Country*
Karnataka	Ashraya	Bangalore	12	14
Karnataka	M/s Canara Bank Relief and Welfare Society	Bangalore	4	1
Karnataka	M/s Child Foundation Karnataka	Bangalore	4	5
Karnataka	M/s Reach Out	Bangalore	3	1
Karnataka	Shishu Mandir	Bangalore	3	1
Karnataka	Vathsalya Charitable Trust	Bangalore	26	12
Kerala	Dinasevanasabha Snehanikatan	Kerala	22	
Maha-rashtra	Bhartiya Samaj Seva Kendra	Pune	104	58
Maha-rashtra	Holy Cross Home for Babies	Amaravati	9	6
Maha-rashtra	Missionaries of Charity	Mumbai	122	22
Maha-rashtra	Vatsalya Trust	Mumbai	24	1
Orissa	Basundhara	Cuttack	21	36
Tamil Nadu	Families for Children	Coimbatore	27	
Tamil Nadu	Guild of Service (Central)	Madras	15	19
Tamil Nadu	Institute of the Franciscan	Madras	10	10
Uttar Pradesh	Uttar Pradesh Council for Child Welfare	Lucknow	8	8
West Bengal	Indian Societies For Sponsorship and Adoption	Calcutta	27	34
West Bengal	Indian Society for Rehabilitation of Children	Calcutta	44	58
West Bengal	International Mission of Hope (India) Society	Calcutta	8	50
West Bengal	Society for Indian Children's Welfare	Calcutta	24	20

The above figures clearly show a trend of increasing number of children being given in inter-country adoptions. Instances are not lacking wherein few of the organizations have given 70 per cent children in inter-country adoption and less than 30 per cent in in-country adoption. It is in this context there is lot of need on the part of the government to have a check and undertake a detailed study as to the factors contributing for giving children in adoptions to the foreign countries and the fate of such children.

Most importantly the government should take up gender sensitisation programmes with the help of its employees and also NGOs working at the grass-root level. People should be sensitised about the evils of dowry, the responsibility of male in the birth of female child, the equality of sexes etc. The Central Government should organise a coordinating meeting with the concerned departmental heads and also the representatives of the State Governments for formulation or replication of successful policies to eliminate female foeticide, infanticide, sale of girls etc. The cradle scheme of Tamilnadu, the allocation of some amount in the fixed deposit in the name of newly born girl child in the State of Haryana may be implemented in other States also. Further without waiting for the Constitutional amendments all the State Governments should implement the compulsory free primary education for all the children in their respective States. The recent clarion call by the religious heads of the Sikh community to all the members of their community to desist from the acts leading to female foeticide and infanticide and declaring it as a great sin should be taken as examples by other community leaders and they may make similar announcements which will have a great impact in saving the lives of girl children and in giving them due recognition in the society.

Legal Framework for Preventing Sale of Girls

The United Nations Conventions strictly prohibit the sale of women and children for any purpose or even without purpose, which include incongruous marriages. These Conventions stipulates norms to be applied to marriage, covering issues of age, consent, equality within marriage, and the personal and property rights of women. These Conventions strictly prohibit the forcible marriage or marriage without consent of the girl. In this context the 1948 *Universal Declaration of Human Rights* (UDHR),[112] the 1966 *International Covenant on Economic, Social and Cultural Rights* and the 1966 *International Covenant on Civil and Political Rights,* the 1956 *Supplementary Convention on the Abolition of Slavery, the Slave Trade, and Institutions and Practices Similar to Slavery,*[113] the 1964 *Convention on Consent to Marriage, Minimum Age for Marriage and Registration of Marriages,*[114] the 1979 *Convention on the Elimination of All Forms of Discrimination against Women,* the 1989 *Convention on the Rights of the Child* (CRC) are in the right direction.

National Legal Framework

India is a founder member of United Nations and has promised to secure the rights of its subjects by ratifying the various conventions and other human rights instruments including the Convention on the Rights of the Child ratified by it on the 11th December 1992. In India the Constitution and other laws prohibit these kinds of practices. The Constitution prohibits traffic in human beings and forced labour[115] and prescribes a duty on all the citizens to renounce practices derogatory to the dignity of women.[116] But a deep examination of the system and various other laws reveals that the existing laws are not as adequate and as stringent as it ought to be.

Sale of Children for Prostitution

The sale of minor girls for purposes of prostitution is a transnational phenomenon where single rural girls from remote areas are lured to the cities by the agents and are consigned to a life of degradation. The provision under the Indian Penal Code prohibits the buying and disposing of any person as a slave and provides punishment for such acts. It also explicitly prohibited sale of minors for purposes of prostitution. In this context sections 372 and 373 of the IPC prohibit the sale, letting out on hire or otherwise disposing of a child for the purpose specified in the sections. Section 372 of the IPC, *inter alia,* reads:

> *whoever sells, lets to hire, or otherwise disposes of any person under the age of eighteen years with intent that such person shall at any age be employed or used for the purpose of prostitution or illicit intercourse with any person or for any unlawful and immoral purpose, or knowing it to be likely that such person will at any age be employed or used for any such purpose, shall be punished with either description for a term which may extend to ten years, and shall also be liable to fine.*

Further Section 373 of the IPC *inter alia* states that:

> *whoever buys, hires or otherwise obtains possession of any person under the age of eighteen years with intent that such person shall at any age be employed or used for the purpose of prostitution or illicit intercourse with any person or for any unlawful and immoral purpose, or knowing to be likely that such person will at any age be employed or used for any such purpose, shall be punished with imprisonment of either description for a term which may extend to ten years, and shall also be liable to fine.*

Besides, the Immoral Traffic Prevention Act, 1986[117] also contain provisions prohibiting the procuring, inducing, aiding or abetting or taking a person for prostitution.[118] However these legal provisions have failed to achieve the desired results. It is hoped that during the Government on priority would look into this area and strengthen the legislations for curbing the sale or use of children for the purpose of prostitution.

Sale of Children in the name of Marriage

The Indian Penal Code[119] provides only narrower definition by which it prohibits sale of minor children for the purposes of prostitution or any other immoral purpose. In some of the cases the parents due to economic and other considerations perform incongruous marriages. In the name of marriage the girls are sold and forced into prostitution. The Child Marriage Restraint Act, 1929, prohibited child marriages and according to the definition given under the Act [120] a 'child' is a person in the case of a girl who has not attained the age of 18 years and in the case of a boy who has not attained the age of 21 years. Even after 50 years of Independence a marriage in breach of the act is not treated as a nullity for reasons of public policy, but is made punishable in respect of those who perform the marriage. The punishment for performing a marriage in breach of this law is just 3 months of imprisonment and fine.[121]

The Law Commission of India felt the need of examining the system, with a view to remedying any deficiency in the existing law that might be discovered as a result of such examination. The Law Commission in its Report [122] observed that while the Indian Penal Code contains a few provisions designed to deal with the disposal of persons below a certain age by way of sale or other mode of transfer, these provisions are confined to cases where the transaction is entered into, for one of the purposes specified in those sections. Where such purpose does not exist or cannot be proved at the trial, these sections cannot be pressed into service. The Commission noted with concern that:

> *no human being can be allowed to be treated as a chattel, in this twentieth century'. Women and children, however, particularly need the protection of the law, because they are peculiarly vulnerable to exploitation. Further it stated that the existing laws does not take care of cases where a sale simpliciter of a person takes place, where there is no object of using the person sold for a purpose not specified in section 372-373 of the Indian Penal Code. In particular, these sections fail to attend to the situation of sale of a minor for marriage.*[123]

The Law Commission of India has made a recommendation for insertion of a new section 373-A under the Indian Penal Code. The new section gives a wider definition to the aspect of sale, lets to hire or otherwise disposing of a woman or giving for all purposes or even without the purpose.

Under this section both selling and buying irrespective of the motives are punishable. Keeping in view the inadequacy of the law and to improve the status and dignity of women in the society the Government should consider the recommendations made by the Law Commission of India, and should make appropriate amendments to the Indian Penal Code, and other legislations.

Apart from the above there are new set of offences committed against children, such as paedophilia, sexual sadism, child pornography, which are developed and widely reported in the recent years. These offences are increased mainly with the advent of sex tourism. The existing laws are inadequate to prevent these crimes. The National Decadal Plan of Action for the Girl Child has also recognized and stressed the need of taking legislative and administrative measures to combat the growing menace of child sexual abuse. The plan recognizes the rights of the girl child to protection from exploitation, assault and physical abuse. The plan aims to utilize intervention strategies to sensitise various agencies on the need to protect the child from assault and physical abuse and exploitation, and adolescent girls from prostitution and rape through legislation, proper enforcement and speedy legal remedies.[124]

Rescue and Rehabilitation of Children in Prostitution

In India there exist skeletal legislations to protect the children from exploitation. The Supreme Court in *Gaurav Jain's case* [125] while dealing with the aspect of rehabilitation of the children of women in prostitution held that ".... such children have right to equality of opportunity, dignity, care, protection and rehabilitation so as to be part of the mainstream of social life without any pre-stigma attached on them. Report submitted by V.C. Mahajan Committee, constituted pursuant to Supreme Court's order, on questions of validity of having separate schools and hostels, existing laws relating to the target group as to who are prostitutes and possibility of evolving a scheme for those children is workable at national level. Segregating the children of prostitutes by locating separate hostels was not accepted by Supreme Court in its earlier order dated

15-11-1989, as it would not be in the interest of the children and society at large. Suggestion, and the report regarding management of child development and care centres require earnest examination to give force and content to them. Children of prostitutes, including child prostitutes, should be treated as 'neglected juveniles' as defined in Juvenile Justice Act and no stigma should be attached to juvenile homes for a short stay to relieve them from the trauma they may have suffered and thereafter they should be rehabilitated in an appropriate manner.

The Court further held that equally, the right of the child is the concern of the society so that fallen women surpass trafficking of her person from exploitation; contribute to bring up the children; live a life with dignity; and not to continue in the foul social environment. Equally, the children have the right to equality of opportunity, dignity and care, protection and rehabilitation by the society with both hands open to bring them into the mainstream of social life without pre-stigma affixed on them for no fault of her/his. The Court for the effective implementation of various provision and also the schemes formulated, further held that it is State's mandatory obligation to establish juvenile homes, and State has also to constitute Juvenile Welfare Board, officers in charge of juvenile homes, welfare officers and probation officers should be made responsible to protect them in the juvenile homes. Rescue and rehabilitation operation should be kept under Ministry of Welfare and Human Resource, Government of India, which has to devise suitable schemes for proper rehabilitation work. Besides the National Commission for Women since its inception in 1992 making recommendations to the government for providing reservation of seats in various schools including residential schools for the children of women in prostitution.

Girls Child's Right to Education

Albeit the Constitution under Directive Principles provided that "the State shall endeavour to provide within a period of ten years from the commencement of this Constitution, free and compulsory education for all the children until they complete the age of fourteen years"[126] the State has failed to fulfil its obligation even after 50 years of coming into force of the Constitution. The Supreme Court while taking into consideration the educational status and also the non-implementation of the various provisions of the Constitution, in *Miss Mohini Jain's case*[127] held that "the directive principles which are fundamental in the governance of the country cannot be isolated from the fundamental rights guaranteed under Part III. These principles have to be read into the fundamental rights. Both are supplementary to each other. The State is under a Constitutional mandate to create conditions in which all could enjoy the fundamental rights guaranteed to the individuals under Part III. Without making "right to education" under Art. 45 of the Constitution a reality the fundamental rights under Chapter III shall remain beyond the reach of large majority which is illiterate." The Government with an aim to fulfil its obligations under the Convention on the Rights of the Child, the Constitutional principles and the judicial decisions has taken recourse to introducing a Constitution (Amendment) Bill making right to education free and compulsory for the children between the age of 6-14 years.[128]

Keeping in view the mounting cases of crimes against women and children the Government has taken up the review of laws as priority under the Common Minimum Programme (CMP). To give a fitting accolade to the SAARC Decade of the Girl Child (1991-2000) and also for setting a platform for action for the realisation of the rights of the child during the Women Empowerment Year 2001 and the proposed Year of Implementation-2002 the Government has enacted the Juvenile Justice (Care and Protection of Children) Act, 2000[129], which contain elaborate provisions for the care and protection of juveniles in tune with the standards prescribed in the Convention on the Rights of the Child, the United Nations Standard Minimum Rules for the Administration of Juvenile Justice, 1985 (the Beijing Rules), the United Nations Rules for the Protection of Juveniles Deprived of their Liberty (1990), and all other relevant international instruments having bearing on juveniles. Though the provisions contained in the

Constitution and the other legislations are high spirited the real protection and empowerment of children lies in their implementation with aplomb and committedness.

In the light of the above facts it is high time on the Union and the State Governments to divert their attention towards this area by declaring it as a drought prone area. The Anganwadi, ANMs and other workers should be sensitised about the various policies and programmes of the government and also the methods of empowering the women and girls in various spheres such as education, politics, administration, better living etc. Gender sensitisation programmes should be conducted to remove gender disparities and to prevent sale and killing of girl children. The government should conduct a survey and allot ration cards to all the villagers. Besides steps should be taken to make health care and educational facilities within the reach of tribals. Since these tribals migrate to other districts for nearly 4 months every year steps should be taken to admit their children in the residential schools. Further the government should create employment generation programmes in the surroundings by introducing watershed and other programmes.

Besides, to take a clear stalk of the situation it is necessary to implement the Registration of Births and Deaths Act 1969, which provides that, all persons have to give information to the Registrar, about the birth, even still-birth. The Act provides that if the birth of a child takes place, if in a house the head of the house, if in a hospital health centre, etc. the medical officer in charge, in a jail the jailor, in a choultry, hotel, etc. the person in charge, in a public place the Sarpanch/police officer, in a plantation, the superintendent. Besides through administrative directives the Government should assign this responsibility also to the VDO's and they should be made accountable.

Need to Strengthen Machinery at the International, Regional and National Levels

Though the UN has adopted the Convention for the Suppression of the Traffic in Persons and of the Exploitation of the

Prostitution of Others in 1949, it served only as a guidance to the nations in enacting legislations prohibiting trafficking. Due to lack of effective machinery to monitor and implement the Convention it has failed to achieve the desired results. Resultantly the UN has adopted the Optional Protocol to the Convention. However, the Convention on the Rights of the Child, the Convention on the Elimination of All Forms of Discrimination Against Women and few other Conventions provide for more accountability on the States by calling for periodic status reports and also have Committees for effective monitoring. In the backdrop of these things and also as suggested by the Special Rapporteur on Sale and Trafficking of Women and Girls it is necessary to have effective machinery to monitor and curb international trafficking.

Besides, the *Organised Crime Branch* of *Interpol,* which has been established in 1989 with the long-term aim of creating an extensive data base of organized criminal enterprises and persons who are engaged in continued, illegal activity in order to generate illicit profits should be strengthened to prevent international trafficking. Since the publication of the *Marco Polo* study in 1997, there has been increased interest in specific aspects such as smuggling, trafficking in persons by organised groups, to identify the members of such groups. Their means of operation and the criminal activities of the illegal migrants etc. These aspects also need to be regulated apart from adopting conventions and resolutions by the United Nations and by the comity of nations.

The legal luminaries, academicians, NGOs and other groups felt it very arduous to attach stigma on the small infants and minors who are sold for purposes other than prostitution by booking their buyers and sellers under the sections related to prostitution. The police officials also expressed their concern over the lacunae in the existing laws and articulated their doubts as to how can they arrest parents who are selling children due to poverty and with a hope that the persons who are taking their children are well off and give their daughters a bright future. The village administrators expressed their apprehension that if they arrest the parents who will take care of the other children?

As rightly felt by the ILO that entirely separate measures need to be envisaged for adult prostitution *versus* child prostitution. Children are invariably victims of prostitution whereas adults could choose sex work as an occupation. "International conventions all treat child prostitution as an unacceptable form of forced labour; the goal is its total elimination." Success in eliminating child prostitution would also reduce the problem of adult prostitution, since many adult prostitutes report having entered the sex sector while they were still underage.

Keeping in view the changing situations and the reported incidents of sale of women and girls as chattel in the open market by auctioning and other modes, The Law Commission has made a recommendation for insertion of a new section 373-A under the Indian Penal Code. The new section gives a wider definition to the aspect of sale, lets to hire or otherwise disposing of a woman or giving for all purposes or even without the purpose. Under this section both selling and buying irrespective of the motives are punishable. Further the National Commission for Women besides enacting a draft Marriage Bill, 1994, in one of its report to the Government has made suggestions for amending the IPC, Child Marriage Restraint Act, 1929 etc., to prevent recurrence of these incidents. Keeping in view the inadequacy of the law and to improve the status and dignity of women and girls in the society the Government should take up a detailed review of the laws and make appropriate amendments to stand the test of time. Besides the government should immediately set up the much-awaited National Commission for Children. Since poverty and gender bias are the root causes of sale of girls and myriad national problems both the Union and State governments should take up poverty alleviation and gender sensitisation programmes in a planned manner.

References

1. Arts. 45, 46, 47 of the Constitution of India.
2. Cardozo, *The Nature of the Judicial Process,* New Haven. Yale University Press, (1966) (25th printing).

3. *Atam Prakash* v. *State of Haryana*, A. 1986 S.C. 854 (864).
4. *Golaknath* v. *State of Punjab* A. 1967 S.C. 1643 (1655).
5. *Gita Hariharan & Anr.* v. *Reserve Bank of India & Anr.* (1999) 1 LRI 366.
6. *Sadhuram* v. *Pulin* A. 1984 S.C. 1471 (paras. 29, 70, 73).
7. *Yusuf* v. *State of Bombay* (1954) S.C.R. 930.
8. *State of W.B.* v. *Anwar Ali*, (1952) S.C.R. 531.
9. *Dasaratha* v. *State of A.P.*, AIR. 1961 S.C. 564.
10. *Air India* v. *Nargesh* AIR. 1981 S.C. 1829: *Muthamma* v. *Union of India* AIR. 1979 S.C. 1868.
11. *Dattaraya* v. *State of Bombay*, AIR. 1953 Bom. 311.
12. *Art 42 of the Constitution of India.*
13. *Art 39(f) of the Constitution of India.*
14. *Devarajiah* v. *Padmanna*, AIR. 1961 Nad, 35 (39).
15. *Samdasani* v. *Central Bank of India*, AIR. 1952 S.C. 59.
16. *Gopalan* v. *State of Madras*, (1950) S.C.R. 88.
17. *Olga* v. *Bombay Corpn.*, AIR. 1986 S.C. 180.
18. *Bandhu* v. *Union of India*, AIR. 1984 S.C. 802.
19. *People's Union* v. *Union of India*, AIR. 1982 S.C. 1473.
20. *Olga Tellis* v. *Bombay Corpn.*, AIR. 1986 S.C. 180.
21. *Shantistar* v. *Narayan*, AIR. 1990 S.C. 630.
22. *Parmanand* v. *Union of India*, AIR. 1989 S.C. 2039.
23. *State of Maharashtra* v. *Chandrabhan*, AIR. 1983 S.C. 803.
24. *Mohini Jain* v. *State of Karnataka*, (1992) 3 SCC 666, at pp. 679-80 (para 12).
25. *Unnikrishnan J.P. and other* v. *State of A.P. and others*, AIR 1993 SC 2178.
26. *Article 23 of the Constitution of India.*
27. *Nihal* v. *Rambai*, AIR. 1987 M.P. 126 (para 12).
28. *People's Union* v. *Union of India*, AIR. 1982 S.C. 1473.
29. *Bandhua* v. *Union of India*, AIR. 1984 S.C. 804 (para. 21).
30. *Article 24 of the Constitution of India.*
31. *People's Union* v. *Union of India*, AIR. 1982 S.C. 1473.
32. *M.C. Mehta (Child Labour Matter)* v. *State of T.N.* (1996) 6 SCC 756.
33. *Article 32(1) of the Constitution of India.*
34. *Gopal Das* v. *Union of India*, AIR. 1955 S.C. 1.
35. *Fertilizer Corporation. Union* v. *Union of India*, AIR. 1981 S.C. 344.
36. *Gupta* v. *Union of India*, AIR. 1982 S.C. 149 (paras. 14, 17, 25, 141, 609).

37. *Minerva Mills* v. *Union of India,* AIR. 1980 S.C. 1789 .
38. *Hanif Quareshi* v. *State of Bihar,* AIR. 1958 S.C. 731.
39. Article 39(c) of the Constitution of India.
40. *Bandhua Morcha* v. *Union of India,* AIR. 1984 S.C. 802 (para. 10).
41. *M.C. Mehta* v. *State of T.N.* (1991) 1 S.C.C. 283.
42. *M.C. Mehta (Child Labour Matter)* v. *State of T.N.* (1996) 6 SCC 756.
43. *Vishaljeet* v. *Union of India,* AIR. 1990 S.C. 1412.
44. *Unnikrishnan J.P. and others* v. *State of A.P. and Others* (1993) 1 SCC 645.
45. *India ratified the Convention on the Rights of the Child* on December 11, 1992.
46. *Article 51-A(e) of the Constitution of India.*
47. Government of India, *Prostitution in Metropolitan Cities of India,* Central Social Welfare Board (1993).
48. *The Times of India,* dated June 24, 1999.
49. UNICEF, *Child File—Reading as Child Rights-4* (1998), New Delhi at p. 12.
50. *Gauravjain* v. *Union of India,* 1998 SCC (Crl.) 25.
51. Beijing Declaration Platform for Action, paragraph 259.
52. Article 1(1) of the 1926 Slavery Convention defines slavery as 'the status or condition of a person over whom any or all of the powers attaching to the right of ownership are exercised.'
53. The Working Group on Contemporary Forms of Slavery in its 1998 session adopted a recommendation that explicitly declared that 'trans-border trafficking of women and girls for sexual exploitation is a contemporary form of slavery and constitutes serious violation of human rights'.
54. Preamble, *United Nations Charter.*
55. The Universal Declaration of Human Rights (UDHR) was adopted by the General Assembly of the United Nations on December 10, 1948, since then the day of its adaptation is celebrated worldwide as 'Human Rights Day'. The Declaration comprises of 30 Articles, which spell out the basic civil, cultural, economic, political and social rights that all human beings around the world should enjoy. The Declaration has been translated into 321 languages and dialects from Abkhaz to Zulu. The Declaration has served as the inspiration not only for the UN in adopting more than 80 Conventions and Declarations on wide range of issues but also stimulated the national governments in incorporation of these principles under their Constitution and other laws. The Indian Constitution, which came into force on January 26, 1950, contains 28 similar provisions out of 30 Articles of UDHR.
56. Adopted by the General Assembly of the United Nations on December 16, 1966 entered into force in January 1976.

57. Adopted by the General Assembly of the United Nations on December 16, 1966 entered into force in March 1976.
58. Adopted by the General Assembly of the United Nations on November 20, 1989. India acceded to the Convention on December 11, 1992.
59. *Id.*, Article 1.
60. See, Articles 34 and 35, Convention on the Rights of the Child.
61. *Id.*, Articles 35.
62. *Id.*, Article 20 and 21. Article 21 mandates the State Parties to recognize and/or permit the system of adoption shall ensure that the best interests of the child shall be the paramount consideration and they shall, among others; (b) recognize that inter-country adoption may be considered as an alternative means of child's care, if the child cannot be placed in a foster or an adoptive family or cannot in any suitable manner be cared for in the child's country of origin; (c) ensure that the child concerned by inter-country adoption enjoys safeguards and standards equivalent to those existing in the case of national adoption; (d) take all appropriate measures to ensure that in inter-country adoption, the placement does not result in improper financial gain for those involved in it. It further obligates the State Parties to promote, where appropriate, the objectives of the present article by concluding bilateral or multilateral arrangements or agreements, and endeavour, within this framework, to ensure that the placement of the child in another country is carried out by competent authorities or organs.
63. A new Optional Protocol to the Convention on the Rights of the Child prohibiting the use of children in armed conflict was adopted in May 2000 and quickly garnered signatures from seventy countries. The protocol, achieved after six years of negotiations, raised the minimum age for compulsory recruitment and participation in armed conflict from fifteen to eighteen. Besides, a working group is currently drafting an optional protocol to the Convention that will explicitly address the sale of children, child prostitution and child pornography.
64. General Assembly Resolution 53/111, Dec. 9, 1998 .
65. The UN General Assembly through its resolution 55/25 of November 15, 2000, adopted the Convention Against Transnational Organized Crime, the Protocol to Prevent, Suppress and Punish Trafficking in Persons, Especially Women and Children, and the Protocol Against the Smuggling of Migrants by Land, Sea and Air. In December 2000, 148 countries gathered in Palermo, Italy to attend a high-level conference opening the new UN Convention Against Transnational Organized Crime to States signature. Of the 148 countries present, 121 signed the new UN Convention Against Transnational Organized Crime, and over 80 countries signed one

of its supplementary protocols—the Protocol to Prevent, Suppress and Punish Trafficking in Persons, Especially Women and Children. Another supplementary Protocol Against the Smuggling of Migrants by Land, Sea and Air was also open for States signature, and a third Protocol on the Illicit Manufacturing of and Trafficking in Firearms is expected to be completed at the end of 2001. The new UN Convention and its supplementary protocol on trafficking in persons have to be ratified by 40 countries before they become instruments of international law.

66. Article 10, the Protocol to Prevent, Suppress and Punish Trafficking in Persons, Especially Women and Children.
67. *Id.*, section 3(b).
68. *Id.*, section 3(a).
69. *Ibid.*
70. *Id.*, Article 9(5).
71. As on June 26, 2001 the Convention (CEDAW) has been ratified by 168 State parties. India has ratified the Convention on July 9, 1993.
72. *Id.*, Article 6.
73. Section 3, Vienna Declaration and Programme of Action, "The Equal Status and Human Rights of Women".
74. This has contributed in subsequent appointment of a special rapporteur. The special rapporteur has laid special attention to the problem of trafficking of women and girls in her report (2000).
75. The Special Rapporteur on the sale of children, child prostitution and child pornography, also gave the issue detailed attention in her 1999 report to the Human Rights Commission.
76. Article 7(2)(c).
77. The International Labour Organization (ILO) was founded in 1919 and is the only surviving major creation of the Treaty of Versailles, which brought the League of Nations into being. The ILO became the first specialized agency of the UN in 1946. Within the UN system, the ILO has a unique tripartite composition with workers and employers participating as equal partners with governments in its various activities including policy formulation. One of the prime objects of the ILO is to promote around the world social justice and recognition for human and labour rights.
78. Recommendation is an instrument adopted by the ILO at the same time as a Convention, which cannot be ratified. It only provides guidance and cannot form obligations.
79. See, Discrimination (Employment and Occupation) Convention, 1958 (No. 111). See also, Equal Remuneration Convention, 1951 (No. 100).
80. Apart from others the Minimum Age Convention, 1973 (No. 138) and the Worst Form of Child Labour Convention, 1999 (No. 182)

are the landmark Conventions in the area of elimination of child labour.

81. *Maternity Protection Conventions of 1919 and 2000, Medical Care and Sickness Benefits Convention,* 1969 (No. 130).
82. *Indigenous and Tribal Population Convention,* 1957 (No. 107).
83. See, *Freedom of Association and Protection of the Right to Organize Convention,* 1948 (No. 87). See also, *Right to Organize and Collective Bargaining Convention,* 1948 (No. 98).
84. See, Forced Labour Convention, 1930 (No. 29). See also, Abolition of Forced Labour Convention, 1957 (No. 105).
85. Conventions No. 29 of 1930 and 105 of 1957.
86. Source: ILO, "Sex industry assuming massive proportions in South-East Asia" (Press release) 19, August, 1998 *(ILO/98/31).*
87. Adopted by the International Labour Conference in its Eighty-Seventh Session held at Geneva on June 17, 1999 and came into force on November 19, 2000. As on April 2001 the Convention has been ratified by 73 nations.
88. The ILO has also launched an International Programme on the Elimination of Child Labour (IPEC), which in its various facets has a specific focus on trafficking. Besides, the Commission on Human Rights at its Fifty-first session in July 1999 adopted the ILO Convention on the worst forms of child labour and its accompanying Recommendation, which identified the sale and trafficking of children as a practice similar to slavery.
89. *Vocational Rehabilitation (Disabled) Recommendation,* 1955, the *Vocational Rehabilitation Employment (Disabled Persons) Convention,* 1983, and its accompanying Recommendation; *Discrimination (Employment and Occupation) Convention,* 1958; *Employment Policy Convention,* 1964; *Maternity Protection Conventions of 1919 and 2000, Medical Care and Sickness Benefits Convention,* 1969 (No. 130). Apart from others the Minimum Age Convention, 1973 (No. 138) and the Worst Form of Child Labour Convention, 1999 (No. 182) are the landmark Conventions in the area of elimination of child labour.
90. The special rapporteur is mandated to work on the aspects enumerated, *inter alia,* under Articles 2, 19, 21, 32, and 34-39 of the Convention on the Rights of the Child.
91. Source: Human Rights Watch, *World Report* (2001).
92. *Ibid.*
93. Government of India, *Annual Report 1998-99. Department of WCD,* New Delhi at p. 33.
94. For example, under the *Maternity Benefits Act, 1961* [(section 3(b)] "Child" includes a stillborn child; under the *Immoral Traffic Prevention Act, 1956* [(section 2(aa)] "Child" means a person who has not completed the age of sixteen years; under the *Child Marriage*

Restraint Act, 1929 [(section 2(a)] "Child" means a person who, if a male has not completed twenty-one years of age, and if a female, has not completed eighteen years of age.

95. UNICEF (1994) *the Right to be a Child,* New Delhi, p. 4.
96. Source: ILO, "Sex industry assuming massive proportions in South-East Asia" (Press release) 19, August, 1998 *(ILO/98/31).*
97. Government of India, *Prostitution in Metropolitan Cities of India,* Central Social Welfare Board (1993).
98. Sec. 376(6) of the *Indian Penal Code,* 1860.
99. *State of A.P.* vs. *Narasimha,* 1994(2) Crimes 263 (SC).
100. *Bhupendra Prakash* vs. *The State,* 1985 (1) Crimes 524.
101. *Andhra Pradesh Devadasi (Prohibition and Dedicated) Act,* 1988.
102. *The Times of India,* Devdasi Culture Continues to Thrive, dated June 24, 1999.
103. *Vishaljeet* vs. *Union of India,* (1990) 3 SCC 318.
104. Sections 370 to 374.
105. Order dated July 23, 2001 in W.P. (C) No. 196/2001.
106. These incidents of sale of girls were not confined to Andhra Pradesh State alone, but similar instances were reported from Karnataka, Orissa States. In these cases babies were purchased from the poor families by luring them for money. The Karnataka State police have registered 19 cases in 45 Tandas of Konchavaram police station limits during 2000-2001.
107. The number of children sold from each village are; Ammula-6, Chandampet-25, Devarakonda-11, Gundlapally- 1, Nidamanoor- 1, Peddavoora -02.
108. First Information Report (FIR) No. 8/2001, March 10, 2001.
109. Source: Government of India, Ministry of Social Justice and Empowerment (September 2001).
110. *Ibid.*
111. Article 16.
112. Article 1(c) specifically states that "Any institution or practice whereby: (i) A woman, without the right to refuse, is promised or given in marriage on payment of a consideration in money or in kind to her parents, guardian, family ..."
113. *Articles 1, 2, and 3.* The Convention mandates that (1) No marriage shall be legally entered into without the full and free consent of both parties, such consent to be expressed by them in person ... as prescribed by law. (2) States Parties to the present Convention shall ... specify a minimum age for marriage ("not less than 15 years" according to the non-binding recommendation accompanying this

Convention). No marriage shall be legally entered into by any person under this age, except where a competent authority has granted a dispensation as to age, for serious reasons; in the interests of the intending spouses ... (3) All marriages shall be registered ... by the competent authority.

114. Art. 23 of the *Constitution of India.*
115. Art. 51-A (e) of the *Constitution of India.*
116. The Government has enacted this Act in pursuance of the International Convention signed at New York on May 9, 1950 for the prevention of immoral traffic.
117. Section 5, Immoral Traffic Prevention Act, 1986.
118. Under Sections 372 and 373 of the IPC.
119. Section 2(a) of the *Child Marriage Restraint Act,* 1929.
120. Sec. 5 *ibid.*
121. 146th *Report of the Law Commission of India,* New Delhi.
122. Government of India, *146th Report of the Law Commission of India.*
123. Government of India, *National Decadal Plan of Action for the Girl Child,* Dept. of WCD (1991-2000 A.D.).
124. *Gaurav Jain* v. *Union of India* (1997) 8 SCC 114. Also see *Gaurav Jain* v. *Union of India,* 1998 SCC (Crl.) 25.
125. Art 45, of the *Constitution of India.*
126. *Miss Mohini Jain* v. *State of Karnataka and Others.* AIR 1992, S.C. 1858.
127. Under Article 21-A of the Constitution (Eighty Third Amendment) Bill it is provided that free and compulsory education is provided to the citizens in the age group of 6-14 years. Whereas it may be stated that education of the child in the present day competitive world starts even at an earlier stage. The enrolment of children should be started at the age of 4 years in the form of play/pre-school, so that they may be segregated from the family work and other home based working environment and for at least one year the concept of "learning while playing" should be followed so as to lessen the burden on the child and also to inculcate an interest and habit of attending the school. Besides, this provision should be made applicable to all the children in the country irrespective of their nationality, citizenship, origin etc.
128. The Act received the assent of the President on December 30, 2000 and came into force on April 1, 2001, vide S.O. 177(E), dated February 28, 2001, published in the Gazette of India, Extraordinary, Pt. II. Sec. 3(ii) dated February 28, 2001.
129. Section 8, Registration of Births and Deaths Act 1969.

17

RIGHTS OF THE CHILD VIS-À-VIS FOREIGN ADOPTIONS IN INDIA

T.S.N. SASTRY

Introduction : International and National Concern for the Rights of the Child

The importance of the welfare of a child need not be over emphasized in any civilized society. The prosperity of any society or a State mainly determined upon the health and well-being of its children. The children must be brought up in an atmosphere of love and affection and under the tender care and attention, so that they may be able to attain full emotional, intellectual and spiritual stability and maturity and acquire self-confidence and self-respect, and a balanced view of life with full appreciation and realization of the role which they should in the nation-building process without which the nation cannot develop and attain prosperity.[1] Hence children constitute as the paramount asset for the well-being of either international community or for a nation.

To protect and promote the rights of children independently as individuals of themselves, abolishing the customary practice of the parents around the world treating children as their property was first recognized by international law through the Geneva Declaration on the Rights of the Child in 1924 by the League of Nations. In order to extend further impetus to the Declaration, the General Assembly of the United Nations in 1959 adopted another Declaration on the Rights of Children. The Declaration aims to promote the well-being of the child without any discrimination to sex, caste, creed, community, religion, race, and, expects States parties to take steps to protect the child by reason of his /her physical and mental immaturity, need special safeguards after birth.[2] Further, in order to promote and to create awareness across the globe about the importance of the rights of the children, the year 1979 was declared as the International Year of Child by the United Nations.

Furthermore, to meet the standards set in and to fulfil the principles proclaimed in the Charter of the United Nations, Universal Declaration of Human Rights, the two Covenants on Human Rights and the Declaration of Children, in the year 1989 the United Nations adopted a Convention on the Rights of Child for the protection and harmonious development of children by the States parties. The Convention apart from recognizing the Civil and Political rights, and, the Economic, Social and Cultural rights of children, mainly aims at extending protection from exploitation and abuse in abnormal or dangerous situations, and to help and promote in the child the sense of security, self-esteem and pride with roots in his native culture and familial surroundings which are highly essential for the development of one's personality.

The Vienna Declaration and Programme of Action, 1993 of the World Conference on Human Rights also highlighted the importance of the rights of children. Accordingly, it has requested all the States parties to ratify the Convention without exception and also made an appeal to take necessary legislative, executive, administrative, economic and other welfare measures be adopted keeping in mind the primary interest of a child.[3]

At the national level, the framers of the Constitution also expressed their concern in no uncertain terms for the upliftment of children in safe, secure and healthy manner through various provisions in the Constitution. Accordingly Article 15 (3) enables the State to make special provisions for children apart from women. Article 24 explicitly prohibits child labour and hazardous employment of children. Article 39 (f) further directs the State in its policy towards the well-being of children. Hence, it is the duty of the State, that children be given opportunities and facilities to develop in a healthy manner and in conditions of freedom and dignity and childhood and youth are protected against exploitation and against moral and material abandonment.

The Government of India in accordance with the provisions of the Constitution and to express its solidarity to the concern expressed by the framers of the Constitution, on the vital role of children in shaping the future destiny of the nation, adopted a National Policy for the Welfare of Children and constituted a National Children's Welfare Board with the Prime Minister as its chairman in 1974. The National Policy in unequivocal words expressing the importance of children as the foundation of the nation states that:

> "The nation's children are supremely important asset. Their nature and solicitude are our responsibility. Children's programmes should find a prominent part in our national plans for the development of human resources, so that our children grow up to become robust citizens, physically fit, mentally alert and morally healthy, endowed with skills, and motivations need by society. Equal opportunities for development to all children during the period of growth should be our aim, for this would serve our larger purpose of reducing in equality and ensuring social justice."[4]

To express the gratitude for the promotion and welfare of children, and taking into account the love and affection of Pandit Jawaharlal Nehru towards children, the Government of India has declared November 14 as Children's Day and celebrates it every year. Perhaps India is the only county to express such a commitment for the well-being of children's rights.

In spite of the lofty efforts both at the international and national mechanisms to protect and promote the welfare of children, not even a single day passes without a notorious abuse of the tender age of children across the globe. Everyday tens and thousands of children are brutally exploited, seriously harmed, crippled, sexually abused, abandoned and sold like sheep and goats and becoming prey to the vicious acts of the unwanted elements and elders of the society. Among the various maladies that are plaguing the children, Foreign Adoptions is one such area wherein a great majority of Indian children are at risk, in spite of the clear-cut guideline laid down by the judiciary and the constitution of the Central Adoption Resource Agency (CARA). Taking into consideration of the maladies involved in foreign adoptions, a modest attempt is made in the chapter to throw light on the concept and necessity of adoptions in general, foreign adoptions in particular, and, to highlight the gray areas that exist in this area and the need for their regulation to protect human rights of the future generations of India from the inimical activities of foster placement agencies.

Concept of Adoption

It is a well established fact that the balanced development of a child in shaping its personality is always available only within the family. The most cordial atmosphere would naturally be that of the family of the child's biological parents. If for any reason, it is not possible for a child, the next best alternative then is familial surroundings. Highlighting the importance of a family in shaping the personality of a child, the World Conference on Human Rights has rightly stated, "the child for the full and harmonious development of his or her personality should grow up in a family environment which accordingly merits broader protection."[5]

Hence, the responsibility for providing care and attention to children, which includes orphaned, abandoned, neglected, and abused, rest mainly with the family. However in view of broad social changes, due to urbanization, industrialization, influence of foreign culture and various other aspects, it is not possible always for a child to have the support of family. In such situations, the next best alternative to a child is an adoptive family. In view of the social and economic character of the Constitution, the responsibility lies upon the government to extend support to destitute children. Hence the Government of India always supports adoption, than placing a child in a foster placement agency.

In the beginning very few countries like, India, France, Rome, Spain and Greece only recognized the institution of adoption. However, today a great majority of States are extending the legal recognition to the institution of adoption. In spite of the recognition by the international community, unfortunately the Muslim world is still out of the purview of adoption, refuses to recognize it either morally or legally.

Traditionally adoption has been widely accepted and followed in India and also recognized by Hindu law and regulated by the Hindu Adoption Act, 1956. Adoption means, "to take into one's family through legal means and bring up as one's own child."[6] The act of adoption creates a legal relationship between a parent and a child, who have had no genetic relationship. Further, it ensures a satisfaction to parents who crave for children for biological, emotional, physical, spiritual and social reasons. Adoption certainly provides a child all the material and other social, emotional necessary security for its proper development. Adoption being an important alternative next to biological family, it extends the care and protection to abandoned, destitute or neglected children. For this reason, the Convention on the Rights of Child, 1989 also recognizes the institution of adoption.[7]

Whenever a child is offered for adoption in the best interest of the child, all efforts should be made to find out adoptive parents within the same country to the extent possible. Because a child can develop quickly in its own cultural, social, religious, and, linguistic background easily. It is, therefore, becomes the responsibility of all the institutions and agencies involved in the welfare activities of abandoned, destitute and neglected children to find out a suitable family for in-country adoption. In case, if all the efforts to place a child with adoptive parents residing in India proved to be unsuccessful, the next best alternative they can resort to is foreign or inter-country adoption as recognized by international law of human rights.

Foreign Adoptions: Indian Scenario

The concept of foreign adoptions is of contemporary origin and recognized by several countries including India. Foreign adoption is an aspect of private international law and also popularly often referred to as inter-country adoption. Foreign adoption means, adoption of a child belongs to one country by the parents of another country. According to the Indian Council of Social Welfare, a foreign adoption means, "...where, the adopters and the child do not have the same nationality as well as in which the habitual residence by the adopters and the child is in different countries."[8] However, a foreign adoption has to be preferred only in the best and future welfare of a child and also meets the safeguards and standards equivalent to that of a national adoption and does not result in improper financial gain for the agencies involved in it.[9] Though it has been recognized by several countries, there are certain issues which are centrifugal to foreign adoptions especially, with respect to choice of law, jurisdiction of the courts and the recognition of foreign adoption orders. In order to remove the difficulties centred round the area, the Tenth Hague Conference of Private International Law had adopted a Convention in 1965, popularly referred to as Hague Convention on Foreign Adoptions.[10]

In India, there is no legislation dealing with foreign adoptions. There is no provision even in the Hindu Adoption and Maintenance Act, 1956, or in the Guardians and Wards Act 1890, or in the Juvenile Justice Act, 2000. However, the courts are guided by Sections 7-11 and 17 of the Guardians and Wards Act, 1890, whenever a foreigner wants to adopt an Indian child and by the Hague Convention on Foreign Adoptions even though India is not a party. Although the said Act, and the provisions of the Convention are guiding the courts in exercising their discretionary powers in passing a foreign adoption order, there exists a difference of opinion among the various High Courts in the country.[11] This is because of the dereliction of the government to regulate the issues involved in the area and to enact a comprehensive legislation. Fortunately even though, there is no legislative regulation on this area, the situation is better than yester years in view of the guidelines laid down by the apex court in *Laxmikant Pandey* v. *Union of India.*[12]

The Guidelines of the Supreme Court

Thanks to the public spirited lawyer, Mr. Laxmikant Pandey on whose initiation, the apex court took a lead role to halt the profiteering motives of various voluntary agencies involved in offering Indian children to foreign parents, and, framed certain guidelines to be followed in the future interest and welfare of children in the absence of a legislation. Since the judgment is too exhaustive, a few specific aspects are only mentioned.

- In view of the malpractices involved in the area, the court held that in future the activities of the agencies involved in foreign adoption be regulated through a permanent mechanism.
- In future the agencies recognized by the Government (which includes Indian as well as foreign) only should participate in foreign adoptions.
- Any prospective applicants opt for adoption the application has to be rooted through a proper foreign agency, along with a home study report and an assessment of the adoptive parent's capacity to handle the trans-racial, trans-cultural, and, trans-national aspects of such adoption.
- The social or child welfare agencies must send progress reports in a quarter to the Indian Social or Child Welfare agencies until the application for guardianship can be declined by the court.
- Natural parents of a child be assisted by the agencies in taking a decision about the relinquishment of the child for adoption be informed of the chances of foreign adoption, and be allowed to review their decision within 90 days.
- If any disruption takes place in the prospective adoptive family of the foreigner before adoption can be affected,

the foreign agencies should find out an alternative family within the same country and report it to the court handling guardianship proceedings.

- If any orphan, destitute or abandoned child has come to any institution, all efforts be made by such agency within three months to trace the biological parents before declaring the child free for adoption after completing the procedures prescribed by the court.
- The foreign social or child welfare agency should have an Indian citizen as its representative with a degree or diploma in social work and in child welfare. The representative should work only for one agency and a paid employee of such organization having power of attorney to act in India on behalf of such foreign agency for all practical purposes.
- All the children offered for foreign adoption must accompany a child study report for the consideration of the prospective parents.
- The courts should take due caution and care before passing an order appointing a foreigner as a guardian keeping in mind the future welfare of the child as a primary aspect.

As rightly pointed out by the apex court, the future welfare of the child is a vital aspect, and always should be borne in mind before appointing any foreigner as a guardian. In the words of Lindely, J., "the welfare of the child is not to be measured by money or by physical comforts only. The word must be taken in its widest sense. The moral and religious welfare of the child must be considered as well as its well-being. Nor can ties of affection be disregarded."[13]

Taking into consideration, the seriousness with which the malpractices are employed by various child and social welfare agencies, and the anguish expressed by Supreme Court on the lackadaisical attitude of the government, the Government of India constituted a Central Adoption Resource Agency (CARA) in 1990, under the supervision of Ministry of Social and Family

Welfare. Accordingly CARA will act as a clearing house to promote in-country adoptions; regulate inter-country adoptions. No child or social welfare agency can process the application in the competent court for inter-country adoption without obtaining the "No Objection Certificate" from CARA. CARA has also been empowered with vast powers to issue guidelines to all the social or child welfare agencies to be followed, to cancel the licences of any agencies, if found guilty to inspect, regulate, monitor and issue directions to all the adoption agencies in the country.[14]

Critical Appraisal

There is no doubt that the continuous judgments and the guidelines issued by the apex court are exhaustive enough to regulate the foreign adoptions in the country. But at the same time, the relaxations given by the court with respect to few aspects as requested by the various organizations need to be regulated. The court in its second judgment considering the difficulties presented by the adoption agencies with respect to the restriction of foreign parents visiting India, before approving the child for adoption as stated in its first judgment has relaxed. The reasons presented before the court and the concession extended by it that the prospective parents need not visit India and stay with the child seems to be right. However, taking into consideration, the future welfare of the child and to access the mentality of the parents, it would have been better at least they are asked to be interviewed personally by the Head of the Indian Mission of the country of the prospective parents. Basing on the assessment of the Head of the Mission, a confidential report can be sent to CARA. Only if the report is positive, CARA should issue a no objection certificate. Instead of prescribing such a safety measure, the court has given a blanket permission to the prospective foreign parents not to visit the country, not to stay with the child and permitted them to adopt an Indian child merely depending on the homestudy report of the foreign adoption agencies. In this type of situation, there is every possibility for obtaining a favourable home study report from a foreign agency by the agencies in India interested in making money illegally.

The court in its second supplemental judgment considering the hardships presented by the applicants with respect to the time limits set by it in the earlier judgments for various categories of children to be declared free for adoption was reviewed and reduced accordingly. But as some of the agencies involved in the process are only interested in making money then considering the future welfare of the child, the procedure prescribed by the court needs certain amendments. First, the court relaxed the rule to obtain a release order by a Juvenile Court or Social Welfare Department or the District Collector that the child is free for adoption in cases where a child is relinquished by its biological parents or an unwed mother. It has been suggested that it would be sufficient to procure an adoption order by simply filing the Deed of Relinquishment before the competent court. In view of the maladies exist in, due to various social, lingual, economic and political factors there is every possibility that some agencies may fraudulently obtain a Deed of Relinquishment from the biological parents or an unwed mother without informing the consequences of relinquishment. To stop such evil designs, it would be better to examine the parents personally by the competent court to satisfy it self that the Deed of Relinquishment has been executed by them voluntarily on their own knowing all the consequènces of executing such a deed. To a certain extent it will act as a guard to reduce the evil designs of the profit-making tendency of the agencies involved in the trade. Secondly, in the case of destitute or abandoned children, it is the responsibility of the child or social welfare agency to lodge a complaint before the local police to trace the natural parents or guardians, the moment they found a child. Basing on the information, the Inspector General or the Commissioner of Police concerned has to conduct an enquiry to ascertain the biological parents within a month. In the meanwhile the social or child welfare agency may approach the Juvenile Court, Social Welfare Department or the Collector of the District to declare the child free for adoption. The above authorities upon the receipt of police report may pass an order that the child is free for adoption, if the biological parents of the child are not traced. The procedure prescribed by the court seems to be sufficient to protect the future welfare of a child still there is every possibility to misuse the norm in various ways and means. At times the agencies may bribe the police or may influence them to issue a report without conducting a proper inquiry. In case if the police took up the case seriously to conduct a proper and thorough investigation, the natural parents may be bribed by the adoptive agencies not to reveal the truth, or through political or any other means may bring in pressure on the police to submit a report that they could not trace the biological parents of the child. In order to prevent the misuse of the provisions, the child's identity be published in newspapers and be telecasted through at least State run television channels for a proper identification of the biological parents. Though this measure is not acceptable to the apex court, in the best interest of the child it should be made compulsory as a part of the inquiry. Further, a high power committee be constituted at district level consisting of the District and Sessions Judge as the Chairman and one or two advocates, academicians or social workers as members to supervise the investigating procedure of the police before they submit the report to the appropriate authorities.

Apart from these measures, another aspect which needs meritorious consideration is that every competent court before passing a foreign adoption order should ask the agencies to produce the child in the court physically or if for any reason, if the child cannot be produced in a court physically, the concerned judge or an advocate appointed by the judge should visit the premises personally to see the child. This step is necessary in view of fake identities and birth certificates of the children produced by several agencies.

Further, though the Government of India constituted CARA empowering with vast powers still maladies exist in this area due to lack of seriousness on the part of the official machinery of CARA in implementing the procedures many of the Indian children's fate is hanging in fire as it is happening in Andhra Pradesh[15] and in other parts of the country[16] at the mercy of powerful voluntary agencies involved in trading or selling babies for hefty sums in the name of doing social service by matching childless couples with abandoned couples.

The pathetic conditions of children and their misuse by the agencies involved in foreign adoptions are presented by the media time and again certainly raises the eyebrows of people about the functioning of and the attitude of the Government of India. The Government should not deter from its commitment in the promotion and welfare of the children by simply constituting CARA and washing off its hands. The Government, especially the Ministry of Social and Family Welfare should review the situation and caution CARA for its lackadaisical attitude in its functioning about the future welfare of children. Furthermore, the Government of India should immediately take steps to establish branches of CARA in every State to monitor effectively the activities of the agencies in each State. If financially the suggestion may not be feasible to have an office of CARA in every State, at least in the Four Regions four Sub-offices can be opened to monitor the activities in that region and to assist the Central Office in New Delhi.

Apart from the above, the CARA has to specify the periodicity of its monitoring functions such as inspection of the social or voluntary agencies, the periodical meeting of Voluntary Coordinating Agencies, evolve suitable programmes to train the social workers and others involved in foreign adoptions with specific modules to tackle the illegalities. The Ministry of Social and Family Welfare should evolve programmes to disseminate in all the national languages through television and radio and distribute pamphlets highlighting the importance of children in the nation building and the responsibility of the community in protecting the future generations and also about the importance of adoptions in general and foreign adoptions in particular with respect to destitute or abandoned children.

Conclusion

As rightly pointed out by the Supreme Court in its second supplemental judgment, it is not possible to eradicate the maladies exist in the field of inter-country adoptions altogether, we can reduce the miseries by acting swiftly. With the co-operation and co-ordination of the governments of Union of India, State and Union Territories and the society it can be curbed to a maximum extent. The need of the hour is to deal sternly with the muscle and money power that is playing a big role and treating children as goods and exporting them to various foreign countries in the name of providing security to their future through the institution of Foreign Adoptions. The Government of India should come forward to enact a legislation taking into consideration of various opinions and suggestions rendered by academicians and people who are interested in the promotion and future welfare of children. Being a party to the international conventions and declarations on human rights in general and of children in particular, and to fulfil its constitutional obligations, is it not the responsibility of the government to enact a comprehensive law to halt the horrors faced by millions of children? If any attempt is made in this direction, such a legislation should be comprehensive enough to cover the interests of children of all the religions including Muslims without any fear or favour to discharge its constitutional mandate under Art. 44 of the Directive Principles of State Policy and should not eliminate or keep postponing things unlike the Children's Bill which was watered down. If legislation is enacted, it should have broad based provisions to constitute monitoring bodies at the Union and State levels empowered to periodically review the activities of CARA, VCA and other agencies and to render suggestions to the government for further steps to be taken to prevent any maladies. Such a body should consist of Judges, Lawyers, Police Officers, representative from Social and Child Welfare organizations, Academicians having expertise in the area, and women representatives, under the chairmanship of the Ministers' of Social Welfare at the Union and State level.

Though it is viewed by a section of scholars and by the Government that the existing guidelines laid down by the Supreme Court and the procedures adopted by CARA are sufficient, in view of the gaps that still exist in the area and the malpractices adopted by various agencies, a legislation with strict penal provisions for the violators certainly go a long way and would deter the agencies in committing grave illegalities. As all of us are well aware that we have inherited this country not from our forefathers but from the future generations, we are answerable to them. And the responsibility further lies on the shoulders of everyone of us that we should hand over this country in the safest form to our future generations to the maximum extent possible, if not at least the way we inherited from our forefathers. Hence in the best interest of the nation and to protect the supreme asset (i.e., the children) of the country, it is necessary to lend a helping hand in moulding their future in a free and evil free society. Let me conclude with a fervent appeal once again,[17] to the Government of India that it should come forward to enact a law at the earliest to see the smiles on the faces of the children of this country.

References

1. Sathyavan Kottarakka v. State, AIR 1977, Ker 133 at 136, 137.
2. *United Nations: The UN and Human Rights,* 110 (1984).
3. World Conference on Human Rights: The Vienna Declaration and Programme of Action, 36 (1993).
4. Government of India, Department of Social Welfare, No. 1-14/74-CDD, August 22, 1974.
5. *Supra* note 3.
6. *Reader's Digest:* Universal Dictionary, 30 (1987).
7. See Arts 20 and 21 of the Convention.
8. Cited *in re* Rasiklal Chhaganlal Metha, AIR 1982, Guj., 193 at 196.
9. Art. 21(c) and (d) of the Convention on the Rights of the Child, 1989.
10. For a detailed and critical discussion on the Convention See: Graveson, "The Tenth Session of the Hague Conference" 14, *International Law and Comparative Law Quarterly,* 537 (1965); also see, Jost Bloom, "Adoption Act, 1968, and Conflict of Laws" 22, *ICLQ,* 109 (1970); T.S.N. Sastry, "Adoption in Private International Law" Research Papers on Some Aspects of International Law, Unpublished Masters of Law Dissertation, Andhra University, Chapter III, 1987.
11. Re Sister Gemma, AIR 1970 Mad, 262; *Trine Holst Thomson* v. *The Children's National Institute,* AIR 1974 All.95; For a detailed discussion, see T.S.N. Sastry "The Need for an Enactment on Foreign Adoption", *The Academy Law Review,* Vol. XII, No. 2, 1988, p. 157 at 159-61.

12. AIR 1984 SC 469; AIR 1986 SC 272; AIR 1987 SC 232; AIR 1992 SC 118. Since the facts and the Judgment of the court are well aware and exhaustive, only important guidelines stated by the Supreme Court are only mentioned.
13. Re McGrath (Infant) 1893, 1 Ch. 148.
14. For further details on CARA see the web site *www/http//cara.nic.in.*
15. Radha Venkatesan "Children as Commodities" *The Hindu,* 16 (March 3, 2002); The news item telecasted by NDTV 24 7 in the first week of July, 2003, that a single child has been given in adoption for two families really heartening and proves the point beyond doubt the maladies exist and the attitude of CARA in protecting the welfare of children.
16. M Siraj Sati: "Babies for Sale" The Hindu, V, (August31, 1997)
17. See T.S.N. Sastry, "Inter-Country Adoptions: Indian Scenario", *Journal of Indian Legal Thought,* Vol. 1, 2003, p. 70 at 80.

18

WHY HUMAN RIGHTS ARE CALLED FOR?

AN INQUIRY INTO KASHMIR MIGRANTS PROBLEM

R. RAMA SUBRAMANIAN

Human Rights in Kashmir

Consider a situation wherein you are born and brought up good part of your life in the lanes and by-lanes of a place. You inherit a great culture from the people of this place. You identify yourself with its land, its air, its trees, its rivers, its mountains, its temples, its shrines, and its way of life. You are planning for the rest of your life in that place. And then a systematic process of *'ethnic cleansing'* starts. Your brother and father are killed mercilessly and women-folk are raped and assaulted. Your old grandfather, who has spent more than 75 years of his life in this place, is manhandled and assaulted. The family is threatened with dire consequences and is forced to follow certain religious rituals. And finally, you are asked to leave your home and hearth within 24 hours. You are given two choices of *either to leave the place* within 24 hours or *get killed* within 24 hours. And keep in mind that these are the only choices. Which one to choose?

The question posed is the same one that the Kashmiri migrants in general and Kashmiri Hindus in particular had to answer in 1989-90 popularly referred to as the issue of Kashmiri Pandits when there was peace prevailing in the homes of

Kashmir. The sudden events landed their lives in lurch and made them refugees in their own country. But for the rest of the world, it was just another *migration* i.e, some 400,000 people from Kashmir valley had migrated to different parts of India. It is violation of their basic right to life and liberty. The UDHR and other covenants and conventions on human rights guaranteed every individual right to life, liberty and security of person at all times and specified the remedies which can be obtained through national tribunals in exercise of their fundamental rights guaranteed to him/her either by Constitution or by law.

In spite of the UN Proclamation to this effect, migrant people are not in a position to exercise their right of freedom; don't have right to life, liberty and security of their person; are subjected to torture and cruel, inhuman and degrading treatment; deprived of their right to an effective remedy by the competent national tribunals. They are also subjected to involuntary exile and alienated from their home land and property. Is the Universal Declaration of Human Rights just a piece of paper or is it something sacrosanct that should be enforced by the United Nations and its member countries? These are some of the issues that one has the responsibility to answer. This study in particular aims at analyzing the problems faced by the Kashmiri migrants. The issue of human rights in Kashmir, therefore, merits detailed treatment.

Multiple Dimensions of the Kashmir Crisis

Events, attitudes, traits and beliefs do not spring from nowhere. They have deep roots. And the seeds of these roots are planted in the past. Some plants bend with age and wither away in course of time; some shed their leaves temporarily but sprout them again under congenial conditions; and some are uprooted totally by the storms and tornadoes of history. But there are others that remain, influencing silently and imperceptibly the social, political and cultural environment. We all live in the social and cultural cage that has been fabricated in the past,[1] though new light and fresh breeze of the present continue to reach us through the gaps in its bars. Viewed in the context of the deeds of its kings and their courtiers, the history of Kashmir, with a few illuminating exceptions is a long and lamentable tale of conspiracies and collusions. It has often been said that history repeats itself. But in the case of Kashmir, history appears to have repeated itself many times over, both as tragedy and as farce. What the future holds for Kashmir and the rest of the country depends upon who would be at the steering wheel of history. The current tornado of mass killings, migration and economic under-development in Kashmir has been caused more by the negative forces in the Indian political, social and moral order, than by the individuals who were the products, and in some way also the *creators*, of these forces.

Strategic Dimension

Kashmir—The name evokes *images of alpine vistas* and *rushing rivers*, gondolas floating on lotus-filled lakes, horse carts loaded with fresh apples and mountains covered with snow. This tiny, isolated corner of South Asia seems *neither southern nor Asian*[2]; its terrain, culture and spiritual traditions are unique. But in the past decade, the name Kashmir has come to evoke very different images: *sand-bagged army bunkers* dominating every street corner in Srinagar, the summer capital; soldiers in camouflage gear patrolling every road; guerrillas detonating landmines and throwing grenades, women in kerchiefs wailing over dead bodies.

On the map of India, the State of Jammu & Kashmir looks like a crown. The State is 640 kms in length from north to south and 480 kms from east to west. The nearness to the boundaries of foreign countries has made the position of the State most important from military point of view. For centuries, Kashmir has struggled against oppressive rule in one form or another. First the Mughal King Akbar invaded the region in the sixteenth century, ending its era as a sovereign State. The Mughals were followed by the Pathans, the Sikhs and then the British, who sold the land, lakes and populace to Dogra rulers for a nominal sum in the mid-nineteenth century. The seeds of the current tragedy were sown half a century ago.[3] The iron-fisted Dogras were forced out, but Kashmir was battered anew by the bloody and confusing events that accompanied the 1947 partition of India and Pakistan and the abrupt withdrawal of Great Britain's colonial rule over the subcontinent.

Geographic Dimension

The State of Jammu Kashmir is a divided entity that got formed into one political unit by *accident of history*. As one travels north from the plains of Punjab, the area up to 4000 metres high Pir Panjal range of mountains is the Jammu division. Linguistically, ethnically and from the historical point of view, the fate of this area was closely linked to that of Punjab and the hill areas of the east. The Kashmir valley at the height of over 5,000 ft that lies beyond the Pir Panjal range is to the north bound by the great Himalayan range and to the east and south by the Ladakh and the Zaskar range. Both these ranges rise above 18,000 ft and are formidable barrier to normal movement. The natural route to the Kashmir valley is through the *Jhelum gorge* that opens up towards the west.

To the east of the valley of Kashmir is the Kargil and Ladakh region. Ladakh is mainly Buddhist, has historical links with Tibet and for over six months remains cut off from the rest of the State. To the north of the valley are the areas of Gilgit and Baltistan with affinity to Central Asian region. West of Kashmir is the district of Mirpur that is Punjabi speaking and more akin to the Jammu division than Kashmir. The Kashmir valley is thus surrounded by areas that are ethnically and linguistically different. The mountain barriers ensured that the Kashmir valley develops in isolation from the rest of the areas. Each defendability and fertile land gave rise to a rich culture that produced some of the best literature in Indian History. Isolation and lack of external threats also made internecine quarrels frequent and the greatest threat to the political stability came from within.[4]

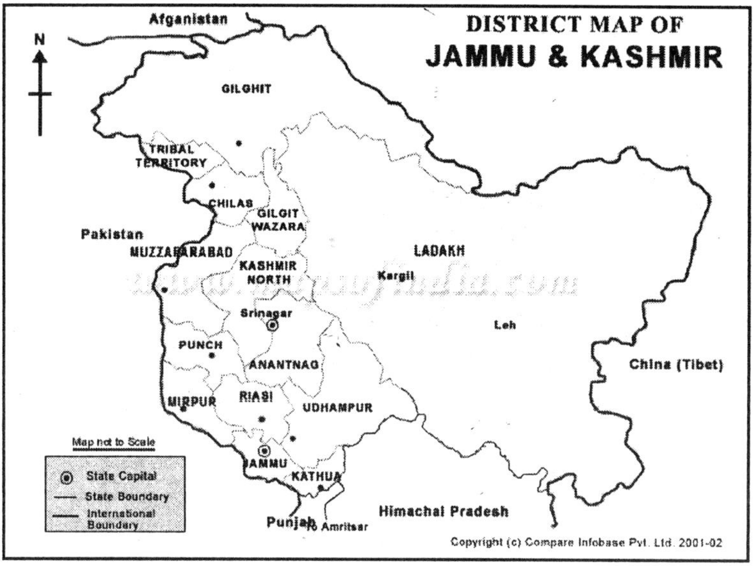

Ethnic Dimension

The various ethnic groups of the Jammu & Kashmir State though intermingled have their areas of high concentration. For example, *Kashmiris* are mainly concentrated in the Valley bottom; *Dards* occupy the valley of Gurez; *Hanjis* are confined to waterbodies of Kashmir; *Gujjars* and *Bakarwals* are living and oscillating in the Kandi areas; *Dogras* occupy the outskirts of the Punjab plain, while *Chibhalis* and *Paharis* live between Chenab and Jhelum rivers. Moreover, there are numerous small ethnic groups like *Rhotas, Gaddis* and *Sikhs*, which have significant concentration in isolated pockets of the State.

Political Dimension

There is no escape from the fact that the Kashmir problem is basically an internal problem of the *failure of the ideology* that underpins the Indian State.[5] It is not just an internal problem; it is also a bilateral problem between India and Pakistan. Kashmir's geography that gives it a border with Pakistan is a major factor of the violence taking place there. An attempt to search for a solution to the Kashmir problem must be preceded by a clear understanding of three dimensions namely – Internal, Bilateral and International. It needs to be clearly understood that there are further causal relationships relating to the economic, social, political, psychological and strategic aspects. It is this multiplicity of causes and their dynamic relationships that make the Kashmir issue neither easy to understand nor to solve.

Displacement of Peoples in the Valley

Ethnic tensions and conflict have caused significant dislocations of people in the region of Kashmir both internally and across the borders. The circumstances that gave rise to displacements include *armed conflicts, human rights violations, economic underdevelopment* and other failures of governance. In other instances individuals decide to migrate for *prosaic reasons*, such as new perceptions of unease or insecurity and fear of future discrimination or simply because of loss of privilege in new social orders. The horrors of mass extermination of people because of their ethnic origins made it clear how important it is to protect the human rights of the vulnerable groups and to eliminate discrimination.

In the case of Kashmir, the real threat to the inhabitant minority is due to the militancy. The State of Jammu & Kashmir is the dwelling place of the Muslims, Kashmiri Pandits and Sikhs. By and large, the society in Jammu and Kashmir remained well knit until 1989 when widespread violence erupted. The uniting factor had been *Kashmiriyat* – a concept of ethnic identity of the Valley. However, this came under serious attack with the supremacy of fundamentalist/secessionist groups like the Hizbul-Mujahideen. Kashmiri Pandits are an *ethno-religious minority* who numbered around 160,000 in the Kashmir valley in 1990. The Islamic organization which was believed to have started as a freedom movement degenerated into a massive operation of loot, extortion and rape. The majority of Kashmiri Pandits having fled, the guns were now turned towards the moderates amongst Muslims and the common village folk.

The reason for the targeted victimization of this particular community by the secessionist groups was due to the overall strategy of evicting those not sympathetic to the cause of an 'independent State'. Besides, the gradual assertion by the Kashmiri Pandits of a distinct identity based on their culture and tradition only increased the militant's ire. Thus, by cleansing of all non-Muslims from the Valley the militants wished to establish an *'Islamic State.'*

Phases of Displacement

The *first phase of displacement* of the Kashmiri Pandits took place from mid 1989 to end 1990. To counter the insurgency forces that proliferated in the valley due to many reasons, the army began its operations in Kashmir in 1990. It suffered from various handicaps. It was like a *blind man trying to fight an unseen enemy in the night.* The ham handed approach alienated the population even further from the government. To counter the pressure from the security forces, the militants turned its ire against 2,00,000 strong Hindu community. Living in isolation and forming less than 3 per cent of the population, the Kashmiri Pandits were vulnerable to terrorists. The ethnic cleansing of the Kashmir valley by the militant organization (like JKLF) began by selective murders of prominent people. The commonly heard cry in the valley was, *'leave your women and property and get out'*. As a result a massive exodus of the Hindus began on January 21, 1990. Many went to New Delhi and other parts of India. The poorer people who had nowhere else to go came to Jammu and began life as refugees in their own country.

This massive tragedy, comparable with the Human rights violations in former Yugoslavia and ethnic cleansing in Bosnia, was largely ignored by the Indian media possibly under pressure from the government. The government's logic was that the news of the exodus of Hindus might provoke reaction against Muslims in other parts of the country. Indian media, though largely independent, has a tradition cooperating with government on sensitive security issues. Even in 1971, the best kept Indian secret was the identity of a majority of the nearly nine million refugees driven out from the erstwhile East Pakistan.[6] Since these refugees were mostly Hindus, this fact was kept carefully hidden from the Indian masses to prevent communal rioting. The same feat was repeated in the case of the Kashmiri refugees. *While the rationale behind this was laudable and even logical, its effect at regional and global levels was disastrous.* The terrorists, who perpetrated one of the biggest post cold war ethnic cleansing and their supporter Pakistan, were left free instead to blame India for the violation of human rights. The West cynically exploited this *faux pas* on the part of India and concerned its ham-fisted and naïve diplomats on various world for. It was only in 1995 that the Indian government woke up to the folly of this approach and began highlighting the plight of refugees from Kashmir. It is noteworthy that despite all the propaganda against the Indian security forces and their alleged atrocities, there has been no influx of refugees into Pakistan from Kashmir.

The *Second Phase* of displacement began in March 1997, with the massacre of seven Pandits by militants at Sangram Pora village in the Budgam district and later with the killing of 23 Pandits in Wandhama village (Ganderbal constituency). Prominent leaders of both Hindu and Muslim communities were killed and their families were threatened.

The *third phase* commenced when 24 Kashmiri Pandits were killed on 23 March, 2003 in Nadimarg village in Pullawa district. The Pandits reportedly migrated to Jammu. The number of Kashmiri Pandits displaced in the second and third phase as a result of the Sangram Pora and Nadimarg incidents is not available.

Migrants or Internally Displaced Persons (IDPs)

First thing that one should keep in mind was to correct us about the use of the term 'Migrant'. The right term to define in case of Kashmiri people is '*displaced*'. Migrants are those who willingly migrate from one place to another. But they are displaced because they were forced to leave their homes. To leave Kashmir was not a voluntary act on their part. The terrorists have unleashed an organized violence and sustained campaign to exterminate and eliminate the people against their ideology in Kashmir supported by foreign mercenaries resulting in killings of thousands of innocent men, women and children continuously for the last ten years, thus contravening the basic principles of equality, liberty, life and due process of law which underline the UDHR, constitutes the "*Gross violation of Human Rights of Minorities*".[7]

Internally displaced persons (IDPs) are generally considered to be persons who have been forced to flee their homes in large numbers, suddenly, as a result of armed conflict, strife, systematic human rights violations or natural or man-made disasters. Some IDPs are concentrated in clearly identifiable camps or shanty towns, but others are more dispersed, moving to larger towns and cities along with the rest of the rural/urban exodus. IDPs are either those who have continued to remain within the territory of their country or who have returned to their own country but have not been able to return to their original places of residence.[8]

Kashmiri Pandits Problems

The Kashmiri Pandits are closely linked to the land of Kashmir, its geography, history and culture for the last 5,000 years. Their shrines scattered all over the Kashmir valley are the integral part of beauty of Kashmir. Kashmiri Pandits as sages, poets, historian, philosophers, artists, lovers of nature and exotic art, have contributed to various branches of science, learnings, art and architecture, iconography and calligraphy, abstract philosophy and theological sciences,[9] thus enriching the broad Indian civilization in its totality. They have contributed a great deal in Indian freedom struggle and in shaping the nations pluralistic constitutional democracy and secularism. In the face of adverse conditions like physical aggression by outsiders and cultural domination by Muslim missionaries this community was reduced to the status of a miniscule religious-cultural minority. In 1947 according to the census figures, there were 15 per cent Kashmir Pandits in the valley. In 1981 there were about 5 per cent and in the 1991 only about 0.1 per cent. 99.9 per cent of this community was forced to flee the valley under the terror tactics of the well-concerted plan by outside forces, executed through militants and mercenaries.

With a view to put the whole scenario in a proper perspective it needs to be said that the fundamental cause necessitating the exodus of Kashmiri Pandits is the *communal bigotry*. As revealed by the telling facts of history the first major exodus dates back to the barbarous times of Sikander Butshikan (1389-1413) who unleashed a reign of terror for conversion of Hindu Kashmir to the Islamic religion. The exodus was so massive in its scale and dimension that only *eleven Kashmiri Pandit families* stayed back in their homeland. The processes of conversion continued without a let up at various stages of Muslim rule.

While the community accommodated, mingled with and absorbed the culture and traditions of all outsiders who came to Kashmir, it was repeatedly rewarded with the most inhuman and brutal treatment. The Kashmiri Pandits in the valley of Kashmir, irrespective of their age, sex, position status or situation became the prime target of the terrorists' onslaught. They were warned and threatened, individually and collectively, through word of mouth, through insinuation and innuendo, through posters and press and over loud speakers installed in thousands of mosques all over the valley. Fear loomed large and the terrorist shadow stalked educational markets and other public places wherever the Kashmiri Pandits had a representation, however small. They were identified and denounced; hit lists were exhibited on electric poles, office doors and entries to numerous institutions; and the public at large was exhorted to watch them and hound them out. They were followed and kidnapped from their homes and places of work and interrogated and tortured. A spree of killings of the intellectuals of the community started. This was followed by *indiscriminate gunning down, hanging, dismembering, tying with grenades and blasting into pieces, skinning, burning and sawing alive the members of this ethnic minority of all walks of life.*

Many of the victims after being butchered were thrown into streets as exhibits for everybody to get terrorized. The bereaved were not permitted to mourn the dead and perform the last rites. Those who dared to attend the funeral were earmarked for reprisals. Molestation and rape was the order of the day. A large number preferred to stay behind, partly hopeful of a let up in the persecution and the frantic killings and partly on account of the reassurances by their friends, neighbours and colleagues of the Muslim majority community. In the present turmoil the strategies used in the terrorist operations against the people in Kashmir are:

1. Extermination of communal enemies—Kashmir Pandits.
2. Subjection of those people to brutal torture to instil fear among them in order to achieve their submission to the terrorists and their exodus from Kashmir.
3. Flushing out such Hindus, Muslims and even Sikhs.
4. Destruction of their residential homes, who migrate and the appropriation of their business establishments to ensure that they do not return.
5. Declaration of religious crusade against the Hindus.

By July-September 1990 more than 2 lakhs people, mainly Hindus had evacuated from their homes leaving their property, land, trade and business behind them.

Human Rights Violation against the Pandits

The last five years have witnessed a perpetuation of human rights' violation against this community, which had to leave the valley helter-skelter and got dispersed far and wide in different parts of the country. Most of the nearly three hundred thousand refugees came out with clothes barely enough to cover their bodies. They came out with the illusion of a return to their homes and hearths in the near future. Families got split and scattered in the scramble for shelter and livelihood. Parents got separated from children, spouses from their partners, and brothers from sisters. They are still on the move from one place to another like wandering nomads looking for help and succour. As a result of this dispersal the social fabric of the community is torn asunder, the economic structure has collapsed, material possessions have vanished and the political base has been overturned.

The old and infirm of the community have met a

premature end, dying for want of health and family support.[10] A large number of youth suffered mental breakdown. Depression, panic attacks, phobias, nightmares and insomnia have seized all age groups. Unnatural deaths in the form of sunstroke, snake and scorpion bites, hydrophobia and accidents have taken a big toll. The terror, a feeling of siege, a sense of rootless ness and loss of identity, the trauma of forced migration, exposure to an alien and hostile environment, problem of acclimatization, poor housing, unsanitary conditions, lack of basic amenities like drinking water, scarce medicare, malnutrition and idleness compounded by hurt and humiliation have orchestrated to result in physical, mental and psychological trauma of unimaginable magnitude. The community has reached the end of the tether and its reserves of patience and hopes have dried up. The spectre of disease, death and extinction are haunting the community. It seems unlikely that the community will ever be able to organize itself again into a cohesive social and political entity, which is vital for its survival and resurgence. Far from regaining its pristine glory, it is hard pressed to keep body, mind and soul together. Let us analyze the problems faced by the displaced Pandits.

The social structure, which was one of the strengths that saw it through centuries of persecution, is now breaking as under. The joint family system has been shattered by the migration and the subsequent *ghetto*-life in tents and tenements. Sometime back surveys had revealed that the community is already running a negative population growth. The family life is under great strain in the community. A report showed that the divorce rate in the couples in the prime fertility age group has seen an alarming increase. A third of all cases before the matrimonial Court are said to be those of Kashmiri Pandits.

An interview with a Kashmiri Pandit revealed, how strong that feeling is when they describe their life in Kashmir. It is not a passionate description. The emotions are overpowering whether it is the description of the scenic beauty of Kashmir, or that of the houses and the land that they left behind, or of the 'earlier times' when everything was normal for them in Kashmir. The irony of time gets unfolded as we mention the limited 'space' which they occupy one room for the livelihood. Apart from perceptible physical dislocation it is the emotional context of displacement that is distressing. While all those who have migrated from Kashmir similarly suffer the *trauma of displacement,* yet there is a context of specificity about the way it has affected different sections of Kashmiri Pandit community.

For the aged, being uprooted at this age is most awful experience. With nothing to look forward to, they not only feel sad and depressed but also alienated. Many of them are forced to live a life of isolation with no communication with the outside world. Not able to converse in any language other than Kashmiri, many of them, especially the old women are virtually forced to remain confined to one corner of the room, which is their abode. The emotional support that the old people used to get is missing because of many factors. The children shifting to different places and the joint family system gets disintegrated etc. Among those who feel the most bitter about their displacement were young at the time of onset of militancy and who were looking forward to their future. Many of them could not complete their education, there are others who were going to start their career are still awaiting their employment.

Large number of Hindu employees working in the State government has been pushed out as a result of migration from Kashmir and the Muslim employees have been appointed and confirmed on the posts of these migrant employees. This has created a new vested interest of employees who work hard for the non-return of Hindus to the valley. The student community of Hindu refugees has been segregated from others and is being refused admissions in Government schools, colleges, university and in the professional colleges. The unemployed educated youths of Kashmiri Pandits are being deprived of any employment in the State government. The temporary employees working in government and corporate bodies funded by State government and the Hindu teachers of Kashmir University have been pushed out of service as a result of migration.

Insufficiency of the living space offered by one room tenement which has been allotted to each family. The average family size taken as 5 members is found to be as high as 8 – 10 for most of the families.

Irregular payment of cash allowance—each migrant family is receiving a monthly subsistence allowance of Rs. 2400. Complaints of delay in disbursement were heard at each camp. It was informed, sometimes accumulated payment is made once in 2- 3 months.

Inadequacy of education facilities for migrant's children. Though schools and colleges have been opened for the migrants children, these are not running effectively due to shortage of accommodation and absence of library and laboratory facilities.

Settlement of property claims and payment of compensation for burnt/damaged houses. No one is satisfied with the government action.

Demands of the government employee—The migrant government employees are receiving full salary with benefits of annual increment and medical allowance. Their period of dislocation is, however, being treated as special leave with the result that they lose the normal benefit of leave encashment. They are also denied House Rent Allowance (HRA) and City Compensatory Allowance (CCA). Though they are considered for promotion, they cannot avail of it. Simply because they are posted on promotion to far flung areas in the valley which they cannot enter for no fault of theirs.

Unemployment of educated migrant youth – Despite repeated announcements and assurances by the government, nothing has been done so far to tackle this problem. Moreover, the migrant student is made to face an uneven and unfair competition with other aspirants because of their poor living conditions, which are not conducive to proper education. The demand for reservations for Kashmiri Pandits in the matter of government services was voiced at each camp.

Inadequacy of medical facilities – Though each camp has a dispensary of its own and medical and para medical staff is held far in excess of requirements, there is acute shortage of medicines and life saving drugs rendering the staff helpless and the patients defenceless. Because of no systematic arrangements for the maintenance of the ambulances, the elementary facility is actually non-functional at most places. These dispensaries manned by qualified staff in good strength can be used to improve the medical cover in the entire area by providing necessary medicines and developing elementary testing facilities.

Camp security–Though no one raised this issue, the absence of any security arrangement appears to be a serious one because no camp has been so far fenced.

Health Trauma–Other reports have pointed to an abnormal increase in the metabolic diseases among the migrant community. Diabetes is said to be rampant, almost of epidemic proportions. Psychosomatic diseases, biophysical effects of stress and strain, cases of cancer all are noticeably evident. The whole community is faced with a despondence with neither a clear direction nor any hope of future. There is a pressing need to rehabilitate this community before the situation takes an irreversible turn.[11] Though there has been talk of certain moves in the direction, they neither display vision nor innovations. They certainly do not appear to take the gravity of the situation into consideration.

Government's Response

The Indian government's response to displaced persons from Kashmir has been significantly different from its response to displaced persons in the North-East. It is said that the Indian government spends rupees 26 million (U.S. $597,000) per month just on financial and food aid for the displaced. In Jammu & Kashmir alone, that has totalled some rupees 2,741 million (U.S. $62.9 million) since 1990. Also the government has spent another rupees 200 million (U.S. $4.6 million) on compensation for displaced persons whose homes were burned down. The Jammu & Kashmir State government's policy toward the displaced is shaped by a high-level committee chaired by the revenue minister. The State government works in collaboration with the national government, *"but as far as implementation of policy, the primary responsibility is vested with the State."*

Of the 29,000 displaced Kashmiri families in Jammu, some 14,200 families (some 59,500 people) receive government assistance as displaced persons. Another 14,800 families (almost all Hindus) are headed by former government workers, to whom the Government of India has continued to pay full salaries (or retirement benefits) since their displacement in 1990. According to Jammu official, those living outside camps who receive government assistance are given a monthly cash payment of rupees 1,800 (U.S. $41) for families of four or more, plus a food-aid package consisting of rice, flour, and sugar. For the first six or seven years after their displacement, most displaced Kashmiris in Jammu lived in tents. Over the years, many obtained rented accommodation in Jammu or Delhi or moved elsewhere in India or abroad. The government constructed some 4,600 one-room, semi permanent houses for those who remained in the camps.

The Jammu government has also built ten primary schools and three high schools for displaced children, and provides medical care to the displaced, including paying for 28 doctors based at the camps. In Muthi camp, for instance it was observed that there is a small dispensary, but that the government doesn't provide any medicines for it. Also the displaced have access to local hospitals, but that, unlike local people, they are not given free medicines.

In New Delhi alone some 21,000 displaced Hindu Pandit families are dispersed throughout the city, living mostly in private accommodations, though some 2,000 to 3,000 continue to live in 14 camps for the displaced. Those living outside the camps receive the same government assistance as displaced Hindu Pandits living outside of camps in Jammu. Those living in the camps receive rupees 1,200 (U.S. $27), plus housing, electricity, and some food aid.

Pandit leaders appear to believe that if the Government of India officially recognizes them as *internally displaced persons,* they might receive some of the protection and assistance that is often provided to internationally recognized refugees. The only difference between a refugee and an internally displaced person is that the displaced person is a refugee in his own country whereas the refugee is in another country.

The government has enacted an Act to protect the immovable property of the displaced. According to 'Jammu & Kashmir Migrant Immovable Property (Preservation, Protection and Restraint on Distress Sales) Act, 1997; "Migrant" means any person who has migrated from Kashmir valley after 1st November, 1989 and is registered as such with the relief commissioner and includes a person who has not been so registered on the ground of his being in service of the government in any moving office, or having left the valley in pursuit of occupation or vocation or otherwise and is possessed of immovable property in the valley, but is unable to ordinarily reside there due to the disturbed conditions.

Conclusion

Terrorism is a violation of human rights, whatever its political objectives.[12] Terrorism in Jammu & Kashmir motivated by ideological commitments to a communal crusade is a greater violation of human rights. The Universal Declaration of Human Rights was adopted by the world community precisely to save mankind from the *scourge of crusades*; the Kashmir carnage was a war of crusades. The degree of crusades is not only in Kashmir but also in other parts of India, like Gujarat, Orissa etc. The 'Subversion and Separatism' is the root cause for all those happenings. There is an imperative necessity for a bold and unconventional endeavour to identify the content and contours of violence which has ravaged Jammu & Kashmir State and describe the perspectives in which the infringements of human rights deserve to be accessed. Human judgments are presumed to be universal, as the UDHR, underline generally accepted norms and standards of human behaviour and not such norms and standards, which are arbitrarily devised.

It is high time that the conscience of mankind awakens to the reality of the situation in Kashmir where the so-called freedom struggle is merely an extension and escalation of the ongoing offensive against a small yet ancient and distinct ethno-religious community which has been turned into a minority—the Kashmiri Pandit (Hindu)—who is being exterminated under a diabolical plan masterminded by religious zealots turned terrorists with the direction, support and connivance of their mentors from across the border in Pakistan.

The human rights aspects should be considered even in 'war zones' like Kashmir (or Punjab sometime back), where the Indian State is fighting secessionists forces aided and abetted from outside. Kashmir today is a battleground for a low intensity or proxy war by Pakistan against India. This distinction between low intensity and normal war is essentially applicable at strategic level. As many of these engagements take place in populated areas, the innocent bystanders suffer. India knows that insurgency is not a matter of search and destroy missions or contests in body count but a struggle for the hearts and minds of the people. Therefore, it is necessary that the armed forces must uphold humanitarian approach even during insurgencies. India has also failed to articulate its position on human rights for long, as the government hid the atrocities committed by the terrorists from public gaze so as to prevent any repercussions in other parts of the country. This has proved counter productive at the international level.

Brave nations do not seek permission from other countries, however powerful, to enact laws, which are in the best interest of the people. It is the Union government's duty under the Constitution to provide security to its citizens, irrespective of caste, creed and religion. Enough of precious blood has been shed, that has flowed down the *holy Vitasta,* meandering through the valley, whose nomenclature has changed to 'Hell upon this earth' from what famous Persian poet Firduos has described as 'Heaven upon this earth'.

Given the fact that this community has been widely dispersed within the country, it is commendable that they have sustained a resolve to return to the motherland. However, it is a great pity that for securing a rightful place in the land of their ancestors the Pandits have focused on demanding a separate demarcated 'homeland' in the valley, which they call *Panun Kashmir.* It is immaterial as to what administrative arrangements are made for such a separate entity, the fact is that it is a *Self-defeating exercise.* There are several reasons for it.

The future of Kashmiri Pandits as well as the Kashmiri Muslims is in *living together,* closely interlinked, no matter what bitter memories the experiences of the past decade or so may have conspired to generate. Viewed with far sight, ethnically diverse communities need each other in order to flourish together. That is imperative of *long-term social development.* This is even truer when religious pluralism exists within cultural similarity or identity. If the two religious communities in the Kashmir were indeed live side by side in demarcated zones or homelands, then the foundations for unending long-term hostility would have been laid. *There would be no peace, only recriminations.* The idea of homeland is also flawed because it would bring economic ruin to the Pandit community. A small land mass will seriously impediment the economic muscle because of small space. *Whereas, world over people look for wider and wider spaces to flap their wings.*

With recent changes in the political dispensation in Kashmir hopes were raised that an acceptable solution to the problems of the Pandits may be found. *Firstly* both Pandits and Muslims of Kashmir will have to accept that two communities must learn afresh the *art of living together in a single larger community without any artificial boundaries. Secondly,* the leadership of the Kashmiri Muslim community, as distinct from the government, must undertake to *guarantee the safety and security of their Pandit Brethren. Thirdly* the government should provide the financial backing to help rehabilitate Kashmiri Pandits in the valley in a manner that suits individual genius and helps to generate self-sustaining resources. A gift of governmental jobs is a sterile arrangement, which, in the present times, is an insufficient lure for the younger generation of Kashmiri Pandits while at the same time becoming an avoidable long term burden on the State exchequer. Instead these young men and women should be encouraged to set up new businesses and enterprises that are self sustaining in the long run and will add to the economy of the State while helping to rehabilitate the Pandit community at places of individual preference within the valley. In order to achieve this objective it is necessary for the many organizations that claim to represent this small community to come together and project this agenda as their common minimum demand.

In order to uphold the human rights of the Pandits, a good number of suggestions have been offered time and again. Apart from the various suggestions offered, the following needs a meritorious consideration.

1. The first and foremost requirement is to count the community as *'Refugees'*, which was demanded time and again. The official status as 'refugees' whether internally displaced or otherwise, instead of the wrong and misleading nomenclature of 'Migrants' will correct the blunder and clear the confusion both at home and abroad.
2. Because of the long-winded intricacies and fallacies that have been generated and introduced into what is called 'Kashmir Question', it is only fair and essential that the Kashmiri Pandit community be made a party in all discussions and decisions on the resolution of the 'Question' at all forum, national and international.
3. Numerically the Kashmiri Pandit community is a small minority in the State of Jammu & Kashmir. That has been at once the cause and the consequence of them be ignored, abandoned and enormously discriminated against in all aspects of life. This long-standing oppression and deprivation can be remedied and a proper balance achieved, only when they are afforded political representation in the nation and the States legislatures and government. This can be arranged in several ways without violating the spirit of the Constitution. India's true democracy offers many examples, such as has been done for *Anglo-Indians and other ethnic minorities* in spite of their being in much better position than us or for under-privileged or historically deprived sections of the Indian society.

Kashmiri Pandits have been reduced essentially to the level of these latter sections and should not be judged by caste alone.

4. Further, another inquiry commission should be set up to identify the prime criminals who indulged in inhuman torture, death, loot and rape should be brought to book and punished under law. There are international and national precedents on this subject.
5. The minorities and nationalist elements in the valley, which were hounded out by terrorist secessionists have been made to suffer untold physical, economic, psychological and cultural devastation. From relatively comfortable homes of their own, they had to find shelter in tents and hovels unworthy of even cattle and in the most inhospitable environs. There seems to be no public hygiene, medical facilities and infrastructure for generation of employment. Above all, these townships need to be build around major cities and should have reliable measures of safety and security.
6. Special provisions must be made on long term basis for admissions of displaced youth seeking education at all levels especially technical, professional, medical courses etc, throughout the country.
7. The educated youth seeking employment should be absorbed on the basis of reservation in all States and central government organizations, public undertakings universities including government aided institutions with age relaxation of 10 years.
8. Where the property has been destroyed or otherwise seized illegally, viz. houses, factories, shops, stocks, agricultural lands etc., compensation at prevailing market rates be given without delay.
9. Life and general insurance facilities should be liberally extended to the displaced persons, without insisting on certain procedures and conventional practices, which cannot be observed in the present situation.

References

1. Victoria Schofield, *Kashmir in the crossfire,* 1996, I.B. Tauris & Co Ltd., London.
2. Abbas, S., Kashmir: Autonomy Demand, *Economic and Political Weekly,* 2000, Vol. 35, issue 49, pp. 4360.
3. Kashmir's greatest historian Kalhan writes about his native land : *"It is a country where the sun shines mildly, being the place created by Rishi Kashyap, for his glory – big and lofty houses, learning, saffron, icy cool water and grapes rare in Heaven are plentiful here – Kailash is the best place in the three worlds (Tri-lok), Himalayas the best place in Kailash, and Kashmir the best place in Himalayas"*
4. Alexander Evans, A Departure from History: Kashmiri Pandits, *Contemporary South Asia,* 11 (1) 2002.
5. Prakash, S, The political economy of Kashmir since 1947, *Contemporary South Asia,* 2000, Vol. 9, issue 3, pp. 315-338.
6. James Thomas, A peace process for Kashmir? *Economist,* 2000, Vol., Issue 22, December, 2000, pp. 20-21.
7. Swami, P., *Clueless in Kashmir,* Seminar, 2001, Vol., issue 497, pp. 59-63.
8. A Report to the people of India, *Blood in the Valley,* 1996, Institute for Kashmir Studies, Srinagar.
9. Khursheed Wani, "Homeless at Home", *The Pioneer,* September 8, 2002.
10. I.B. Tauris, *'Kashmir in the Crossfire'.*
11. K.L. Kaul and M.K. Teng, "Human Rights Violations of Kashmiri Hindus" in G.C. Raju Thomas (ed.) *Perspectives of Kashmir* (London: Westview Press, 1992).
12. Government of India, Ministry of Home Affairs, *Annual Report* 2001-02.

THE CONTRIBUTORS

Dr. A. David Ambrose, Lecturer, Department of Legal Studies, University of Madras, Chennai.

Dr. B. Krishnamurthy, Reader and Coordinator, Centre for Nehru Studies, School of Social Sciences and International Studies, Pondicherry University, Pondicherry.

Dr. D. Surya Prakasa Rao, Associate Professor, Dr. B.R. Ambedkar College of Law, Andhra University, Visakhapatnam.

Dr. D.S.N. Somayajulu, Prof. of Law (Retd), Dr. B.R. Ambedkar College of Law, Andhra University, Visakhapatnam.

Dr. (Justice) David Annousamy, Retd. Judge, High Court of Madras, Pondicherry.

Mr. K. Ramachandra Reddy, Advocate, High Court of Andhra Pradesh, Hyderabad.

Dr. K.N. Chandrasekharan Pillai Director, Indian Law Institute, New Delhi.

Dr. Lalit Dadwal, Lecturer,Regional Centre, Dharmasala, H.P.

Dr. N. Balu, Prof. and Head, Department of Legal Studies, University of Madras, Chennai.

Mr. R. Rama Subramanian, Research Scholar, Centre for South Asian Studies, S.I.S. Jawaharlal Nehru University, New Delhi.

Dr. R. Venkata Rao, Prof. of Law,and Principal, Dr. B.R. Ambedkar College of Law, Andhra University, Visakhapatnam.

Dr. Raghunath Patnaik, Professor, P.G. Department of Law, Utkal University, Vani Vihar, Bhubaneshwar.

Dr. Ranbir Singh, Director, NALSAR University of Law, Hyderabad.

Dr. S.S. Rama Rao Pappu, Professor of Philosophy, Miami University, Oxford, Ohio, USA.

Mr. Sadiq A. Jilani Syed, Associate Human Rights Officer, UN Mission of Support in East TIMOR, Australia.

Dr. Subhash C. Kashyap, Former Secretary General, Lok Sabha and Member, National Commission to the Working of the Constitution, New Delhi.

Dr. Sunil Deshta, Associate Professor, Department of Law, Himachal Pradesh University, Shimla.

Dr. T.S.N. Sastry, Reader and Coordinator, Centre for Human Rights, School of Social Sciences and International Studies, Pondicherry University, Pondicherry.

Dr. V. Hemalatha Devi, Prof. and Head, PG Department of Law, Sri Venkateswara University, Tirupathi.

Dr. Vijaya Lakshmi, Reader, Department of Law, Kakatiya University, Warangal.

INDEX

content and thrust to the development of human rights jurisprudence in post Maneka Gandhi era. The Court has maintained that the State has no right to take any action which may deprive the citizen of the enjoyment of his basic fundamental rights except in accordance with a law which is reasonable, fair and just.[44] It is heartening to state that the apex court did not allow the legal technicalities to come in its way for granting relief to the victims of State terrorism or of State lawlessness, otherwise it would have amounted to surrendering to State lawlessness, or showing cold indifference to the personal liberty of the individual or its immense indifference to sufferings not contemplated by the Constitution.

The apex court considered the question of giving compensation to a person who has unduly suffered detention and bodily harm. In *Khatri* v. *State of Bihar (Bhagalpur Blinding Case)*,[45] the question was whether the State was liable to pay compensation for the alleged blinding of certain prisoners by the police. Dealing with the question of granting relief to the person who has suffered deprivation of his life or liberty guaranteed under the Article 21 Bhagawati J. held[46]:

> *"Why should the court not be prepared to forge new tools and devise new remedies for the purpose of vindicating the most precious of the precious fundamental right to life and personal liberty."*

Addressing the leading question, i.e "Would the State be liable to pay compensation for acts of its servants outside the scope of their power and authority affecting life or personal liberty of a person and thus infringing Article 21?" Answering in affirmative, the Court held that[47]:

> *"If it were not so, Article 21 would be reduced to a nullity, a mere rope of sand, for in this view, if the officer is acting according to law there would be no breach of Article 21 and if he is acting without the authority of law, the State would be able to contend that it is not responsible for his action and therefore there is no violation of Article 21."*

Rudul Sah exposed "a sordid and disturbing state of affairs" for which the responsibility was squarely on the administration. Petitioner was acquitted by Muzaffarpur Sessions Court on June 3rd 1968, but he was released on 16th October 1982 on a *habeas corpus* petition. The question before the court was whether it could grant some compensation under Article 32 for his wrongful detention. The Court held that[48]:

> *"It is true that Article 32 cannot be used as a substitute for enforcement of rights and obligations which can be enforced efficaciously through the ordinary process of courts civil and criminal.*

Referring to the fact, that the petitioner was detained illegally in the prison for over 14 years after his acquittal in full dressed trial, the Court felt that[49]:

> *" If it refused to pass an order of compensation in favour of the petitioner, it will be doing merely lip service to the fundamental right to liberty which the State government has so grossly violated. It would denude their right to life and liberty under Art. 21 of its significant content if the power of the court was limited merely to passing orders of release from illegal detention."*

Further, it observed:

> *" One of the telling ways in which the violation of that right can reasonably be prevented and due compliance with the mandate of Art. 21 secured, is to mulct its violators in the payment of monetary compensation. Administrative sclerosis leading to flagrant infringements of fundamental rights cannot be corrected by any other method open to the judiciary to adopt. The right to compensation is some palliative for the unlawful acts of instrumentalities which act in the name of public interest and which present for their protection the powers of the State as a shield...."*

Besides the State Government is also empowered under the Orphanages and other Charitable Homes (Supervision and Control) Act, 1960 to levy penalties and initiate legal proceedings for those who run orphanages and other children's homes without following the prescribed norms.

After visiting the tribal villages and inspecting few of the orphanages in Hyderabad we had visited Tandur for inspecting an orphanage being run by John Abraham Bethelaham Home, the next day. Unlike the Devarakonda Revenue Divison roads, which are broken and seems to be temporary the Tandur roads are well maintained. On our way we could find big farmhouses, residential colleges, schools etc. We reached Tandur at around 2.30 p.m., to inspect John Abraham Memorial Bethany Home, (R.R. District) accompanied by the police officials, RDO, NGOs and other officials. There we were shocked to see the deplorable conditions prevailing in the orphanage. We came to know from the police that all the members of the Managing Body had run away and were not traceable for the last few days. We [illegible]

[illegible]

the files we found astonishing facts even to the extent of issuing of adoption clearance certificates by the VCA after death of the children. Out of nearly 90 available files of case history of children inspected, we were surprised to read that 16 infants were died during the year 2000 alone.

The situation being so grave, our immediate priority shifted from investigation to the care of the children. We have, therefore, instructed the RDO, Vikarabad, to give immediate medical aid to the children and to post two *Anganwadi* workers with the orphanage on a 24-hours basis and also two police officials for security of children and also guarding the seized files and other documents. We have further instructed that the *Anganwadi* workers should start taking care of the children with whatever feeding material was immediately available in the stock. However, the stocks are found to be sufficient only for about [illegible] days. Therefore, we sent SOS letters to the Chief Minister of Andhra Pradesh and other concerned officials in